Critique of
Economic Reason

Critique of
Economic Reason

ANDRÉ GORZ

Translated by
Gillian Handyside and Chris Turner
(Material Word)

V
VERSO

London · New York

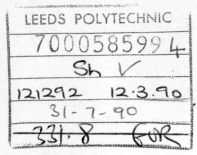
First published as Métamorphoses du travail: Quête du sens, Galilée, 1988
This edition published by Verso 1989
© Éditions Galilée 1988

Verso
UK: 6 Meard Street, London W1V 3HR
USA: 29 West 35th Street, New York, NY 10001-2291

Verso is the imprint of New Left Books

British Library Cataloguing in Publication Data

Gorz, Andre
  Critique of economic reason.
  1. Work & leisure. Social aspects
  I. Title   II. Metamorphoses du travail. *English*
  306′.36

  ISBN 0-86091-253-1
  ISBN 0-86091-968-4 pbk

US Library of Congress Cataloging-in-Publication Data

Gorz, André.
    [Métamorphoses du travail.   English]
    Critique of economic reason / André Gorz ; translated by Gillian
Handyside and Chris Turner.
        p.   cm.
    Translation of: Métamorphoses du travail.
    ISBN 0-86091-253-1 — ISBN 0-86091-968-4 (pbk.)
    1. Quality of work life.   2. Leisure.   3. Hours of labor.
  4. Marxian economics.   I. Title.
  HD6955.G6713   1989
  331′.01—dc20

Typeset in 10/12 point Times by Leaper & Gard Ltd, Bristol
Printed in Great Britain by Bookcraft (Bath) Ltd

À Dorine

Contents

What I propose in the following is a reconsideration of the human condition from the vantage point of our newest experiences and our most recent fears. This, obviously, is a matter of thought, and thoughtlessness ... seems to me among the outstanding characteristics of our time. What I propose, therefore, is very simple: it is nothing more than to think what we are doing.

Hannah Arendt

Introduction

What we are experiencing is not the crisis of modernity. We are experiencing the need to modernize the presuppositions upon which modernity is based. The current crisis is not the crisis of Reason but that of the (increasingly apparent) irrational motives of rationalization as it has been pursued thus far.

The current crisis is not an indication that the process of modernization has reached an impasse and that we shall have to retrace our steps. It is rather an indication of the need for modernity *itself to be modernized*, to be included reflexively in its own sphere of action: for *rationality itself to be rationalized*.[1]

Indeed, if we define modernization as the cultural differentiation of the spheres of life and the secularization of their corresponding activities, then the process is far from complete. The process of modernization, as it has evolved up to now, has created its own myths, sustaining a new credo which has been shielded from reasoned enquiry and rational criticism. The limits to rationalization which have thus been set down have become indefensible. What 'post-modernists' take to be the end of modernity and the crisis of Reason is in reality the crisis of the quasi-religious irrational contents upon which the selective and partial rationalization we call industrialism – bearer of a conception of the universe and a vision of the future which are now untenable – is based.

As long as we remain bound by this vision, we will continue to cling to individual pursuits and nostalgic views of the past, incapable of giving either meaning or direction to the changes which have caused the destruction of our past beliefs.

I do not mean to insinuate by such statements that rationalization could, or should, be extended indefinitely until it absorbs everything which has thus far escaped its grasp. On the contrary, I hope to demonstrate that rationalization has ontological and existential limits, and that these limits can only be crossed by means of pseudo-rationalizations, themselves irrational, in which rationalization becomes its opposite.

One of my principal objectives here will be to delimit the sphere of what can be rationalized. As starting point I will take a commentary on a text which unintentionally brings us straight to the heart of the crisis of that particular form of rationality we call economic, a rationality unaware of how narrow its proper limits are. I shall then turn to the examination of the ideological and ethical presuppositions which have enabled it to expand beyond the practical sphere in which it is applicable.

In an article which is characteristic of the prevalent economic thinking, Lionel Stoleru writes:

> A wave of technological advances has rendered a whole series of jobs unnecessary and reduced employment on a huge scale without creating an equivalent number of jobs elsewhere. . . . It will enable us to produce more and better with less human effort: savings in manufacturing costs and in working time will increase purchasing power and *create new areas of activity elsewhere in the economy (if only in leisure activities).*[2]

Stoleru later returns to this last point to make it clear that these new activities will be *paid* activities, *jobs* although they will not be properly 'work' as it has been understood up to now:

> The substitution of robotics and computer communications for human labour . . . allows a value to be released which is greater than the wages previously paid out. . . . This value is then available *for remunerating those who have lost their jobs.* Unemployment constitutes a displacement of activity rather than the abolition of jobs.

The interest of this apparently economic text lies in the wealth of different explicit and implicit meanings it contains. To begin with, Stoleru, by contrast with the majority of political leaders and apologists for the employers, admits that the current technical changes save on working hours *across the whole of society* and not just on the scale of particular enterprises: they allow more and better production using fewer working hours and less capital; they allow not only wage costs to be reduced but also costs in capital per unit produced.[3] Computerization and robotization have, then, an economic rationality, which is characterized precisely by the desire to *economize*, that is, to use the factors of production as efficiently as possible. We shall return to this type of rationality later on, to examine it in greater detail. For the moment, suffice it to say that a rationality whose aim is to *economize* on these 'factors' requires that it be possible to *measure, calculate and plan* their deployment and to express the factors themselves, whatever they may be, in terms of a single unit of measurement. This unit of measurement is the 'unit cost', a cost which is itself a function of the working time (the number of hours worked) contained in the product and the means (broadly speaking, the capital, which is accumulated labour) used to produce it.

From the point of view of economic rationality, the working time saved across the whole of society, thanks to the increasing efficiency of the means used, constitutes working time made available for the production of additional wealth. This is precisely the point made by Stoleru (indeed, he returns to it twice to stress his point). The working time saved, he writes, 'allows for the remuneration of those who have lost their jobs' by employing them to perform other economic activities, or by paying them to perform activities which were previously neither paid nor considered to be part of the economy. It allows for new jobs to be created 'elsewhere in the economy, if only', as Stoleru makes clear, 'in leisure activities'.

The model implicitly envisaged here is consequently one of an economy which is continually absorbing new spheres of activity at the same time as working time is being liberated in spheres that were previously part of the economy. This expansion in the scope of the economy will nonetheless lead, according to its own rationality, to new savings in time. Economicizing, that is, including within the economic sphere what was once excluded, means that time-generating economic rationalization will gain ground and release increasing quantities of free time.

This can well be seen in the directions most often suggested to ensure 'new growth': they concern, on the one hand, the computerization and robotization of household tasks (for example, 'telephone shopping', automatic, computer-programmed cooking, the electronic cottage), and, on the other, the at least partial industrialization and computerization of services providing catering, cleaning, bodily care, education, childcare and so on. Economic rationalization appears thus destined to penetrate the sphere of 'reproduction' in which domestic labour, which is neither remunerated nor accounted for, nor, more often than not, even measured as regards the time spent on it, is still dominant. The explicit goals of the innovations proposed are to save time, and, more especially, to liberate women or households from household chores.

To say that they will 'create jobs' is a paradoxical way of denying the economic rationality which is, in other respects, their justification: the aim of fast-food chains, domestic robots, home computers, rapid hair-dressing salons and the like, is not to *provide work* but to save it. Where paid labour (that is, jobs) is really necessary in these areas, the quantity of paid labour provided is much lower than the quantity of domestic labour saved. If this were not the case, these products and services would be financially inaccessible and devoid of interest for the vast majority of people: in order to obtain an hour of free time, the average wage earner would have to spend the equivalent of – or possibly more than – the wage she or he earned in one hour of work; he or she would have to work at least an extra hour in order to gain an extra hour of free time; the time saved in performing domestic tasks would have to be spent working (or working extra time) at the factory or the office, and so on. Now the use value of domestic appliances and industrialized services lies precisely, by contrast, in the *net* time they gain for us, and their exchange value in their high productivity per hour: the user spends less time working in order to earn enough to purchase these products or services, than she or he spends in providing these services for him- or herself. This is indeed a liberation of time across the whole of society.

The question we must ask, then, is what meaning we wish to give this new-found free time and what content we wish to give it. Economic reason is fundamentally incapable of providing an answer to this question. To consider, as Stoleru does, that it will be filled by activities 'elsewhere in the economy, if only in leisure activities', is to forget that when the time saved in traditional economic activities is used to economicize activities previously excluded from the economic sphere, additional time will be saved as a result of this displacement. The expansion of the sphere of economic rationality, made possible by savings in working time, leads to savings in time even in activities which were previously not counted as work. 'Advances in technology' thus inevitably pose the question of the meaning and content of free time; better still, of the nature of a civilization and a society in which there is far more free time than working time and in which, therefore, economic rationality ceases to govern everyone's time.

Including leisure activities within the economic sphere and assuming that their expansion will generate new economic activities appears at first to be a paradoxical way of avoiding the above question. The rationality governing leisure activities is, in fact, the opposite of the rationality governing economic activities: such activities consume rather than create free time; their aim is not to save time but to spend it. This is holiday time, time for extravagance, time for gratuitous activity which is an end in itself. In short, such time has no utility, nor is it the means to any other end and the categories of instrumental rationality (efficiency, productivity, performance) are not applicable to it, except to pervert it.

To state, as Stoleru does, that leisure activities generate, that they indeed demand, new paid activities is not, however, totally absurd, provided that society is viewed not as a single but as a dual economic entity. And this is, in effect, what the majority of writers do. The continued division of society as they conceive it will be inevitable. The reason for this division will be (as it is already) the unequal distribution of the savings made in working hours: an increasingly large section of the population will continue to be expelled, or else marginalized, from the sphere of economic activities, whilst another section will continue to work as much as, or even more than, it does at present, commanding, as a result of its performances or aptitudes, ever-increasing incomes and economic powers. Unwilling to give up part of their work and the prerogatives and powers that go with their jobs, the members of this professional elite will only be able to increase their leisure time by getting third parties to procure their free time for them. Therefore they will ask these third parties to do in their place all the things everyone is capable of doing, particularly all labour referred to as 'reproduction'. And they will purchase services and appliances which will allow them to save time *even when producing these services and appliances takes more time than the average person will save by using them.* They will thus foster the development, across the whole of society, of activities which have no economic rationality – since the people performing them have to spend more time in doing them than the people benefiting from them actually save – and which only serve the private interests of the members of this professional elite, who are able to purchase time more cheaply than they can sell it personally. These are activities performed by *servants*, whatever the status of the people who do them or method of payment used.

The division of society into classes involved in intense economic activity on the one hand, and a mass of people who are marginalized or excluded from the economic sphere on the other, will allow a sub-system to develop, in which the economic elite will buy leisure time by getting their own personal tasks done for them, at low cost, by other people. The work done by personal servants and enterprises providing personal services makes more time available for this elite and improves their quality of life; the leisure time of this economic elite provides jobs, which are in most cases insecure and underpaid, for a section of the masses excluded from the economic sphere.

Stoleru makes no reference to this division but it appears, thinly disguised, in the following analysis by Edmond Maire:

There will be a progressive decrease in the industrial products we purchase, not in terms of quantity but in terms of value, because automation will reduce the price of most of these products. The purchasing power released in this way, combined with the purchasing power arising from future growth, will allow for the expansion of the so-called neighbourhood services to be financed. . . . Even now certain users already have the purchasing power available to do this.[4]

This analysis is based entirely on the fact, nowhere admitted in the text, that automation is able to produce a reduction in price *because it reduces wage costs* or, in other words, the number of paid workers. Obviously, the people who will enjoy this additional purchasing power as a result of prices coming down will be the ones who can retain well-paid, permanent jobs and not the workers who will be expelled or excluded from production. *They alone* will be able to afford the neighbourhood market services whose development Edmond Maire predicts will create 'millions of jobs'. The people paid to do these jobs will be, directly or indirectly, in the service of the privileged sections of society who will benefit from automation.

The unequal distribution of work in the economic sphere, coupled with the unequal distribution of the free time created by technical innovations thus leads to a situation in which one section of the population is able to buy extra spare time from the other and the latter is reduced to serving the former. Social stratification of this type is different from stratification in terms of class. By contrast with the latter, it does not reflect the laws immanent in the functioning of an economic system whose impersonal demands are made as much on managers of capital and company administrators as on paid workers. For a section at least of those who provide personal services, this type of social stratification amounts to subordination to and personal dependence upon the people they serve. A 'servile' class, which had been abolished by the industrialization of the post-war period, is again emerging.

Certain conservative governments, and even a number of trade unions, justify and promote this formidable social regression on the pretext that it permits the 'creation of jobs', that is, that servants increase the amount of time their masters can devote to activities which are highly productive in economic terms – as if the people who do 'odd jobs' were not also capable of productive or creative work; as if those who have services done for them were creative and competent every minute of their working day and were thus irreplaceable; as if it were not the very conception the latter have of their function and rights which is depriving the young people who deliver their hot croissants, newspapers and pizzas of chances of economic and social integration; as if, in a word, the differentiation of economic tasks required such a degree of specialization that the stratification of society – into a mass of operatives, on the one hand, and a class of irreplaceable and over-worked decision-makers and technicians who need a host of helpers to serve them personally in order to do their jobs, on the other – were inevitable.

Certainly, the existence of a servile class is less obvious today than it was during the periods when the affluent classes employed a large number of domestic servants (according to British censuses – in which they were categorized as 'domestic and personal servants' – the latter represented 14 per cent of the working population between 1851 and 1911). The difference is that nowadays these personal services are to a large extent socialized or industrialized: the majority of servants are employed by service enterprises which hire out labour (insecure, part-time employment; piecework; and so on) which is then exploited by private individuals. But this does not alter the basic fact that these people are doing servants' work, that is, work which those who earn a decent living transfer, for their personal advantage and without gains in productivity, on to the people for whom there is no work in the economy.

We are thus faced with a social system which is unable to distribute, manage or employ this new-found free time; a system fearful of the expansion of this time, yet which does its utmost to increase it, and which, in the end, can find no purpose for it other than seeking all possible means of turning it into money: that is, monetarizing, trans-forming into jobs and economicizing, in the form of increasingly special-ized services for exchange on the market, even those previously free and autonomous activities capable of giving meaning to it.

To postulate, as is generally done, that the total amount of free time created by current rationalization and technicization can be re-employed 'elsewhere in the economy', as a result of the infinite expansion of the economic sphere, amounts to saying that there is no limit to the number of activities that can be transformed into paid services which generate employment; or, in other words, that in the end everyone, or nearly everyone, will have to sell a specialized service to others and buy from them everything they do not sell themselves; that the market exchange of time (without the creation of value) can absorb with impunity all areas of life, without destroying the meaning of the free, spontaneous activities and relations whose essential characteristic is to *serve* no purpose.

It is [writes Hannah Arendt] a society of laborers which is about to be liberated from the fetters of work, and this society does no longer know of those other higher and more meaningful activities for the sake of which this freedom would deserve to be won. . . . What we are confronted with is the prospect of a society of laborers without labor, that is, without the only activity left to them. Surely nothing could be worse.[5]

Except, perhaps, disguising private activities and leisure activities themselves as work and jobs. This state of affairs, to which I will return later, is not such a distant possibility.

This crisis is, in fact, more fundamental than any economic or social crises. The utopia which has informed industrial societies for the last two hundred years is collapsing. And I use the term utopia in its contemporary philosophical sense here, as the vision of the future on which a civilization bases its projects, establishes its ideal goals and builds its hopes. When a utopia collapses in this way, it indicates that the entire circulation of values which regulates the social dynamic and the meaning of our activities is in crisis. This is the crisis we are faced with today. The industrialist utopia promised us that the development of the forces of production and the expansion of the economic sphere would liberate humanity from scarcity, injustice and misery; that these developments would bestow on humanity the sovereign power to dominate Nature, and with this the sovereign power of self-determination; and that they would turn work into a demiurgic and *auto-poietic* activity in which the incomparably individual fulfilment of each was recognized – as both right and duty – as serving the emancipation of all.

Nothing remains of this utopia. This does not mean that all is lost and that we have no other option but to let events take their course. It means we must find a new utopia, for as long as we are the prisoners of the utopia collapsing around us, we will remain incapable of perceiving the potential for liberation offered by the changes happening now, or of turning them to our advantage by giving meaning to them.

Notes

1. The idea of reflexive rationalization comes from Ulrich Beck, *Risikogesellschaft*, Suhrkamp, Frankfurt-am-Main 1986.
2. Lionel Stoleru, 'Le chômage de prospérité', *Le Monde*, 31 October 1986. My italics.
3. This fact is still frequently contested on the grounds that fixed capital *per job* shows a tendency to increase rapidly in industry and industrialized services, with no concomitant sudden decrease in the number of jobs. The fact is, however, that neither the capital immobilized per job nor the actual number of jobs tell us anything about the way in which the quantity of work absorbed by the economy is evolving: the only significant figure is the total number of hours worked in a year in the economy as a whole or, in other words, the 'volume of work'.

The West German statistics, which (unlike the French) measure this annual volume of work on a regular basis, provide the following data on the subject: the German GNP grew by a factor of 3.02 between 1955 and 1985; the annual volume of work diminished by 27 per cent during the same period. From 1982 to 1986, it diminished by a little over one billion hours, that is to say, by the equivalent of 600,000 full-time jobs. From 1984 to 1986, despite a decrease in the volume of work of 350 million hours, that is to say, the equivalent of more than 200,000 full-time jobs, the number of people in employment rose by 200,000. This increase in the number of active workers was due to a reduction in the collectively agreed working week and an increase in the number of part-time jobs.

This is to say, as I repeat, that the figures relating to the number of people out of work and the number of people gainfully employed do not provide us with the information necessary to measure the evolution of productivity or of the quantity of work utilized by the economy.

4. Edmond Maire, 'Le chómage zéro, c'est possible'. *Alternatives économiques*, 48, June 1987.

5. Hannah Arendt, *The Human Condition*, 5th edn, Chicago and London 1969, p. 5.

PART I

Metamorphoses of Work

1

The Invention of Work

'Work' as we know it, is a modern invention. Work in the form in which
we recognize and perform it, and to which we give a central place in the
life of the individual and of society, was invented, then subsequently
generalized only with the coming of industrialism. 'Work', in the modern
sense, bears no relation to the tasks, repeated day after day, which are
indispensable for the maintenance and reproduction of our individual
lives. Neither should it be confused with the toil, however demanding it
may be, which individuals undertake in order to complete tasks of which
they, or their family, are the sole beneficiaries; nor with what we undertake on our own initiative, without counting the time and effort it takes
us, for a purpose of no importance to anyone other than ourselves and
which no one can do in our place. If we do happen to refer to these
activities as 'work' – 'housework', 'artistic work', 'work of self-
production' – it is in a fundamentally different sense from the work
around which society revolves, and which is both its chief means and its
ultimate goal.

For the essential characteristic of such work – which we 'have', 'seek'
or 'offer' – is that it is an activity in the *public* sphere, demanded,
defined and recognized as useful by other people and, consequently, as
an activity they will pay for. It is by having *paid* work (more particularly,
work for a wage) that we belong to the public sphere, acquire a social
existence and a social identity (that is, a 'profession'), and are part of a
network of relations and exchanges in which we are measured against
other people and are granted certain rights over them in exchange for
the duties we have towards them. It is because work paid and determined socially is by far the most important factor of socialization –
even for those who are seeking it, preparing for it or who lack it – that
industrial society views itself as a 'society of workers' and distinguishes

13

itself, on these grounds, from all earlier forms of society.

This demonstrates that the work on which social cohesion and citizenship are based cannot be reduced to 'work' as an anthropological category or as the need for Man to produce his means of subsistence 'by the sweat of his brow'. Indeed, labour, that is, work carried out in order to ensure survival, was never a factor of social integration. It was rather a criterion for exclusion: in all pre-modern societies, those who performed it were considered inferior. They belonged to the realm of Nature, not the human realm. They were slaves to necessity and therefore incapable of the high-mindedness and disinterestedness which would have rendered them capable of taking charge of the affairs of the city-state. As Hannah Arendt demonstrates at length,[1] in an argument based substantially on the research of Jean-Pierre Vernant, in Ancient Greece the labour necessary to satisfy vital human needs was considered a servile occupation incompatible with citizenship, that is, with participation in public affairs. Labour was considered unworthy of a citizen not because it was reserved for women or slaves; on the contrary, it was reserved for women and slaves precisely because 'to labour meant to be enslaved by necessity'.[2] And only those who, like slaves, had chosen to live rather than be free – thus proving their servile nature – could accept this enslavement. This is why Plato classes peasants with slaves, and why artisans (*banausoi*) insofar as they did not work for the city-state or in the public sphere, were not full citizens: 'their chief interest being their craft and not the market place'.[3] The free man refused to submit to necessity. He controls his body so he will not be a slave to his needs and, if he labours, he does so only in order not to be dependent on what he cannot control, that is, in order to ensure or increase his independence.

The idea that liberty, that is, the human realm, only begins 'beyond the realm of necessity', that Man is only capable of moral conduct when his actions cease to express his pressing bodily needs and dependence on the environment and are solely the result of his sovereign determination, is one which has persisted since the time of Plato. It reappears, in particular, in Marx in the famous passage in *Capital* Volume 3 in which he appears to contradict what he writes elsewhere by locating the 'realm of freedom' beyond economic rationality. Marx observes in this passage that capitalism's 'development of the productive forces' creates 'the embryonic conditions' which will make possible a 'greater reduction of time devoted to material labour'[4] and adds,

> In fact, the realm of freedom actually begins only where labour which is determined by necessity and mundane considerations ceases; thus in the very nature of things it lies beyond the sphere of actual material production. . . . Beyond it begins that development of human energy which is an end in itself, the true realm of freedom . . .[5]

In this passage, Marx does not consider the labour which consists of producing and reproducing the material requirements of life as belonging to the sphere of freedom, any more than Greek philosophy did. There is, however, a fundamental difference between labour in capitalist society and labour in the ancient world: in the former it is performed in the public sphere, whilst in the latter it was confined to the private sphere. Most of the *economy* in the ancient city-state consisted in private activity performed, not in public, in the market place, but within the sphere of the family and household. The organization and hierarchy of the latter was determined by the necessities of subsistence and reproduction. 'Natural community in the household therefore was born of necessity, and necessity ruled over all activities performed in it.'[6] Freedom only commenced outside the private, *economic* household sphere. The sphere of freedom was the public sphere of the *polis*. 'The *polis* was distinguished from the household in that it knew only "equals" whereas the household was the center of the strictest inequality.'[7] It had to 'master . . . the necessities of life'[8] so that the *polis* could be the sphere of freedom, that is, the sphere of disinterested quest for the common good and the 'good life'.

> What all Greek philosophers, no matter how opposed to *polis* life, took for granted was that freedom is exclusively located in the political realm, that necessity is primarily a prepolitical phenomenon, characteristic of the private household organization, and that force and violence are justified in this sphere because they are the only means to master necessity – for instance, by ruling over slaves – and to become free. . . . [Violence] is the prepolitical act of liberating oneself from the necessity of life for the freedom of the world.[9]

Thus the private sphere of the family coincided with the sphere of economic necessity and labour, whilst the public, political sphere, which was the sphere of freedom, rigorously excluded activities which were necessary or useful from the domain of 'human affairs'. All the citizens belonged simultaneously to these carefully separated spheres, passing continually from one to the other, and endeavouring to minimize the burden of the necessities of life, shifting it on to their slaves and their wives on the one hand, and controlling and limiting their needs by adhering to the discipline of a life of frugality on the other. The very notion of the citizen as 'worker' was inconceivable in this context: the worker was doomed to servitude and confined to the household sphere. Far from being a source of 'social identity', 'labour' defined private existence and excluded those who were enslaved by it from the public sphere.

The modern notion of labour only appeared, in fact, with the advent of manufacturing capitalism. Until that point, that is, until the eighteenth century, the term 'labour' (*travail, Arbeit, lavoro*) referred to the toil of serfs and day-labourers who produced consumer goods or services necessary for life which had to be recommenced day after day without ever producing any lasting results. Craftworkers, on the other hand, who created durable objects which could be accumulated and which the people who acquired them more often than not bequeathed to posterity, did not 'labour', they 'produced works' [*œuvraient*], possibly using in their 'work' the 'labour' of unskilled workers whose job it was to do menial tasks. Only day-labourers and unskilled workers were paid for their 'labour'; craftworkers were paid for their 'works' [*œuvre*] according to a price-list fixed by the professional trade unions – the corporations and guilds – which strictly forbade all innovations and forms of competition. In seventeenth-century France, new techniques and machines had to be approved by a council of elders composed of four merchants and four weavers, and then authorized by the judges. The wages earned by day-labourers and apprentices were fixed by the corporation and protected from all attempts to bargain over them.

'Material production', therefore, was not on the whole governed by economic rationality. Nor would it become so with the expansion of merchant capitalism. For example, in textile production, until around 1830 in Great Britain, and around the end of the nineteenth century in the rest of Europe, manufacturing capitalism, and then industrial capitalism, coexisted with cottage industry, the greater part of which was undertaken by individuals working from home. As with the cultivation of the soil for the peasant, weaving was, for the home weaver, not just a means of earning a living: it was a *way of life* governed by traditions which, while they might have been irrational from an economic point of view, were respected by the capitalist merchants. These merchants, participants in a system of life that looked after the respective interests of both parties, did not even contemplate rationalizing the *labour* of the home weavers, putting them in competition with each other or striving to achieve maximum profit in a rational and systematic way. Max Weber's description of the system of domestic production and its ultimate destruction by the manufacturing system is instructive in this regard:

> Until about the middle of the past century the life of a putter-out was, at least in many of the branches of the Continental textile industry, what we should today consider very comfortable. We may imagine its routine somewhat as follows: The peasants came with their cloth, often (in the case of linen) principally or entirely made from raw material which the peasant himself had

produced, to the town in which the putter-out lived, and after a careful, often official, appraisal of the quality, received the customary price for it. The putter-out's customers, for markets any appreciable distance away, were middlemen, who also came to him, generally not yet following samples, but seeking traditional qualities, and bought from his warehouse, or, long before delivery, placed orders which were probably in turn passed on to the peasants. Personal canvassing of customers took place, if at all, only at long intervals. Otherwise correspondence sufficed, though the sending of samples slowly gained ground. The number of business hours was very moderate, perhaps five to six a day, sometimes considerably less; in the rush season, where there was one, more. Earnings were moderate; enough to lead a respectable life and in good times to put away a little. On the whole, relations among competitors were relatively good, with a large degree of agreement on the fundamentals of business. A long daily visit to the tavern, with often plenty to drink, and a congenial circle of friends, made life comfortable and leisurely.

The *form* of organization was in every respect capitalistic; the entrepreneur's activity was of a purely business character; the use of capital, turned over in the business, was indispensable; and finally, the objective aspect of the economic process, the bookkeeping, was rational. But it was traditionalistic business, if one considers the *spirit* which animated the entrepreneur: the traditional manner of life, the traditional rate of profit, the traditional amount of work, the traditional manner of regulating the relationships with labour, and the essentially traditional circle of customers and the manner of attracting new ones. All these dominated the conduct of the business, were at the basis, one may say of the *ethos* of this group of business men.

Now at some time this leisureliness was suddenly destroyed, and often without any essential change in the *form* of organization, such as the transition to a unified factory [*geschlossener Betrieb*], to mechanical weaving, etc. What happened was, on the contrary, often no more than this: some young man from one of the putting-out families went out into the country, carefully chose weavers for his employ, greatly increased the rigour of his supervision of their work, and thus turned them from peasants into labourers. On the other hand, he would begin to change his marketing methods by so far as possible going directly to the final consumer, would take the details into his own hands, would personally solicit customers, visiting them every year, and above all would adapt the quality of the product directly to their needs and wishes. At the same time he began to introduce the principle of low prices and large turnover.

There was repeated what everywhere and always is the result of such a process of rationalization: those who would not follow suit had to go out of business. The idyllic state collapsed under the pressure of a bitter competitive struggle, respectable fortunes were made, and not lent out at interest, but always reinvested in the business. The old leisurely and comfortable attitude toward life gave way to a hard frugality in which some participated and came to the top, because they did not wish to consume but to earn, while others who wished to keep on with the old ways were forced to curtail their consumption.

And, what is most important in this connection, it was not generally in such cases a stream of new money invested in the industry which brought about this revolution – in several cases known to me the whole revolutionary process was set in motion with a few thousands of capital borrowed from relations – but the new *spirit*, the spirit of modern capitalism, had set to work.[10]

All that remained to be done was to construct the factory system on the ruins of the system of domestic production. As we shall see, this was no easy business.

We shall return later to the question of the underlying motivations which led the capitalist merchants to break with tradition and rationalize production with a cold and brutal logic. For the moment, it is enough to point out that these motivations, according to Max Weber, contained an 'irrational element'[11] whose decisive importance tends to be under-estimated. The *interest* for the capitalist merchants in rationalizing weaving, controlling its cost and making it possible to calculate and predict this cost with precision, was by no means a new development. What was new was that at a particular point in time the merchants attempted to impose it on their suppliers, whereas they had previously refrained from doing so. Max Weber puts forward a convincing argument to show that their earlier restraint was not for legal, technical or economic reasons but for ideological and cultural ones: 'one may – this simple proposition, which is often forgotten, should be placed at the beginning of every study which essays to deal with rationalism – rationalize life from fundamentally different basic points of view and in very different directions.'[12] What was new about the 'spirit of capitalism' was the one-dimensional, narrow way in which the capitalist entre-preneur, concerned only with financial factors, pushed economic rationality to its extremes:

> Similarly, it is one of the fundamental characteristics of an individualistic capitalistic economy that it is rationalized on the basis of rigorous calculation, directed with foresight and caution toward the economic success which is sought in sharp contrast to the hand-to-mouth existence of the peasant, and to the privileged traditionalism of the guild craftsman and of the adventurers' capitalism . . . but it at the same time expresses what is, seen from the view-point of personal happiness, so irrational about this sort of life, where a man exists for the sake of his business, instead of the reverse.[13]

In other words, economic rationality was, for a long time, held in check not only by tradition, but also by other types of rationality, other goals and interests which set limits that were not to be exceeded. Industrial capitalism was only able to take off when economic rationality freed itself from all the other principles of rationality and submitted them to its dictatorial control.

Indeed, Marx and Engels say the same thing themselves in the *Communist Manifesto*, although they have a somewhat different approach: according to them, the bourgeoisie had finally torn away the veil which had hitherto masked *the reality* of social relations: 'It has pitilessly torn asunder the motley feudal ties that bound men to his "natural superiors", and has left remaining no other nexus between man and man than naked self-interest . . . for exploitation, veiled by religious and political illusions, it has substituted naked, shameless, direct, brutal exploitation.' It has 'torn away from the family its sentimental veil, and has reduced the family relation to a mere money relation . . . It has been the first to show what man's activity can bring about . . . [During] its rule of scarce one hundred years, [it] has created more massive and more colossal productive forces than have all preceding generations together.' Whereas

> [conservation] of the old modes of production in unaltered form, was . . . the first condition of existence for all earlier industrial classes . . . [The] bourgeoisie cannot exist without constantly revolutionizing the instruments of production, and with them the whole relations of society . . . All fixed, fast-frozen relations, with their train of ancient and venerable prejudices and opinions, are swept away, all new-formed ones become antiquated before they can ossify. All that is solid melts into air, all that is holy is profaned, and man is at last compelled to face with sober senses, his real conditions of life, and his relations with his kind.

In short, they maintained that the one-dimensional reductionism of economic rationality characteristic of capitalism would have potentially emancipatory implications, in that it swept away all values and purposes that were irrational from an economic point of view, leaving nothing but money relations between individuals, nothing but power relations between classes, nothing but an instrumental relation between Man and Nature, thus giving birth to a class of completely dispossessed worker-proletarians, reduced to nothing more than an indefinitely interchange-able labour power and divested of any particular interest: '[The] work of the proletarians . . . has lost all charm for the workman. He becomes an  appendage of the machine, and it is only the most simple, most monotonous, and most easily acquired knack, that is required of him.' These 'privates of the industrial army . . . placed under the command of a perfect hierarchy of officers and sergeants' embody a human race stripped of its humanity, a human race which can only gain access to this humanity by seizing all the forces of production developed by society – the implication being that it will have to revolutionize society completely. According to Marx, the seeds of Universal Man are to be found within abstract labour.

It is, then, according to the Marxian view, this self-same process of rationalization which, on the one hand, engenders a demiurgic, *poietic* relationship between Man and Nature as a result of mechanization and, on the other, bases the 'colossal' power of the forces of production on an organization of labour which strips both work and worker of all their human qualities. The direct agent of the domination by machines of Nature and the *auto-poiesis* of mankind is a proletarian class of individuals who are 'stunted' and 'crippled', stupefied by their labour, oppressed by hierarchy and dominated by the machinery they serve. Herein lies the contradiction which is to become the meaning and motor of history: as a result of capitalist rationalization, work ceases to be an individual activity and a submission to basic necessities; but at the precise point at which it is stripped of its limitations and servility to become *poiesis*, the affirmation of universal strength, it dehumanizes those who perform it. Industrial labour, which is both a triumphant domination over basic necessities and a submission to the instruments of this domination more constricting than Man's earlier subservience to Nature, shows evidence, in the works of Marx as in the great classics of economy, of an ambivalence which we should keep constantly in mind. The apparent contradictions in Marx, as indeed in most of us, are explained by this ambivalence. And it is this ambivalence which misleads Hannah Arendt.[14] We must examine it in greater detail.

The economic rationalization of labour was by far the most difficult task industrial capitalism had to accomplish. In the first volume of *Capital*, Marx refers frequently to the wealth of literature describing the resistance, for a long time insurmountable, which the first industrial capitalists came up against. It was essential for their enterprise to calculate and forecast labour costs accurately, since it was on this condition alone that the volume and price of the merchandise produced and the expected profit could be calculated. Without these forecast figures, the risk involved in making investments was too great. To make the cost of labour calculable, it was necessary to make its output calculable as well. It had to be possible to treat it as a quantifiable material unit; in other words, to be able to measure it in itself, as an independent entity, isolated from the individual characteristics and motivations of the worker. But this also implied that the workers would enter the process of production stripped of their personality and individuality, their personal goals and desires, as simple *labour power*, which was interchangeable and comparable to that of any other workers and which served goals which were not their own and, moreover, meant nothing to them.

The scientific organization of industrial labour consisted in a constant effort to separate labour, as a quantifiable economic category, from the workers themselves. This effort initially took the form of the mechaniz- ation, not of labour, but of the actual workers: that is, it took the form of output targets imposed by the rhythm or rate of work. Indeed, piece- work, which would have been the most economically rational method, proved from the beginning to be impracticable: for workers at the end of the eighteenth century, 'work' meant the application of an intuitive know-how[15] that was an integral part of a time-honoured rhythm of life, and they would not have dreamt of intensifying and prolonging their efforts in order to earn more. The worker 'did not ask: how much can I earn in a day if I do as much work as possible? but: how much must I work in order to earn the wage, $2^{1}/_{2}$ marks, which I earned before and which takes care of my traditional needs?'[16]

The unwillingness of the workers to do a full day's labour, day after day, was the principal reason why the first factories went bankrupt. The bourgeoisie put this reluctance down to 'laziness' and 'indolence'. They saw no other means of overcoming this problem than to pay the workers such meagre wages that it was necessary for the latter to do a good ten hours' toil every day of the week in order to earn enough to survive:

> It is a fact well known . . . that the manufacturer [worker] who can subsist on three days' work will be idle and drunken the remainder of the week . . . The poor . . . will never work any more time in general than is necessary just to live and support their weekly debauches . . . We can fairly aver that a reduction of wages in the woollen manufacture would be a national blessing and advantage, and no real injury to the poor.[17]

In order to cover its need for a stable workforce, nascent industry in the end resorted to child labour as being the most practical solution. For as Ure observed, writing of workers from rural or artisanal backgrounds, 'it is found nearly impossible to convert persons past the age of puberty into useful factory hands'.[18] Ure found that after the factory owner's initial struggle to break their habits of nonchalance or idleness, they either spontaneously left his employ or were dismissed by the overseers for lack of attention to their duties.

The economic rationalization of labour did not, therefore, consist merely in making pre-existent productive activities more methodical and better adapted to their object. It was a revolution, a subversion of the way of life, the values, the social relations and relation to Nature, the *invention* in the full sense of the word of something which had never existed before. Productive activity was cut off from its meaning, its motivations and its object and became simply a *means* of earning a wage. It ceased to be part of life and became the *means* of 'earning a living'. Time for working and time for living became disjointed; labour, its tools, its products acquired a reality distinct from that of the worker and were governed by decisions taken by someone else. The satisfaction of 'producing works' together and the pleasure derived from 'doing' were abolished in favour of only those satisfactions that money could buy. In other words, concrete labour could only be transformed into what Marx called 'abstract labour' by turning the worker/producer into a worker/consumer: that is, the social individual who produces nothing she or he consumes and consumes nothing he or she produces; for whom the essential objective of work is to earn enough to buy commodities produced and defined by the social machine as a whole.

The economic rationalization of work will thus sweep away the ancient idea of freedom and existential autonomy. It produces individuals who, being alienated in their work, will, necessarily, be alienated in their consumption as well and, eventually, in their needs. Since there is no limit to the quantity of money that can be earned and spent, there will no longer be any limit to the needs that money allows them to have or to the need for money itself. These needs increase in line with social wealth. The monetarization of work and needs will eventually abolish the limitations which the various philosophies of life had placed on them.

Notes

1. Hannah Arendt, *The Human Condition*, (HC) 5th edn, Chicago and London 1969, ch. 3.

2. HC, p. 83.

3. HC, p. 81

4. Karl Marx, *Capital* Volume 3, London 1972 p. 819.

5. Marx, p. 820.

6. HC, p. 30.

7. HC, p. 32.

8. HC, pp. 30–1.

9. HC, p. 31.

10. Max Weber, *The Protestant Ethic and the Spirit of Capitalism*, London/Sydney 1985, pp. 66–8.

11. Weber, p. 78.

12. Weber, pp. 77–8.

13. Weber, pp. 76, 70.

14. Hannah Arendt (*The Human Condition*) argues that Marx reduces work to *labour* while at the same time continuing to view it in some places as 'making works' and, at others, to forecast its abolition.

15. This is not to say it did not demand an apprenticeship but that this apprenticeship did not demand a formalized standard knowledge.

16. Weber, p. 60.

17. J. Smith, 'Memoirs of Wool', quoted by Stephen Marglin in André Gorz, ed., *The Division of Labour*, Hassocks 1976, p. 34.

18. Andrew Ure, *Philosophy of Manufacturers*, London 1835, p. 16, quoted by Marx, *Capital* Volume 1, Harmondsworth 1976, p. 549.

2

The Utopia of Work in Marx

These developments had been anticipated by Marx as early as the *1844 Manuscripts* in which the 'worker' (*Arbeiter*: which we ought to translate as 'labourer', if usage did not dictate otherwise) – and work too – are presented as 'products of capital':[1] work being 'work in general', any sort of work, irrespective of its determinations which, from the worker's point of view, are always 'accidental' and alien. This latter therefore no longer has any determinate, 'natural' place in society, nor, as a consequence, any particular interest. Her or his work reflects '*universal* dependence, that natural form of the universal collaboration of individuals', and it is, according to Marx, the abstraction of this work and the individuals that it defines which contains the germ of their universality. The division of labour into an infinite number of inter-changeable tasks of an indifferent, 'accidental' character, which is now seen as social (and no longer natural), suppresses the 'limited relationship of men to Nature' and their 'limited relationship to one another' and, as 'the universal development of the productive forces', engenders a '*universal* intercourse between men', 'which itself implies the actual empirical existence of men in their *world-historical*, instead of local, being'.[2]

Certainly, from the *1844 Manuscripts* onwards, Marx observed, following J-B. Say, that 'The division of labour is a *convenient* and *useful* method, an intelligent use of human forces for increasing social wealth, but it diminishes *the capacity of each man* taken individually'.[3] He pushes this point to even more radical conclusions in *The German Ideology*:

> Never, in any earlier period, have the productive forces taken on a form so indifferent to the intercourse of individuals *as* individuals, because their inter-

course itself was formerly a restricted one. On the other hand, standing over against these productive forces, we have the majority of the individuals from whom these forces have been wrested away, and who, robbed thus of all life-content, have become abstract individuals . . .

The only connection which still links them with the productive forces and with their own existence – *labour* – *has lost all semblance of self-activity* and only sustains their life by stunting it.[4]

Even more scathing characterizations of the nature of industrial labour and its debilitating character are found in the *Grundrisse* and, subsequently, in *Capital.* But for Marx this dehumanizing, debilitating, idiotic, exhausting labour nevertheless represents a form of objective progress to the extent that it substitutes 'general workers' – the proletarians – for private producers – artisans – thus giving birth to a class for whom *work* is directly *social* labour determined in its contents by the functioning of society *as a whole* and which, consequently, has a vital, overriding interest in taking over the social process of production in its totality.

In order better to understand how Marx, after 1846, conceives the proletariat as a potentially universal class, divested of any particular interest and therefore in a position to appropriate for itself and rationalize the social process of production, we should look first of all at a much more explicit passage which he devotes in the *Grundrisse* to market production as a *private* activity.[5] He insists at length in this passage on the fact that the product an individual manufactures for the market only acquires its exchange value, and therefore is only of advantage to its producer, on condition that it finds a place in the *social* process of production, within which it alone becomes exchangeable. Now, adds Marx, if it becomes exchangeable, it does so because it is a particular concretization, of use to others, of a *general labour* contributing to social production as a whole. The work of production is socially divided into a multiplicity of complementary instances of production for the market, each dependent upon the other, each determined in its nature and its content by the functioning of society as a whole (*'gesellschaftlichen Zusammenhang'*). But this division of labour, this coherence of complementarities 'remains an external and, as it seems, accidental thing' to the individuals who confront each other on the market.

> The social interrelation [*Zusammenhang*], which results from the encounter [*Zusammenstoss*] of independent individuals and appears to them as both a material necessity and an external bond, represents precisely *their independence, for which social existence is indeed a necessity, but only as a means, and therefore appears to individuals as something external.*[6]

The situation is quite different for the proletarians who, being directly tied to collective labour in general have a direct interest in uniting together as a collective worker and, by their union, in subordinating the social process of production to their common control, by substituting voluntary collaboration for socially divided work. The proletarianization of the producers therefore promises to be merely one facet of a grandiose and potentially emancipatory enterprise of rational unification of the social process.

There is no question, therefore, of going back to the past, of seeking, by '[setting] factories ablaze, . . . to restore by force the vanished status of the workman of the Middle Ages.'[7] Quite the reverse. The point is to see how individuals, at last freed from their 'limited relations' and now directly geared in to the 'universal intercourse between men' may – no longer being anything determinate – 'become all', may become the universal subjects of a total activity because they are no longer engaged in an individual private activity of any kind.

The philosophical context and reasoning which led Marx to this dialectical overturning are presently of little relevance to us. All that matters here is its utopian content, because it is this utopian vision which has penetrated the labour movement and which still today provides the energy behind the ideology of work shared by the various strains of the classical Left. We must, therefore, first of all, understand the contents to which the Marxian utopia owes its lasting attraction and then examine to what extent these contents still exist today and still have their original meaning.

When, in 1845–46, he formulated it for the first time in *The German Ideology*, Marx clearly had difficulty in giving his utopian conception, communism, a compelling rational coherence. Unlike the utopians whose visions of a future society express ideals deriving from ethical exigencies, Marx is seeking to show that there is no need for communism to pre-exist in the consciousness of the proletariat for it to be realized; it is 'the movement of the real' itself. Marx does not as yet base the necessity of its advent on the internal contradictions of capitalism's development, as he was to do after 1856; he bases it on the fact that, for the proletariat, the revolution is – or will become – essential for their survival. The 'absolute inexorable necessity' in which they find themselves, of having to destroy the old society merely 'to ensure their continuing existence', serves in a sense as a transcendental guarantee of their ultimate victory. This conception of the necessity of the communist revolution corresponds, all in all, to a period in which the labouring masses, reduced to the most extreme poverty, were rising up in the cause of the right to life.

Within these labouring masses, there remained however a high proportion of ruined artisans and homeworkers who still kept alive the memory of a craft system based on the freedom and dignity of work. The communist utopia had therefore to guarantee the workers 'not only their material existence', but also the autonomy and dignity which capitalist rationalization had removed from work. Autonomy and dignity of work must not however be *restored* in the name of an individual and subjective ethical exigency opposed to economic rationality. It must, on the contrary, be shown that capitalist rationality is simply a limited rationality which inevitably produces overall effects which are contrary to its objectives and which it is incapable of controlling. True rationality consists in transforming work into a 'personal activity' but at a higher level at which 'the voluntary union' of individuals will put 'voluntary collaboration' in the place of capitalist division of labour and will subordinate the social process of production to the control of the associated producers. Each individual will 'as an individual' be master of the totality of the productive forces by means of voluntary collaboration. His 'work' will become his 'self-activity' (*Selbsttätigkeit*) as a 'total individual'.

The contradiction which so troubled Hannah Arendt no longer exists therefore: 'work' (*Arbeit*) in the sense that it was defined in the previous chapter will be eliminated (*beseitigt*) by rational social collaboration between individuals; in its place, we shall see the triumph of a collective *poiesis* which is no longer the labour of serialized and specialized individuals but the self-activity of individuals collaborating consciously and methodically. We here encounter once again the utopia of worker self-management and of workers' control; the unity of work and life; working activity as the total all-round development of the individual, a utopia which has remained alive right up to our own day.

It remains, however, for us to examine the rationalization of social collaboration envisaged by Marx from the point of view both of its possibility and of the rationality of the political and existential postulates on which it rests.[8]

Its principal utopian content is that within it the proletariat is destined to realize the unity of the real as the unity of Reason: individuals divested of any individual interest as they are divested of any individual trade, are to unite universally in order to make their collaboration rational and voluntary and to produce together, in a single common praxis, a world which is totally theirs: nothing shall exist there independently of them. This triumph of the unity of Reason obviously presupposes the reunification of the existential and social dimensions which modernization has differentiated to the point of making them autonomous (which does not mean independent) one from another. For to render impossible everything which exists independently of individuals means also abolition of the state as an apparatus of law and administration standing outside the control of individuals; abolition of political economy with its own laws that impose themselves upon social actors; abolishing the social division and specialization of labour which to the extent that these 'subject individuals' to a 'limited instrument' make of them 'limited individuals', each locked into a limited function, and therefore incapable of perceiving and controlling social production as a whole through universal and voluntary collaboration. The generalized self-management of material production is thus supposed to make redundant not only the separate apparatus of management, administration and co-ordination, but also the political sphere itself. The universal voluntary collaboration of 'the united individuals' is supposed to be direct and transparent; it neither requires nor tolerates any mediation, for each individual 'as total individual' assumes the whole totality of social production as her or his personal task. This task allows each to accede to the dignity of universal subject and total personal development through the development of all his or her faculties.

The two basic presuppositions of this utopia are:

1. *On the political level,* that the physical rigidities and constraints of the social machine can be eliminated. All juridical regulation and codification of individual conduct can be abolished; the whole of individual actions and interactions can recover a lived intelligibility and meaning and therefore become based upon the individuals' own motivation to understand one another and collaborate rationally. It is this presupposition – the elimination, in Habermas's terminology, of the 'systemic constraints of the autonomized economic process' and its 'reintegration into the lifeworld'[9] – which Marx will ultimately have expressly rejected in the passage from *Capital* Volume 3 cited above. We shall return to this later.

2. *On the existential level,* that personal self-activity and social labour may coincide to such a degree that they become one and the same. Each individual must be able, by and in her or his work, to identify personally with the undivided totality of all (with the collective productive worker) and find his or her total personal fulfilment in that identification. All in all, a thoroughgoing socialization (in the sense of *Vergesellschaftung,* not *Sozialisierung*) of personal existence must correspond to the complete personalization of social existence, the whole of society possessing in each member its conscious subject and each member recognizing in it her or his unification with all the others.

The Marxian utopia – communism – therefore presents itself as the achieved form of rationalization: total triumph of Reason and triumph of total Reason; scientific domination of Nature and reflexive scientific mastery of the process of that domination. Not only will the collective end-product of social collaboration, which was previously 'left to chance' because this collaboration was not voluntary, be 'subordinated to the power of united individuals'; their union in 'voluntary collaboration' will itself be based upon the rational will of each and will ensure that the will of each coincides with the will of all, and that the individual worker is one with the collective worker.

This triumph of Reason very clearly presupposes the total rationalization of individual existence: the unity of Reason and life. And this total rationalization demands, for its part, an individual asceticism which, in certain respects, recalls Puritan asceticism: it is as universal individual, stripped of all individual interests, attachments and tastes, that each will accede to the true unity of the meaning of life and of history.

> . . .the sharp condemnation of idolatry of the flesh and of all dependence on *personal* relations to other men was bound unperceived to direct this energy into the field of objective (impersonal) activity. The Christian . . . acted in the service of God's ends, and these could only be impersonal. Every purely emotional, that is not rationally motivated, personal relation of man to man easily fell in the Puritan, as in every ascetic ethic, under the suspicion of idolatry of the flesh. In addition to what has already been said, this is clearly enough shown for the case of friendship by the following warning: 'It is an irrational act and not fit for a rational creature to love any one farther than *reason* will allow us . . . It very often taketh up men's minds so as to *hinder* their love of God. (Baxter, *Christian Directory*, IV, p. 253.)

One only has to replace 'Christian' by 'Communist', 'idolatry of the flesh' by 'petty-bourgeois individualism' and 'God's ends' by 'the meaning of history' in this passage quoted by Max Weber[10] to arrive at an accurate characterization of communist morality as it developed historically in Stalinism, Maoism and even Castroism. This resemblance between Puritan ethics and communist morality is mainly attributable to the fact that both the adaptation of life to the order of the world desired by God (Puritanism) and the tailoring of the conduct of each to the transpersonal goals of collective efficiency and history demand total rationalization of human conduct. Yet observations of this type explain nothing. We shall, rather, have to ask ourselves what deep motivations underlie the attraction which pan-rationalist asceticism has persistently exercised in its religious, political and – now, in its latest incarnation – technocratic forms. And we shall have to try and understand why the ideal of modernity, as expressed in its most complete form in the

Marxian utopic vision of a coincidence of social labour and personal activity, has produced disastrous results wherever efforts have been made to implement it on a macro-social scale.

Notes

1. 'The worker produces capital, capital produces him – hence he produces himself, and man as *worker*, as a *commodity*, is the product of this entire cycle. To the man who is nothing more than a *worker* – and to him as a worker – his human qualities only exist in so far as they exist for capital *alien* to him. Because man and capital are foreign to each other, however, and thus stand in an indifferent, external and accidental relationship to each other . . . As soon, therefore, as it occurs to capital (whether from necessity or caprice) no longer to be for the worker, he himself is no longer for himself: he has *no* work, hence *no* wages . . .' Karl Marx, *Economic and Philosophic Manuscripts of 1844*, ed. D.J. Struik, trans. M. Mulligan, London 1970, p. 120. [Marx's emphasis.]

2. Karl Marx and Frederick Engels, *The German Ideology*, trans. W. Lough, in Marx and Engels, *Collected Works*, vol. 5, 1845–1847, London 1976, pp. 86–7.

3. Marx's emphasis.

4. My emphasis.

5. *Grundrisse*, German edn, Berlin 1953, p. 909. [Our translation G.H./C.T.]

6. The same analysis can be found in Émile Durkheim, *De la division du travail social*, Paris 1930, pp. 242 and ff.

7. Marx and Engels, *The Communist Manifesto*, Harmondsworth 1967.

8. The main passage in *The German Ideology* devoted to the question of 'necessary' collective appropriation and voluntary collaboration comes at the end of a section in which Marx demonstrates that the productive forces (which include labour itself) 'appear as a world for themselves, quite independent of and divorced from the individuals . . .' who, as a result of being split off from one another, have no purchase upon those forces, even though they have created them. 'Thus things have now come to such a pass', continues Marx,

that the individuals must appropriate the existing totality of productive forces, not only to achieve self-activity, but, also, merely to safeguard their very existence . . . The appropriation of these forces is itself nothing more than the development of the individual capacities corresponding to the material instruments of production. *The appropriation of a totality of instruments is, for this very reason, the development of a totality of capacities in the individuals themselves . . .*

All earlier revolutionary appropriations were restricted; individuals whose self-activity was restricted by a crude instrument of production and a limited intercourse, appropriated this crude instrument of production, and hence merely achieved a new state of limitation . . . they themselves remained subordinate to the division of labour and their own instrument of production . . . *in the appropriation by the proletarians, a mass of instruments of production must be made subject to each individual, and property to all.*

It is precisely because they are 'shut off from all self-activity' that 'the proletarians of the present day . . . are in a position to achieve a complete and no longer restricted self-activity, which consists in the appropriation of a totality of productive forces', an appropriation which demands a 'universal union'.

Only at this stage *does self-activity coincide with material life, which corresponds to the development of individuals into complete individuals* and the casting-off of all natural limitations. *The transformation of labour into self-activity corresponds to the transfor-*

mation of the earlier limited intercourse into the intercourse of individuals as such. (*The German Ideology*, pp. 92–3, my emphasis).

See also *Grundrisse*, German edn, p. 505.

9. Jürgen Habermas, *Theorie des Kommunikativen Handels*, vol. 2, Frankfurt/Main, 1981, p. 500. Subsequent extracts are taken from the English version, entitled *Theory of Communicative Action*, Cambridge 1987.

10. Max Weber, *The Protestant Ethic and the Spirit of Capitalism*, London/Sydney 1985, p. 224.

3

Functional Integration or the Divorce between Working and Living

In order to exist and to keep going, an industrial enterprise needs more than machines, raw materials and labour; it also needs to be able to calculate its costs in advance, anticipate the demand for its goods and programme its production, investments and amortization. In other words, it needs to render calculable the factors on which the economic rationality of its management depends. And these factors are not exclusively internal to its functioning. There are also external factors, that is, factors determined by the enterprise's political, legal, administrative and cultural environment. The greater the amount of capital immobilized, the greater the length of time required for it to produce a profit and the more important it becomes for the enterprise that the conduct, not only of its employees but also of the government, the administrative bodies and the courts, be predictable and reliable. '. . . modern capitalist enterprise . . . presupposes a legal and administrative system whose functioning can be rationally predicted . . . just like the expected performance of a machine.'[1] The conduct of the enterprise can only conform to economic rationality if all spheres of society and even the life of the individual are conducted in a rational, predictable and calculable way.

Hence the importance Max Weber and his descendants, even distant ones like Habermas, attribute to capitalism's rootedness in culture: the rationalization of spheres of activity leading to their differentiation; this demanding in its turn a rationalization of the politico-juridicial sphere incompatible with the arbitrary exercise of power of an absolutist state; and ultimately resulting in the differentiation and complexification of the economic, administrative, scientific and artistic spheres and in their relative autonomy.

As the economy, administrative bodies, the state and science become differentiated and give rise to complex apparatuses, their development and functioning demand an increasingly complex division of skills and competences, an increasingly differentiated *organization* of increasingly specialized *functions*. The overall working of these apparatuses is beyond the comprehension of the individuals within them and even of the individuals (ministers, managing directors, departmental heads and so on) who (formally) bear institutional responsibility for them.

As it becomes more complex, the organization of specialized functions, for the purpose of accomplishing a task which exceeds the comprehension of any individual, is increasingly unable to rely on the agents' own motivations for accomplishing this task. Their favourable disposition, personal capacities and goodwill are not enough. Their reliability will only be ensured by the formal *codification* and *regulation* of their conduct, their duties and their relationships. I term *functional* any conduct which is rationally programmed to attain results beyond the agents' comprehension, irrespective of their intentions. *Functionality* is a type of rationality which comes from the *outside* to the conduct determined and specified for the agent by the organization in which she or he is subsumed.[2] This conduct is the *function* which the agent has to perform unquestioningly. The more it grows, the more the organization tends to function like a machine.

Once the process has been set in motion, it develops its own dynamic: each step in the differentiation of competences produces an increase in bureaucratization which permits an increase in the differentiation of competences and so on. The economic and administrative apparatuses become differentiated, more complex and bureaucratized in synergy. The result of this, for individuals in their work, is that their *field* of responsibility and scope for initiative (but not necessarily their responsibility and initiative as such) are narrowed and, what is more, the coherence and goals of the organization – within which they are more or less consenting cogs – become less and less intelligible.

I term *sphere of heteronomy* the totality of specialized activities which individuals have to accomplish as functions co-ordinated from outside by a pre-established organization.[3] Within this sphere of heteronomy, the nature and content of tasks, as well as their relations to each other, are hetero-determined in such a way as to make individuals and organizations – which are themselves complex – function like the cogs of a huge machine (be it industrial, bureaucratic or military); or, which amounts to the same thing, to make them accomplish in isolation from each other specialized tasks demanded by a machine which, because of its dimensions and the number of attendants needed, deprives the workers of any possibility of co-ordinating their activities through procedures of self-regulated co-operation (through workers' self-management). This is the case, for example, not only in postal, rail and air networks and in power generation, but also in all industries which make use of a large number of specialized plants, often situated very far apart, to supply the components for a single final product.

The kind of collaboration and integration found in the sphere of heteronomy differs radically from the co-operation and integration found between members of a work group or work community. Undoubtedly, hetero-determined collaboration, such as the kind organized by Taylorism or 'scientific work organization' still involves, necessarily, a minimum of self-regulated co-operation, a minimum of agreement and cohesion between the members of the small teams of people engaged in the same task and, therefore, a minimum of social integration. Yet nevertheless, this collaboration is itself functionally integrated as a cog in a more complex machinery.

There is an obvious relationship between what I term sphere of heteronomy and functional integration and what Habermas calls 'system' and 'systemic integration' on the one hand, as opposed to 'lifeworld' and 'social integration'[4] on the other. The latter 'is integrated through consensus, whether normatively guaranteed or communicatively achieved.'[5] 'Systemic integration', on the other hand, 'is integrated through the non-normative steering of individual decisions not subjectively co-ordinated.'[6] Habermas insists forcefully, on several occasions, on the fact that society has to be viewed as pertaining to both the 'system' and the 'lifeworld', that is, as being socially *and* functionally integrated, without ever being *entirely* either the one or the other: it could only coincide with the 'lifeworld' if all the systemic interrelations between individuals' relations with each other could become an integral part of their intuitive knowledge – in other words, be self-regulated by them with the purpose of pursuing a common aim and, therefore, abolished precisely as heteronomous ('systemic') imperatives. Conversely, society could only coincide with the 'system' if it were able to function like a mechanism determining for all its components a way of functioning that is strictly hetero-regulated from outside.

To put it another way, self-regulated ('social') integration refers to the ability of individuals to self-organize by co-ordinating their conduct with a view to obtaining a result by their collective action. This is what Sartre describes as a 'group' (not only a 'fused group' but also a group in the process of differentiating into 'specialized sub-groups' co-ordinated by a 'regulatory third party' who has been appointed for the purpose).[7] Hetero-regulated integration, by contrast, in which 'goal-directed actions are co-ordinated not only through processes of reaching understanding, but also through functional interconnections that are not intended by them and are usually not even perceived within the horizon of everyday practice',[8] refers to what Sartre describes as the external totalization of the actions of serialized individuals.

There are, however, two types of hetero-regulation or totalization which are conflated in Habermas's system: first, one which derives from a totalization (which no one wanted, anticipated or planned) of serialized actions by the material field in which they inscribe themselves; and secondly, one which involves organized programming, an organization chart drawn up for the purpose of getting individuals, who are neither able to communicate nor to arrive at a mutual agreement, to realize a collective result, which they neither intend nor are, in many cases, even aware of.

The former type of hetero-regulation corresponds more particularly to regulation by the *market*. There is a tendency to consider this kind of hetero-regulation as self-regulation. In fact, it is a pure 'systemic mechanism' (Habermas) which imposes its laws from without on individuals who are then ruled by them and are forced to adapt and to modify their conduct and projects according to an external, statistical and totally involuntary balance of forces. The market *for them* is, then, an a-centred, *spontaneous hetero-regulation.*[9] It can only be regarded as a form of self-regulation if the social whole is viewed from the outside as a *purely material system* whose constituent parts, like the molecules of an inert gas or liquid, are only externally related to each other and, since they lack the capacity to pursue any goal, are individually of no interest.

The spontaneous hetero-regulation of serialized actions – notably by the market – has no *meaning* to individuals pursuing their own individual goals, independently of – and oblivious of – each other. In their external resultant, these actions have a certain coherence but that coherence is a product of chance: like thermodynamics, it is of the order of statistical laws and thus has neither meaning nor ultimate goal. Spontaneous hetero-regulation does not, properly speaking, produce the *integration* of individuals: what it integrates, as Sartre has shown very well, is the external materiality of actions insofar as it is beyond the grasp of the action and, far from corresponding to individuals' *own intentions*, it designates these individuals as *others*. These alienated actions are not functional to anything. One could only speak of functionality if their resultant were someone's goal. Now, the movements of prices which the buyers and sellers, each pursuing their own interests, bring about within a perfect market, do not, by definition, respond to the intention of any one of them and their behaviour is not therefore functional in relation to anything (except, in certain cases, in relation to the goals of someone secretly manipulating them by spreading false information and thereby distorting the market). Similarly, the market itself is not the goal of any of the actors who confront one another there; it is the space that results from their confrontation, just as 'traffic' is the external resultant of all those who are driving their cars at any particular moment and have – each of them as an 'other' – an average speed imposed upon them by all the other drivers, none of whom has actually chosen it.

If we say, however, that the market is also an *institution* whose operation demands the respecting of certain rules, just as traffic can only flow well if the conduct of each driver is regulated by a 'highway code', speed limits, a signalling system and so on, then we leave the ground of *spontaneous* hetero-regulation and come on to that of *programmed* control or hetero-regulation.

In practice, every modern society is a complex system in which sub-systems of 'communicational' self-organization, spontaneous hetero-regulation and programmed hetero-regulation interact. In the process of giving birth to gigantic technical installations and tentacular organiz-ations, economic rationality has conferred increasing importance upon sub-systems functioning by programmed hetero-regulation: that is to say, upon administrative and industrial machineries in which individuals are induced to *function* in a complementary manner, like the parts of a machine, towards ends that are often unknown to them and *different from those offered to them as personal goals.* These ends, which are to *motivate* individuals to work towards alien goals, constitute one of the two types of regulatory instruments [*Steuerungsmedien*] which, though conflated in Habermas's work, have to be differentiated: the most important of the first type being the money, security, prestige and/or power attached to the various functions, in terms of a carefully worked out hierarchical graduation. Alongside these *incentive regulators*, *prescriptive regulators* force individuals, on pain of certain penalties, to adopt functional forms of conduct – most often laid down and formal-ized as proper procedure – which are demanded by the organization. Only incentive regulators ensure functional *integration*, by inducing individuals to lend themselves of their free will, to the instrumental-ization of their predetermined activity.

The expansion of the larger apparatuses functioning by programmed hetero-regulation will produce an increasingly deep division within the social system. On the one hand, the mass of the population, doing increasingly specialized and predetermined work, are motivated by incentive goals that have no coherence whatever with the ultimate objec-tives of the organizations into which they are functionally integrated. On the other hand, a small elite of organizers attempt to ensure the co-ordination, the operating conditions and the overall regulation of organ-izations, determine the final objectives and structures (the organigramme) of the corresponding administrations, and define the most functional regulatory mechanisms – both incentive and prescriptive. There is therefore a split between an increasingly functionalized and manipulated society and a public and private administration that is increasingly invasive; there is a rift between an ever-smaller self-regulated civil sphere and a state equipped with increasingly extensive powers of hetero-regulation as required both by the operation of the great industrial machines and the administrative and public service machines which belong to the state itself.

To this split between the auto-regulated sphere of civil society and the hetero-regulated sphere of the industrial–state megamachine, there correspond two different rationalities: the rationality of individuals pursuing ends which, even if they motivate functional patterns of conduct, are irrational in regard to the ultimate objectives of the organizations in which they work; and the rationality of these organizations which have no meaningful relation with the goals motivating the individuals involved.

This splitting of the social system and this divorce between different rationalities produces a split within the lives of individuals themselves: their professional and private lives are dominated by norms and values that are radically different from one another, if not indeed contradictory. Within large organizations, professional success requires a will to succeed according to the purely technical efficiency criteria of the functions one occupies, irrespective of content. It demands a spirit of competition and opportunism, combined with subservience towards superiors. This will be recompensed – and *compensated* – in the private sphere by a comfortable, opulent, hedonistic lifestyle. In other words, professional success becomes the *means* of achieving private comfort and pleasures that have no relation with the qualities demanded by professional life. These qualities are not connected with personal virtue, and private life is sheltered from the imperatives of professional life.

Thus it is that the private virtues of being a good father and husband, or being liked by one's neighbours, can be combined with the professional efficiency of the civil servant who moves without difficulty from serving a republic to working for a totalitarian state, or vice versa; or that the mild-mannered collector of *objets d'art* and protector of birds can work in the manufacture of pesticides or chemical weapons, and in a general way, that the high-ranking or middle manager, after putting in a day's work serving the economic values of competitiveness, productivity and technical efficiency, wants nothing more, when his work is finished, than to go home to a little haven where economic values are displaced by the love of children, animals and the countryside, or doing little jobs about the house. We shall return to this later.

Long before the creators of contemporary scientific dystopias, Max Weber thought that bureaucratization and the onward march of machines would progress to the point where society would become a single megamachine which its human cogs 'would be forced to serve, as powerless as the fellah of Ancient Egypt. This might happen *if* a technically superior administration *were to be the ultimate and sole value* in the ordering of their affairs, and that means: a rational bureaucratic administration with the corresponding welfare benefits.' He was to equate the 'mind objectified' (*geronnener Geist*) of 'inanimate machines' with that of 'the animated machine, the bureaucratic organization, with its specialization of trained skills, its division of jurisdiction, its rules and hierarchical relations of authority.'[10] He also compared the industrial–bureaucratic machine to a 'shell of bondage' (*Gehäuse der Hörigkeit*) protecting us against insecurity and anguish, but at the cost of deprivation of meaning and freedom and a general 'dehumanization' of

> that colossal universe that is the modern economic order, founded upon the technical and economic bases of a machinist–mechanical production which, through its oppressive constraints determines now, and will continue to determine, the lifestyle of all individuals – and *not* just economically active individuals – precipitated since birth into the cogs of this machine, until the last hundredweight of fossil fuel has been used up.

'Material goods' have acquired over men

> an increasing and finally an inexorable power . . . as at no previous period in history . . . No one knows who will live in this cage in the future, or whether at the end of this tremendous development entirely new prophets will rise, or there will be a great rebirth of old ideas and ideals, or, if neither, mechanized petrification, embellished with a sort of convulsive self-importance. For of the last stage of this cultural development, it might well be truly said: 'Specialists without spirit, sensualists without heart; this nullity imagines that it has attained a level of civilization never before achieved.'[11]

In fact, history was both to confirm and invalidate Max Weber's prophecy: the weight of bureaucracy has indeed increased, programmed hetero-regulation has become more and more dehumanizing, and the 'shell of bondage' has become at the same time increasingly constraining and increasingly comfortable. But, for precisely that reason, the system has reached a crisis point: the operation of the bureaucratic–industrial megamachine and the need to motivate its 'fellahs' to function as cogs, have confronted it with problems of regulation that are increasingly difficult to solve. No rationality and no totalizing view or vision have been able to provide it with an overall meaning, cohesion and directing goal.

Notes

1. Max Weber, *Economy and Society: An Outline of Interpretive Sociology*, eds Guenther Roth and Claus Wittich, New York 1968, vol. 3, p. 1394.

2. Cf. André Gorz, *Farewell to the Working Class*, London 1982, ch. 5.

3. Cf. André Gorz, *Farewell to the Working Class*, chs 8 and 9.

4. Jürgen Habermas, *Theory of Communicative Action*, Cambridge 1987, vol. 2, p. 117.

5. Habermas, p. 150.

6. Habermas, p. 150.

7. Jean-Paul Sartre, *Critique of Dialectical Reason: 1 Theory of Practical Ensembles*, ed. Jonathan Rée, trans. Alan Sheridan-Smith, London 1976, p. 379.

8. Habermas, p. 150.

9. This notion is borrowed from Edgar Morin, *La Vie de la vie*, Paris 1980.

10. Max Weber, *Economy and Society*, vol. 3, p. 1402 (translation modified).

11. Max Weber, *The Protestant Ethic and the Spirit of Capitalism*, London/Sydney 1985, pp. 181–2.

4

From Functional Integration to Social Disintegration (And from Compensatory Consumption to the All-Embracing State)

For a long time, the revolutionary workers' movement and the socialist regimes believed they could avoid or reverse these developments. The 'collective appropriation of the means of production' would reconcile the workers with their function – and not just with their work – and prompt them *to assume that function willingly,* fully aware of its importance. Collective appropriation would cause individual goals and collective aims to coincide, the interests of each to equate with the interests of all. The collective task would become sufficiently motivating for the individual, on account of the hopes and the promise it held out for society as a whole, for personal incentive regulators – 'material incentives' or individual rewards – to become as superfluous as prescriptive regulators.

Individuals would develop a 'socialist consciousness' and with it the conviction that private and public interest were one and the same and that, by devoting themselves entirely to the task they were assigned, each would ultimately be working for her- or himself and would derive both personal fulfilment from their work and a feeling of oneness with society and the movement of history. In short, 'socialist consciousness', constituted the set of moral and intellectual qualities, by virtue of which each individual would *experience* and *desire* functional integration as a form of social integration.

In fact, the merging of functional and social integration has constantly been postulated, but it has never proved possible to achieve. For it presupposed that the definition of collective aims and the distribution and division of tasks which enabled these aims to be achieved, would be formulated first on the basis of collective decisions and agreement and, subsequently, of the self-organization of specialized sub-groups, so that each person would come to feel that they belonged both to a work community and to the society which unified all these sub-groups in a common project. This project was to find its concrete expression in the Plan. The Plan would consist of the rationally formulated set of objectives which would grant society, in each of its individual members, mastery both of Nature and of the social enterprise that was developing that mastery. The Plan would in some way be society's reflexive consciousness of itself as a collective enterprise based on voluntary collaboration.

But the dimensions, the complexity and the rigidity not just of the apparatus of production as a whole but also of the economic units (firms, trusts, combines) of which it was composed, prevented any one individual gaining lived experience of the collaboration that could exist between the thousands of teams, sub-groups and groups specialized in tasks which were themselves subdivided. They could, at best, have an abstract knowledge of such collaboration (based on statistics, inter-industrial exchanges, physical productivity figures, and so on) but they could never gain lived experience of it from the actual collaboration they were each involved in, through their work, within their teams, workshops and so on.

Various attempts to make the individual worker internalize the objectives of the Plan changed nothing. The most developed of these attempts (most notably the 'Nazarova method') split up the Five-Year Plan adopted by (or prescribed for) each enterprise into as many partial-year plans as there were work stations. These annual plans were themselves then split up into weekly plans, and the daily work norms of these were pinned up in each station. But each of the individual operators, working for example in a chemical complex employing thirty thousand people, was appointed to perform only one of thousands of operations relating to thousands of products and, being often the only person at her or his station, was prevented by the compartmentalized and often routine nature of his or her job from having an overview or any concrete experience of the purpose of the task in which she or he was supposed voluntarily to have collaborated. This task could not, *a fortiori*, be the subject of collective decision-making and collective self-organization.

Society's self-awareness, in the form of the Plan, thus remained a *separated external consciousness*, embodied in a specialized sub-group (itself subdivided): the authorities of the Party or, which amounts to the same thing, the State. And socialist ethics, which presented the realization of the Plan as a moral imperative, demanded of 'conscious' workers nothing less than that they should desire the functional integration demanded of them, *as* their social integration and personal fulfilment. In short, they had *to desire to be the active instruments* by means of which a transcendent will (that of the Plan and the Party) would achieve transcendent aims (those of socialism, history and the revolution); it was through their devotion to the Party, their *faith* in the revolution and in socialism that the specialized, abstract, obscure tasks assigned to them by the Party would acquire a meaning. Faith and revolutionary enthusiasm would compensate for the fact that lived experience could not provide them with any understanding or awareness of the Plan's objectives.

Socialist morality thus exhibited a striking similarity to the 'professional ethic' (*Berufsethik*) described by Max Weber. For the Puritan too could not experience his divine election by means of a methodical devotion to the practice of his profession: on no account would he be 'saved by his works'. Only his hope that the Lord would show him he had been chosen to ensure the reign of His order in the world by crowning him with success, could give meaning to his desperately hard toil. The meaning of his methodical striving after success was not, therefore, to be found in the actual practice of his profession. Rather, this practice had a transcendent significance, which was not accessible to consciousness. What motivated Puritanical ascesis was the faith that God desired this rational ordering of the world and saw in it His glorification. Similarly, what motivated the socialist 'Hero of Labour' was the faith that the labour required by the Plan was – with the Party playing a mediating role – an instrument used by History to bring about the triumph of universal Reason.

For its methodical implementation socialist pan-rationalism (the Plan) thus had to draw on an irrational motivation on the part of the individual: faith in the Reason of which the Party was both incarnation and instrument. And as soon as faith became the indispensable vehicle of the reign of Reason, it was not surprising that that faith should be offered (and itself seek to invest itself in) a charismatic, omniscient guide, or that the quasi-religious cult of that guide should go hand in hand with other irrational and anti-modern types of motivation such as chauvinism and anti-Semitism. As it had not been possible to bring about social integration through the rational identification of workers with their work, the exaltation of traditional, nationalistic values was called upon to compensate for the disintegration of the other social bonds – a disintegration for which cosmopolitan intellectuals, Jews, foreign agents and the influence of Western culture were held to blame on account of the 'corrosive influence' attributed to them. The complete, planned rationalization of the social relations of productive collaboration, resulted, in the end, in dictatorial rule by the state apparatus – which (particularly in the Soviet Union, Poland and Romania) invoked pre-modern, traditional values in order to reinforce its legitimacy.

Soviet-style socialism thus offered a sort of caricatural magnification of the basic features of capitalism. Pursuing accumulation and economic growth as its principal goals, it attempted to rationalize this pursuit by replacing spontaneous hetero-regulation by the market with methodically programmed, centralized hetero-regulation of the economy as a whole. It thus divorced – in all spheres of activity – the functional conduct demanded by the overall rationality of the system from the rationality of individuals' self-regulated modes of conduct. Because it was divorced from the intuitive understanding of their surroundings and relations with one another of which individuals were capable, this methodically programmed rationalization established Reason as a separate power exercised *over* them and not *by* them and established the realm of Reason as the dictatorial rule of those who, as a result of their functions, were its custodians.

It was as if the social system of the factory (the despotism of the factory), with its caste of reputedly omniscient managers and its functional hierarchy, had seized hold of society as a whole in order to strangle its living, self-regulated social relations or else manipulate them for ends that were not their own. This factory-society could not permit any kind of opposition or democratic debate, any more than the factory system itself could; there could only be one truth, one form of rationality, one form of power. The political, administrative, legal and economic powers – that is, the party, the bureaucracy, the law and the economic apparatus – tended, as a consequence, to fuse into a single state machine, governed from the centre by the same instrumental criteria. It was inevitable that this power apparatus should become autonomous and corrupt; but even if the party-turned-bureaucracy had remained faithful to the puritan ethic, the programmed hetero-regulation of all activities and relations would have led inevitably to social disintegration, that is, to individuals' loss of motivation vis-à-vis their functionalized work and to their withdrawal from the regulated social world. Beneath the surface of this bureaucratized 'society' an informal society – based on moonlighting, the black market, barter, mutual aid groups and networks – began to re-form, a society which the bureaucratized system eventually came to rely on to make up for its own failings.

Historical and empirical reasons alone cannot explain the failure of socialist pan-rationalism. The underlying reason for its failure is ontological: the Marxian utopia by which functional work and personal activity could be made to coincide is ontologically unrealizeable *on the scale of large systems*. For, in order to function, the industrial–bureaucratic megamachine requires a subdivision of tasks which, once put into effect, is self-perpetuating and *has to be* self-perpetuating by inertia, if the functional capacity of each of its human cogs is to be made reliable and calculable. The definition and distribution of these partial tasks are thus determined by the material matrix (as shown in the organigramme) of the megamachine whose functioning they are to ensure. It is strictly impossible subsequently to reinterpret this functionalization of hetero-determined activities in terms of voluntary social collaboration. On the contrary, the *functional* integration of individuals will prevent their social integration: the functional predetermination of their relations with each other will exclude them from forming reciprocal relations based on co-operation, for the purpose of achieving common objectives according to common criteria. It will prevent the execution of their tasks from being lived by them as co-operation and group membership. Their 'organic solidarity' (even Durkheim acknowledged this in the end) does not exist *for them* as a lived relationship. It only exists as such for the outside observer, who sees self-regulated collaboration in what is, in reality, a military-style organization, divided in advance into complementary tasks.

In practice, this amounts to saying *there cannot and must not* be voluntary self-regulated collaboration if the megamachine is to function without hitches, in a strictly foreseeable and calculable way. Both economic rationality and the functioning of the megamachine require the 'human factor' to be eliminated and living labour and free workers to be replaced by strictly programmed labour and workers. Both require the submission of the living to the inert, of living labour to dead labour (that is, to machines and capital). In both, the techniques of domination and the imperatives of rationalization are inextricably linked, to the extent that one may consider rational organization to be the goal of domination or, inversely, domination to be the goal of rational organization.

An organizational model based on the functional subdivision of tasks cannot therefore appeal to the workers' sense of responsibility, nor to their spirit of co-operation. It must resort initially to force – by passing laws against 'vagrancy' and begging, and by obliging people to accept the work they are proposed on pain of deportation, hard labour or death by starvation – and bring into play what I have called 'prescriptive regulators': mandatory working hours and work norms, and technical procedures which it is imperative to respect. It can only loosen its constraints if it can motivate the workers by means of 'incentive regulators' to accept work, the nature, rhythm and duration of which have been programmed in advance by the factory or office organization, work they can never *love*. These incentive regulators can only therefore offer, *within the framework* of the functional organization of subdivided tasks, compensations *outside work* for the constraints, frustrations and suffering inherent in functional labour itself. There are two prerequisites, therefore, for the functional integration of the workers to be achieved and the constraints forcing them to work relaxed: first, society must be sufficiently wealthy for the workers to be offered material compensation; and, secondly, the workers must agree to view their work as a means of procuring such compensation.

As we have seen, this second condition has been difficult to fulfil:[1] it assumes workers spontaneously prefer to earn more rather than to work less. It assumes, therefore, that they are conditioned and socialized in such a way that they take their salary and what it allows them to buy as their principal goal and their work as a means of achieving that goal.[2] Socialization must, therefore, operate in two different directions at the same time: it must condition individuals to adopt an instrumental attitude towards their work, of the 'What counts is getting paid at the end of the month' kind; and it must condition them, as consumers, to desire commercial goods and services as both the purpose of their efforts and the symbols of their success.

What French economists have termed 'Fordist regulation' would have been impossible without educating the worker/producer into becoming a worker/consumer. The supply of increasing amounts of so-called 'labour-saving' goods has never sufficed to bring about this conversion. Even during the early fifties, both in Europe and the United States, the extension of forms of 'scientific work organization' derived from Taylorism met with resistance from workers.[3] This resistance, which has never totally disappeared, was only overcome by recruiting an inexperienced workforce of young rural and immigrant workers, that is, groups of people who, by virtue of their social and cultural uprootedness, were more susceptible to the lure of consumerism than the traditional working class.

To move from a regime of work governed by constraint to one governed by incentives is therefore no small undertaking. The difficulties, delays and failures of the 'economic reforms' attempted within the Soviet bloc are evidence of this. It is not enough to produce growing amounts of compensatory goods and services; it is also necessary simultaneously to impose working conditions which will create the 'compensatory' need for these goods,[4] while at the same time 'educating' the workers to *prefer these compensations to the relatively comfortable working conditions* which, in the Soviet Union for example, they have succeeded in procuring under a regime of bureaucratic constraint.

This conditioning of people to accept consumerism cannot be successfully achieved either by the party-state or by any other political authority. Persuading individuals that the consumer goods and services they are offered *adequately compensate for the sacrifices they must make* in order to obtain them and that such consumption constitutes *a haven of individual happiness which sets them apart from the crowd* is something which typically belongs to the sphere of commercial advertising. However, such advertising is only effective if it is issued by private enterprises addressing private individuals. Indeed, there is an essential difference between commercial advertising and propaganda. The latter appeals to us in the name of the public interest with the aim of persuading us it is in our own personal interest to behave in accordance with the higher interest of the state or the nation. Propaganda urges us to conduct ourselves (for example, don't smoke, don't drink, keep to the speed limit) in a way which does not immediately and intuitively correspond to our own individual interest, and whose necessity or advantages must be explained to us by the state in its role as the repository of Reason. It thus urges us to follow a course of action we would not spontaneously adopt and designates us as collective individuals who share with everyone else an all-embracing reality – the public interest – and who, for reasons of convenience, laziness, selfishness or stupidity, are loath to take account of it.

In commercial advertising, on the other hand, a private supplier, selling, for example, cigarettes, alcohol or fast cars, offers us some private satisfaction or pleasure which is strictly and immediately individual. The message of advertising tends to establish a sense of complicity between seller and potential buyer, by suggesting that both are exclusively pursuing their own private advantage and share an interest in ignoring any broader considerations: the seller's only objective is to procure some form of pleasure for the potential buyer which will encourage the latter to make a purchase she or he is under no obligation to make, and the buyer's only objective has to be that of obtaining the greatest possible pleasure.

Compensatory goods and services are, therefore, by definition, neither *necessary* nor even merely *useful.* They are always presented as containing an element of luxury, or superfluity, of fantasy which, by designating the purchaser as a 'happy and privileged person', protects him or her from the pressures of the rationalized universe and the obligation to conduct themselves in a functional manner. Compensatory goods are therefore desired as much – if not more – for their *uselessness* as for their use value; for it is this element of uselessness (in superfluous gadgets and ornaments, for example) which symbolizes the buyer's escape from the collective universe into a haven of private sovereignty.

It is easy to understand, therefore, why regulation by market forces, and not a relaxation of bureaucratic regulation, is the only successful way to replace constraint by incentives. Functional workers, who accept alienation in their work because the possibilities for consumption it offers are adequate compensation for them, can only come into being if they simultaneously become socialized consumers. But only a market economy sector and the commercial advertising that goes with it can produce these socialized consumers.

In the following chapter I will return to the fact that incentive regulation by consumerism can only ever give rise to an extremely unstable form of workers' functional integration. The compensations offered to them will never reconcile them with their condition or be sufficient to make them accept that condition in the long term. The system is continually forced to raise the stakes and offer ever-increasing financial compensation. And it is precisely this increasing monetarization of needs, pleasure and satisfactions which characterized 'Fordist regulation'.

The important thing to note here is that this process of monetarization, the effects of which are added to those of the functional predetermination of subdivided tasks, is a powerful factor of social disintegration. Indeed, offering financial incentives for functional work presupposes the conviction, sustained by commercial advertising, that everything we can do, money does better and that the goods and services provided by paid professionals are essentially superior to those we can provide for ourselves: they incorporate that element of magic, fantasy and non-utility which confers on them a compensatory value (and therefore an exchange value) which is far superior to their actual use value. Thanks to the constant barrage of commercial advertising, the need for money will thus increase as social wealth does, prompting the previously unpaid strata of society to seek waged work. This in turn will further increase the need for compensatory consumption.

Compensatory consumption, originally offered to the workers as a means of persuading them to accept the functionalization of their labour, thus becomes the objective which prompts non-workers to seek functionalized work. We no longer want commercial goods and services to compensate for functional work, we want functional work so that we can afford commercial goods and services. The efficiency of incentive regulation by consumerism thus causes the latter to exceed its initial function and causes a cultural transformation. The satisfaction afforded by earning money is more important than the loss of freedom entailed by accepting functional work. Getting paid becomes the primary objective of the activity to the extent that any activity which does not have financial compensation ceases to be acceptable. Money supplants other values and becomes their only measure.

Now, as we know, compensatory consumption is offered to the *private* individual as a form of protection and refuge from the collective universe. It constitutes an incentive to withdraw into the private sphere and give priority to the pursuit of 'personal' advantages, and thus contributes to the disintegration of networks of solidarity and mutual assistance, social and family cohesion and our sense of belonging. Individuals socialized by consumerism are no longer socially integrated individuals but individuals who are encouraged to 'be themselves' by distinguishing themselves from others and who only resemble these others in their refusal (*socially channelled* into consumption) to assume responsibility for the common condition by taking common action.

The paradoxical and perfectly predictable consequence of this *a-social socialization* will be that the state will find it necessary to reinforce its prescriptive powers. Indeed, the pursuit of personal advantage could only produce a collective optimum in an environment in which there were no shortages, in which sufficient resources existed for there to be unlimited increase in overall wealth and in which, in the absence of all forms of rigidity and inertia in the material sphere, the advantages reaped by one sector of society were never gained at the long-term expense of another. Glimmerings of this world of 'unlimited opportunities', which forms the basis of the liberal utopia, have been seen on a number of occasions throughout history, particularly during the colonization of North America. Otherwise, we know that in an environment where there is scarcity, the actions of individuals each pursuing their own immediate advantage produce in the material sphere an overall result which frustrates the aims of each and, in the words of Marx, 'thwarts their calculations and destroys their hopes'. Sartre calls the way in which the collective effect runs counter to the individual strivings which have produced it 'counter-finality': for example, the actions of individual farmers each clearing trees in order to increase the amount of cultivable land they have, leads to soil erosion and catastrophic flooding.[5]

Along the same lines of thought, one of the most pertinent rebuttals of the virtues of regulation by market forces was made by Garrett Hardin in a well-known game-theory scenario entitled, 'The Tragedy of the Commons.'[6] In this scenario, each farmer is free to pursue his own personal interest and graze the maximum number of animals on the common land. When the pasturelands start to become overcrowded, each additional cow grazed on them will reduce the milk yield per head. However, this reduction will be *at the expense of all*, whereas *each* farmer may expect to increase the amount of milk he produces by increasing the size of his herd. It will therefore be in his interest to enlarge his herd as fast as possible and 'faster than everyone else. Thus the pursuit of each individual of his own advantage will lead inexorably to the ruination of all. Only by imposing an obligatory limit on the total number of animals and also, in practice, on the number of farmers allowed to own animals, can such an outcome be prevented.

Prescriptive regulation thus reappears in the wake of incentive regulation by personal interest. The regulation of traffic, interest rates and pollution standards; land-use plans; speed limits; compulsory insurance; taxes, anti-fraud measures, public services; and so on are so many obstacles to the individual's pursuit of her or his own interest, and represent so many ways in which the state takes charge of the collective dimension of individual endeavours in order to limit their adverse effects and prevent their leading to the ruination of all. Thus the use of incentive regulators to achieve functional integration by appealing to individual interest, will require responsibility for the collective interest to be assumed by a separate authority – the state – whose powers will be widened and whose legitimacy will be based on the mandate received – and solicited – from its citizens to take charge of public affairs on their behalf.

The consequence of this will be an aggravated division between society and state, between the sphere of self-regulated relations and relations established on the basis of prescriptive hetero-regulation. Once public interest is taken on by a separate authority, public affairs will tend to become the sole domain of the managers of these apparatuses. Politicians and the political sphere will thus gain increasing autonomy from social and cultural life. 'Political power', that is, the right to administer the apparatuses of the state, will become the principal stake in political struggles and these struggles will tend to take place essentially between political parties which base their suitability to govern on their competence in public affairs and which seek a mandate from the electorate to assume control of these affairs. Those who stand for public office will not seek such a mandate by outlining their conception of administration and the political ends it should serve – and submitting this to public debate – but by showing their concern for the individual and sectional interests of voters they consider incapable of making decisions in terms of the general interest and social issues. In other words, they will appeal to the voters as *consumers* and *customers* by means of electoral propaganda which will increasingly come to resemble commercial advertising: as well as proving their competence in affairs of state, candidates will have to demonstrate by their private lives and public conduct that they are 'close to the people', that is, that they will defend the latter's most particular individual interests against any possible public encroachments. They will have to show the voter/customer the same *concern* – as described by Jean Baudrillard in *La société de consommation*[7] – as commercial advertising does. They will have to propose to the electorate that the state take care not just of their sectional interests, but also of the risks entailed for them by a dependency-creating functionalization of their activities.

Functionalization of this sort can be made acceptable, and functional integration made effective, on one condition alone: the protective state, the welfare state, must offer the functional worker/consumer social compensations for the loss of his or her autonomy. These compensations take the form of the right to benefits and social services. They must compensate for the withering away of self-regulated social relations and family ties implied in this process of socialization by consumerism. By taking on the services which people previously provided for themselves and satisfying the needs they catered for individually, the welfare state does more than provide them with a considerable degree of security; it also increases the amount of time they can devote to socialization (schooling), waged work and commodity consumption.

Thus, the increasing subdivision and functionalization of tasks entail concomitant developments – in the other spheres of social life – which hold their own logics and dynamic. The development of functional work requires the development of compensatory consumerism if it is to remain efficient. The latter accelerates the development of functional work and creates new compensatory needs, some of which can only be catered for by the state. The fact of the state's assuming responsibility for meeting these needs fosters the development of functional work and compensatory consumption, causes the networks of solidarity to wither away faster and gives rise to an increasing demand for the state to assume these responsibilities. It thereby further increases dependency on the state and a clientelist relationship between the state and the public. The gulf between public life and social life widens as does that between the general interest and individual interests, and between electoral themes and systemic constraints, bringing about a continual expansion of the spheres of competence of the civil service and the regulatory powers of the state, whilst the parliamentary institutions become a mere shadow theatre. This state of affairs is not far from the 'plebiscitary democracy' (*Führerdemokratie*) predicted by Max Weber, in which a society which has disintegrated and been replaced by an industrial–bureaucratic megamachine, can only gain the loyalty of the masses through the person of a charismatic leader. This leader must possess both the majestic authority that befits the driver of the state machine (according to Weber, he must correspond to the model of the *Führer mit Maschine*) and a sympathetic concern for the interests and everyday problems of the people called upon to leave the management of the state in his hands.

George Orwell's nightmare, of which John Brunner has produced a contemporary version,[8] emerges as a logical progression of these developments: the nightmare of a society in a state of total disintegration, in which social relations have given way to functional relations between programmed individuals who have no shortage of amusements – individuals programmed through the very amusements they are induced to participate in. The Weberian vision of a completely bureaucratized, rationalized and functionalized machine-society, in which each individual functions as a cog without attempting to understand the meaning (if there is one) of the partial task she or he performs, is a dystopia that is tending to be realized in a cybernetic form in which indoctrination and militarization are replaced by caring computer networks providing a 'personalized' service for looking after individuals. The goal is the same and the results are no different in nature, but only in the sophistication of the means employed: instead of being imposed by propaganda and the 'thought police', the functional rationalization of individuals' behaviour takes the form of a subtle and insidious manipulation which instrumentalizes non-economic values for economic ends.

Notes

1. See Chapter 1, pp. 29–33.
2. Striking accounts of this instrumental approach to work can be found in a collection of interviews published in Britain by Ronald Fraser. For example, Dennis Johnson, a worker in a cigarette factory says, 'The modern worker neither gives anything to work nor expects anything (apart from his wages) from it. Work, at factory level, has no inherent value. The worker's one interest is his pay-packet.' The same insistence on the absence of any intrinsic value in work is also found most strikingly in a clerk, Philip Callow ('. . . it has no value as work . . . you feel dispensable, interim: automation will take over one day, the sooner the better. You are there for the money, no other reason') or in an advertising copywriter. See Ronald Fraser, *Work*, vol. 1, Harmondsworth 1968.

During the same period, this was a very common attitude among workers in America (a Congress report and a series of articles in *Fortune* magazine entitled 'Blue Collar Blues' described their disaffection with work and the increase in incidents of sabotage), Italy (the left-wing group *Potere Operaio* coined the slogan: 'A salario di merda, lavoro di merda') and France (see in particular, Alexis Chassagne and Gaston Montracher, *La fin du travail*, Paris 1978).

3. Cf. Stephen Marglin, 'What Do Bosses Do?' in André Gorz, ed., *The Division of Labour*, Hassocks 1976.
4. The notion of compensatory needs is borrowed from Rudolf Bahro, *The Alternative in Eastern Europe*, trans. David Fernbach, London 1978.
5. Jean-Paul Sartre, *Critique of Dialectical Reason: 1 Theory of Physical Ensembles*, ed. Jonathan Rée, trans. Alan Sheridan-Smith, London 1976, p. 162.
6. Garrett Hardin, 'The Tragedy of the Commons', *Science*, no. 162, 1968.
7. Jean Baudrillard, *La société de consommation*, Paris 1970.
8. John Brunner, *The Shockwave Rider*, London and New York 1975.

The End of Working-Class Humanism

Who decides what work we do and how we do it? In the industrialized countries the answer is: capital (in the person of its administrators and/ or owners). Production techniques and domination techniques are, as we have already seen,[1] inextricably linked. Stephen Marglin has shown that, contrary to what Adam Smith believed, the subdivision of labour (for example, in the manufacture of pins) was not inspired by the need to increase productivity but by the need to dominate the workers.[2] It was necessary to separate the workers from the means of production and from what they produced in order to be able to dictate to them what the nature, hours and productivity of their labour should be and prevent them from producing or undertaking anything by or for themselves.

Does this mean that if the workers regained ownership – or command – of the means of production, they would be freed from domination by capital and thus able to decide for themselves what work to do and how to do it? The answer to this may, in certain cases, be in the affirmative, but as a general rule it will be in the negative. This is so for the following reason: if, from the outset, the development of the means of industrial production had been in the hands of 'associated producers' in workers' co-operatives, enterprises might have been managed and controlled by the people working in them, but *industrialization would not have taken place.* What we call 'industry' is, in fact, a technical concentration of capital which has only been made possible by the separation of the worker from the means of producing. It is this separation alone which made it possible to rationalize and economize labour, to make it produce surpluses in excess of the producers' needs and to use these growing surpluses to expand the means of production and increase their power.

Industry arose from capitalism and bears its indelible mark. It could not have come into being but for the economic rationalization of labour – which necessarily implied its functionalization – and in its functioning it perpetuates this latter as an essential requirement built into the physical structures of its machinery. Industrial machinery, the result of the separation of the workers from 'their' products, and the means of producing them, renders this separation necessary, even when it was not originally designed to that end. It cannot, by its very nature, be appropriated by the workers[3] and this will continue to be the case even when private ownership of the means of production is abolished and, with it, the supreme importance of profit. There are two closely linked reasons for this:

1. Firstly, the industrial means of production function as fixed capital, whatever the nature of the economic system or the system of property ownership. Fixed capital, as Marx has shown, is essentially 'dead labour', that is, the material result of a past *poiesis* which continues to operate on and through living labour, both by increasing the latter's efficiency and imposing constraints upon it. This past, 'dead' labour which is built into the material structures and continues to operate through living labour – which it conditions – was described by Sartre as 'passivized practice'[4] and by Max Weber as 'mind objectified':

> An inanimate machine is mind objectified. Only this provides it with the power to force men into its service and to dominate their everyday working life as completely as is actually the case in the factory. Objectified intelligence is also that animated machine, the bureaucratic organization, with its specialization of trained skills, its division of jurisdiction, its rules and hierarchical relations of authority.[5]

The important thing here is that the inert materiality of the machinery (or the organization which imitates it) affords past *poiesis* (dead labour or the organization) a lasting hold over the workers who, in *putting it to use*, are forced to *serve it*. The greater the amount of fixed capital (that is, of dead labour and dead knowledge) per work station, the more unyielding this hold. Let me clarify this point: *I am not saying* that the *way* in which industrial labour is carried out cannot be 'humanized', that is, self-determined and 'self-managed', nor that machines cannot be designed and adapted so as to *increase the margin of self-determination left to the worker,* make work stimulating and establish labour relations based on co-operation. What I am saying is that 'dead labour', 'mind objectified', comes between the worker and the product and prevents work being lived as *poiesis,* as the sovereign action of Man on matter. Marx demonstrates this quite remarkably in the *Grundrisse,*[6] and it is something to which we shall have to return, in more concrete terms, with reference to the process industries or those which are robotized. According to Marx, as long as the means of labour is still a tool in the hands of the workers, 'it undergoes a merely formal modification' by the fact that it is also fixed capital.

> But, once adopted into the production process of capital, the means of labour passes through different metamorphoses, whose culmination is the *machine*, or rather, an *automatic system of machinery* . . . set in motion by an automaton, a moving power that moves itself; this automaton consisting of numerous mechanical and intellectual organs, *so that the workers themselves are cast merely as its conscious linkages* . . . In no way does the machine appear as the individual worker's means of labour. Its distinguishing characteristic is not in the least, as with the means of labour, to transmit the worker's activity to the object; this activity, rather, is posited in such a way that it merely transmits the machine's work, the machine's action, on the raw material – supervises it and guards against interruptions. . . . Rather, it is the machine which possesses skill and strength in place of the worker, is itself the virtuoso, with a soul of its own . . . The worker's activity, reduced to a mere abstraction of activity, is determined and regulated on all sides by the movement of the machinery, and not the opposite. The science which compels the inanimate limbs of the machinery, by their construction, to act purposefully, as an automaton, *does not exist in the worker's consciousness, but rather acts upon him through the machine as an alien power, as the power of the machine. The appropriation of living labour by objectified labour,* . . . which lies in the concept of capital, *is posited, in production resting on machinery, as the character of the production process itself* including its material elements and its material motion . . . [A.G.'s italics]

Labour appears merely 'scattered, . . . subsumed under the total process of the machinery itself' which confronts the 'individual, insignificant doings' of the living worker 'as a mighty organism': the worker is transformed into 'a mere living accessory of this machinery', her or his 'labour capacity is an infinitesimal, vanishing magnitude' and, similarly, '*every connection of the product with the direct need of the producer,* and hence with direct use value' *is also destroyed.* The labour process has been transformed 'into a scientific process, which subjugates the forces of nature and compels them to work in the service of human needs' and '*individual labour* . . . *is productive* . . . *only in these common labours* which subordinate the forces of nature to themselves.'

To put it plainly, if Nature is indeed dominated, it is so now in the sense that it is *in the service of a scientific process*; but this process itself *is not dominated by the worker or workers.* On the contrary, this process dominates the workers 'as an alien power, as the power of the machine', since the science within the latter 'does not exist in the worker's conscience' and, quite obviously, cannot be mastered by him or her in, or through, her or his work. In short, *the process of the domination of Nature by Man (by science) turns into a domination of Man by the process of domination.*

The reader will see that this admirably perceptive description still remains valid in its entirety, whatever the system of property ownership; and whether machinery functions as fixed capital within the framework of social relations of capitalism or not. It remains valid even if the ownership of capital is abolished and, with it, the goals (profit, accumulation) it assigns to production. Thus, when Marx concludes his exposition with the observation that:

> The hand tool makes the worker independent – posits him as proprietor. Machinery – as fixed capital – posits him as dependent, posits him as appropriated. This effect of machinery holds only in so far as it is cast into the role of fixed capital, and this is only because the worker relates to it as wage-worker, and the active individual generally, as mere worker[7]

he is making a superfluous addition to an analysis which refutes such a statement – superfluous specifically in that it in no way derives from the argument which precedes it. Indeed, it is not at all clear how refinery workers or train drivers in rolling mills could be anything other than wage-workers; how the products of their labour could relate directly to their needs; how they could look on their plant as their means of labour; how, instead of feeling they *belonged to* the refinery or steelworks, they could look on this industrial plant as their property, and so on.

I shall return later to the nature of this type of work which has ceased to have any but a distant connection with working-class labour as it is traditionally understood.

The brief allusions Marx makes to science in this passage show that machinery is inappropriable from another point of view: the mass of necessarily specialized skills combined in social production are equally impossible to appropriate.

2. Originally, the principal aim of the subdivision of labour was to dominate the workers. Once in place, however, this subdivision was to lead to the progressive specialization of the means of production themselves and promote the mechanization and automation of these means. As a result, technical and scientific skills and disciplines would become increasingly specialized; there would be a growing wealth of knowledge in increasingly narrow fields; and it would be necessary for the specialized, partial forms of production that make up the social process of production as a whole to be subject to increasingly laborious external

co-ordination. We shall call this fragmentation of production into productive activities with no individual value except when in combination with other activities the macro-social division of labour. It should not be confused with the Taylorist fragmentation of jobs on the level of the enterprise or the workshop. The fragmentation of jobs can be overcome – by restructuring and reskilling the work process, and allowing autonomous or semi-autonomous teams to manage the technical aspects of complex tasks themselves – but its macro-social division cannot be reversed. This is due essentially to the fact that the amount of know-how needed to produce an industrial product – even an everyday one – far exceeds the capacities of the individual, or indeed of thousands of individuals. The wealth of industrialized societies rests precisely on their unprecedented ability to combine, by means of pre-established organizational procedures, an immense variety of specialized knowledge which it would be impossible for their possessors to co-ordinate through mutual understanding and conscious, voluntary self-regulated co-operation.

If we consider the diversity of specialized knowledge needed to produce a bicycle, for example (I am deliberately using the example of a relatively simple product instead of a complex one such as a television or a car), we must take into account not only the skills employed by the various industries which provide the components but also, prior to these, the knowledge needed to produce the specialist machines used by these industries: machines for wiredrawing, casting tubes in particular alloys, cutting cogs, manufacturing chains, electrolyzing, machining ball-bearings, manufacturing paint, and so on. All this know-how must be developed, taught and renewed by a network of schools, universities, research centres and so on. Each worker, group of workers and production unit can only master a fraction of the knowledge employed in the factories, often hundreds of miles apart, which supply components to the cycle factory (and to factories of other products too, of course).

The individuals who make up the 'collective production worker' are therefore in no position to become the subjects of bicycle manufacture or to appropriate the process – which is both technical and social – of their production. They can obtain *some* powers of self-determination and workers' control, but these powers in the manufacture of ball-bearings, chains, tubes, tyres and so on, will not give them control over the intended purpose and *meaning* of their work. This work may be – or be made – fascinating and stimulating but it will never ensure the 'total self-realization of individuals' in and through their social co-operation. Worse still, it will never produce that *working-class culture* which, together with a *humanism of labour*, constituted the great utopia of the socialist and trade-union movements up until the 1920s.

The fact is that the specialization of skills has caused the foundations upon which a work culture could be elaborated to crumble. What potentially united all workers within a common culture – that is, in interpretations of the world, which were derived from what was thought of as common experience and which, in return, enabled what was in fact an extremely differentiated working-class condition to be unified through common practices – was the consciousness of their common *poietic* power: whether they were miners, masons, navvies, casters or tool-makers, their different professions had in common a direct contact with the material world in which *a manual intelligence which was impossible to formalize* affirmed itself. This was what was meant by *knowing one's craft*: an ability to judge and react faster than speech, an immediate, synthetic grasp of the situation that was immediately controlled by manual know-how. The work situation presented a challenge to human abilities and *good workers* could be proud of their ability to take up this challenge and prove, in doing so, Man's sovereign power over matter. This was truer of heavy manual labour – mining, iron and steel, boilermaking, road and railway building, construction and shipbuilding – *which moreover employed the largest number of workers*, than it was in machine tending.

The fact that production depended – as far as quality, quantity and cost were concerned – on the non-formalizable abilities of the workers, was obviously unacceptable from the point of view of economic rationality. If it was to be possible to calculate and plan production, it had to cease to depend on the labour of workers producing with varying degrees of speed and efficiency. The productive activities of different individuals had to be made strictly identical; it had to become possible to interchange their performances and measure them by the same yardstick, and to compare their output. To do this it was necessary (as Max Weber so clearly saw) to detach labour from the actual workers, to rationalize and reify it in such a way that the same performance could be provided by any worker in any of the factories set up in any part of the country, or even, indeed, in any of the four corners of the earth. The rationalization of labour called for the rationalization, and then the standardization, of machines. This in turn demanded the standardization of products, and that called for the standardization of workers. It was essential that identical products be everywhere manufactured by identical 'motions', following identical procedures, on machines with identical parameters, so that nuts manufactured in Bucharest would match up with bolts manufactured in Billancourt, micro-circuits from Singapore with appliances assembled in Eindhoven or Nuremberg.

Originally a necessity of economic rationality, the reification of labour or the destruction – ever more complete without ever being either definitive or total – of crafts has finally been rendered largely irreversible as a result of the division of labour and trade on a worldwide scale. It is built into production techniques and product design. It is no longer due uniquely, as Lukács believed, to the fact that capital treats labour power as a commodity. It would persist even if the labour market were to be abolished (as a number of contemporary socialists have proposed[8]) in favour of a guaranteed income for life – even though industrialized and rationalized commercial production may cease, on this hypothesis, to be the principal form of production.

With the destruction of craft skills, working-class culture and pride in one's work were condemned to disappear. The Taylorized factory realized the ideal of the eighteenth-century factory owners, for whom 'semi-idiot workers' constituted the best type of manpower imaginable.[9] The idea of a work ethic became impossible under these conditions, except for an increasingly reduced stratum of craft workers, who continued to dominate the labour organizations. But by the very fact that this stratum could no longer claim to embody the future of the working class and of society itself, its work ethic ceased to be humanist and acquired a corporatist, elitist, conservative character in the eyes of the mass of worker/consumers for whom Taylorized industry was a form of hell (as indeed was office work). In as much as it did survive, working-class culture was no more than a relic of the past and did not constitute *the future of workers* in general; it was no more than a technical culture, a *craft* culture, what the Germans call an *Experten-kultur*, that is, a set of specialized, technical, partial skills without roots or use value in day-to-day relations.

The splits within trade unionism in the 1965–75 period came as a consequence of this fragmentation of the world of labour into a *class* of worker/producers and a *mass* of worker/consumers: semi-skilled workers who 'no longer identified with anything, especially not their work.' As the authors of *Le travail et après. . .*[10] demonstrate, semi-skilled workers could no longer think of themselves as *producers* nor therefore 'agree to be defined uniquely by their role in production', 'so clear is it that this role is meaningless: semi-skilled worker, unskilled worker, pure labour power . . . zero, work, home, bed.'

> The wage cannot be viewed as the price of labour, since this labour obviously has no individual reality. What is being paid for is the work station not the labour . . . that is, the machine, not the person . . . And there couldn't be any attachment to the work station or the company here either . . . The mass worker does not sell the value of his concrete labour – of whose uniform, universal nature he is well aware. He demands the maximum payment for his labour power as an undifferentiated element in a collective wealth-producing

process . . . 'We all do the same job so we want to be paid equally and as
much as possible . . .' He asks the right to enjoy some of the general wealth he
helps to create through the socially necessary activity that is his abstract
labour.[11]

In short, for the mass of workers, it is no longer 'the power of the
workers' that constitutes the guiding utopia, but the possibility of ceasing
to function as workers; the emphasis is less on liberation *within* work
and more on liberation *from* work, with full income guaranteed.[12]

Throughout the industrialized world, the rebellion of semi-skilled
workers against 'scientific work organization' – that is, against the
extreme forms of Taylorist fragmentation of jobs – caused the disruption
of entire industries and produced a rapid rise in wage costs. The motives
for this rebellion could not be expressed – or could only be expressed
with difficulty – in terms of negotiable trade-union demands. Therefore,
a mass of workers withdrew from the class logic of the labour organizations as well as the attempts made by political parties and governments
at mediation or repression. This was the period of wildcat strikes, mass
absenteeism and sabotage. The most rational organization of labour
from an economic point of view had produced a result which was the
opposite of its intended aim. It had been intended that it would make
labour costs and productivity strictly predictable and programmable. To
this end, labour had been broken down into itemized 'movements',
timed to the nearest hundredth of a second. In this way, the rationality
of labour would have an autonomous organizational basis and no longer
depend in any way on the subjective dispositions of the workforce.
Factories would function all the better since their functioning *no longer
relied on the spirit of co-operation* of the workers. The hetero-regulation
of the workers' behaviour would be obtained 'scientifically' by what
appeared to be totally anonymous, imperious demands of the
machinery.

This kind of programmed hetero-regulation became, progressively,
even less bearable since the incentive regulation intended to comple-
ment it appealed to desires which were in contradiction with the
demands of work. As we have seen, these incentive regulators took the
form of compensatory consumer purchases which consumer society
painted in glowing colours to its workers. In short, this society promoted
the hedonistic values of comfort, instant pleasure and minimal effort,
while at the same time requiring its semi-skilled workers to behave
according to diametrically opposed values in their work, and this in a
context of economic growth and ostentatious wealth. Life at work
became the negation of life outside work, and vice versa. For consumer
society, the objective of work was not to work. The motivations which

were to ensure the workers' functional integration instead motivated their rejection of this integration: the rejection of work.

The rationalization of labour had thus gone as far as it could. The rebellion of the semi-skilled workers revealed that optimum economic efficiency could not be attained by pushing economic rationality to its limits. The strategy had to be revised on a number of different levels simultaneously, the aim of which would be to bring into being a new work ethic, by enabling workers to identify with their work. The efforts made to that end were to appeal to a variety of motivations:

1. Work was·to be made more gratifying and autonomous thanks to a certain restructuring of tasks. Relatively complex tasks would be undertaken by semi-autonomous teams who could divide the work between themselves as they thought best, vary the rhythm of work throughout the day and monitor the result. This organization, while increasing the workers' interest in a job which was once more experienced as an *activity*, as *co-operation*, was intended to increase productivity, reduce absenteeism, and, above all, render impossible the disruptive strikes which had previously allowed a few dozen workers to paralyse large factories.

2. A reorganization of labour of this kind would only have had a limited effect if it had not been accompanied by a technological revolution and economic crisis which combined to produce a rapid growth in unemployment[13] and caused a very marked differentiation between the various strata of waged workers. In industry and industrialized services, technical restructuring and the contraction of employment allowed for very selective reductions in the number of waged workers: repetitive jobs were progressively automated or computerized, semi-skilled workers and unskilled employees were dismissed, retired early or encouraged to retrain. A stable job in a large company became a privilege that had to be earned; especially since large-scale enterprises were beginning to adopt the Japanese system of subcontracting as much manufacturing and services as possible to satellite companies which were often tiny (consisting in the most extreme case of a single 'entrepreneur'/craftworker working exclusively for that large-scale enterprise with capital borrowed from the latter), sometimes clandestine, and set up by former employees of the parent company at its instigation.

Thus the parent company, again on the Japanese model, could keep on just a core of permanent workers chosen for their skills, their ability to learn and adapt to technical change, their willingness to co-operate and their loyalty to the company. One single response would enable the economic crisis to be confronted and the crisis of work overcome: the recreation of an elite of skilled workers and the rehabilitation of craft values.

We have come full circle: this is nothing less than the restoration of the unity of life and work which economic rationalization had contrived to abolish in order to replace it with an instrumental conception of work. Thanks to the crisis, technical innovations and the growth in competition, the enterprise is to cease to be a site of functional integration and become a site of social integration and professional development. Such, at least, is the new ideology, the so-called ideology of 'human resources'. In certain respects, it seems to be gaining ground on economistic pan-rationalism. It implicitly acknowledges that labour power is not an instrument like any other, and that its efficiency and performance depend on factors which are not calculable and do not derive from economic rationality, such as the working environment, job satisfaction and the quality of social relations of co-operation, and so on.

In other respects, the ideology of 'human resources' is preparing the ground for the instrumentalization – or, as Habermas has it, the colonization – of non-economic aspirations by economic rationality: the new type of enterprise will strive to take these aspirations into consideration but only because they are factors of productivity and 'competitiveness' of a particular kind. The question is whether this consideration will lead to a greater exploitation and manipulation of workers or to an autonomization of non-quantifiable, extra-economic values, to such an extent that these will restrict the rights of economic logic in order to impose their own claims.

Notes

1. See above, p. 43.
2. Stephen Marglin, in André Gorz, ed., *The Division of Labour*, Hassocks 1976.
3. Cf. André Gorz, *Farewell to the Working Class*, London 1982, chs 2 and 4.
4. Jean-Paul Sartre, *Critique of Dialectical Reason: 1 Theory of Practical Ensembles*, ed. Jonathan Rée, trans. Alan Sheridan-Smith, London 1976, p. 162.
5. Max Weber, *Economy and Society: An Outline of Interpretive Sociology*, eds Guenther Roth and Claus Wittich, New York 1968, vol. 3, p. 1402.
6. The extracts which follow are taken from the English edition, *Grundrisse*, Harmondsworth 1973, pp. 692–5.
7. Karl Marx, *Grundrisse*, p. 702.
8. Bellamy in the United States, Popper-Lynkeus in Austria at the beginning of the century and Jaques Duboin in France in the 1930s.
9. In his *History of Civil Society*, Adam Ferguson writes, 'Manufactures, accordingly, prosper most where the mind is least consulted, and where the workshop may . . . be considered as an engine, the parts of which are men.' Marx, who quotes this passage in *Capital*, Volume 1, ch. 14, follows it by quotes from Adam Smith, G. Garnier and D. Urquhart (*Familiar Words*) from whom he borrows the phrase, 'The subdivision of labour is the assassination of a people'.

10. Danielle Auffray, Thierry Baudouin and Michèle Collin, *Le travail et après . . .*, Paris 1978. This work presents, in a more accessible fashion, the rather difficult works of Italian theoreticians (most notably Mario Tronti and Antonio Negri) on the mass-worker and 'worker autonomy', works which, from 1968 onwards, inspired the activists of *Lotta Continua* and *Potere Operaio*.

11. Auffray *et al.*, pp. 13, 152–3, 170.

12. For all the above, see Gorz, *Farewell to the Working Class*, ch. 6; 'The Non-Class of Post-Industrial Proletarians'.

13. I am not saying the economic crisis was deliberately provoked in order to bring the working class into line. It has complex causes – one of which was the explosion of labour costs without a corresponding rise in productivity levels, in spite of an increase in the amount of fixed capital per work station – which I have summarized in *Paths to Paradise*, trans. Malcolm Imrie, London and Sydney 1985, pp. 7–13 (theses 6 to 8).

6

The Ultimate Ideology of Work

In contrast to the supporters of the fragmentation of jobs, who maintained that workers performed better if forced to function as though they were machines, a minority of 'humanists' have always maintained the opposite point of view – human beings are not machines: they must be able to enjoy their work and espouse the aims of the enterprise in which they work if they are to give of their best.

If this theory has never been put into practice in large-scale industry, it is because a whole *series* of reasons made it difficult to apply: the different workshops and departments of large factories had to synchronize their functions, each producing just enough components to supply the workshops assembling the final product. Calculability and reliability were just as important as actual output, or even more so. Hence the importance of the 'time and motion' men, who defend their control over the finest details of the labour process by resisting even minimal worker autonomy. As William F. Whyte notes in his excellent *Money and Motivation,*

> management is so preoccupied with its efforts to establish control over the workers that it loses sight of the presumed purpose of the organization. A casual visitor to the plant might indeed be surprised to learn that its purpose was *to get out production.* Certainly, if it had been possible to enforce some of the rules described by Roy, the result would have been a slowing down of production.[1]

However, this is only one aspect of the issue. Obsession with control and calculability is, in practice, only rarely motivated by insurmountable technical and economic requirements. Such requirements are always *equally* excuses employed by capital to disguise its wish to dominate labour: that is, excuses for the basic distrust, on the management's part, of a workforce held to be 'inherently' allergic to work and which the representatives of capital suspect of being all the more willing to 'skive' since the objectives of the enterprise are structurally alien, if not indeed antagonistic, to it and, therefore, loftily shrouded in secrecy.

The necessity – from a technical point of view – for control and, consequently, for domination, can be overcome without too much difficulty in small and medium-sized enterprises; it cannot be overcome in large enterprises except by effecting changes which are all the more difficult to implement since they affect both the enterprise's hierarchical staffing structure and its technical (and spatial) organization. William F. Whyte provides a number of examples to show that organizations can be modified so that workers enjoy their work, espouse the aims of the enterprise and mobilize the reserves of productivity and skill they usually keep to themselves. The success of this kind of reorganization necessarily presupposes, first, a relationship of mutual confidence between management and organized labour, second, recognition of the workers' ability to organize themselves, take the initiative and participate in decision-making, and, third, financial involvement of the workers in the results of their labour.

Sooner or later, however, this policy of 'participation' or co-management – of which the Scanlon Plan was one of the best example; and one in advance of the 'quality circles' of thirty years later[2] – meets with the following difficulty: for job security to be guaranteed, the volume of sales must increase at the same rate as the productivity of labour. A duly motivated workforce, however, can achieve staggering increases in productivity (increases of 20 per cent per annum over a period of several years in the examples cited by Whyte[3]). The volume of sales, however, cannot continue to increase at such a rate. The point inevitably comes when management decides to reduce the workforce in order to reduce costs, thus regaining sole ownership of the enterprise's decision-making power. The 'partnership' of labour and capital is thus destroyed at one fell swoop; the workers realize their co-operation with the management has been a swindle; and antagonistic class relations are re-established.[4]

A system of co-operation between workers and management cannot survive, therefore, unless management effectively guarantees its employees job security, by which I mean *employment for life*. It is on this condition alone that there can be social *integration* on the Japanese model within the enterprise. Yet large Japanese firms are only able to guarantee their employees jobs for life by subcontracting out the manufacturing and services which they, as parent companies, have no vital interest in undertaking themselves, to a vast network of satellite companies.

These subcontracting enterprises cushion the parent company from fluctuations in economic conditions: they employ and dismiss their workers according to changes in demand, and the fact that their employees often have no union or social protection whatsoever means this can be accomplished with great speed. *Job security in the parent companies is matched by unstable employment and social insecurity throughout the rest of the economy.* Employment for life and social integration are *privileges reserved for an elite* (about 25 per cent of Japanese employees in 1987, a figure which is decreasing markedly as older workers are encouraged to retire early and are not replaced). They are only compatible with economic rationality within the framework of a dual society. This social division (or 'dualization') has been the dominant characteristic of all the industrialized societies since the mid seventies.

Indeed we are now faced with a situation throughout the world in which there is, on the one hand, a privileged stratum of permanent workers attached to the enterprises in which they work and, on the other, a growing mass of casual labourers, temporary workers, the unemployed and 'odd jobbers'. The integration of a hard core of elite workers into the enterprise, a process which had a solid cultural basis in Japan, has become a technical necessity for all industries undergoing robotization. The question is no longer whether, instead of using compulsion, management prefer to motivate the workers by building up a relationship of confidence and co-operation with them. It no longer has any choice in the matter: it can only reduce its costs by replacing the Taylorized production line and its semi-skilled workers by robotized installations which, in certain departments of the factory at least, require workers of a new type.

The new-style workers, to whom we shall turn our attention shortly, must be able to manage the running of an automated manufacturing system as part of a multi-skilled team. They must be capable of reacting rapidly, must co-operate with their fellow workers sharing out tasks between them as they themselves see fit in response to different situations, and must show both independent initiative and a sense of responsibility. Management is, therefore, physically incapable of commanding, monitoring and supervising the multi-skilled teams which, in the car industry, for example, control certain departments. It must win the loyalty of these new-style workers, build them up socially and psychologically, and create a new image of the factory and its 'operators' who, clad in orange overalls, with clean hands and alert minds, no longer bear any resemblance to the traditional image of the worker.

Hence the ideology of 'human resources' typified – almost caricatured – by the 'integrated, multi-dimensional, human enterprise, conceived as a site for the blossoming of individual and collective initiatives and thus as the engine of social and economic progress' whose virtues are extolled by Danièle Blondel, a university professor.[5]

> [The] social partners now have to accept this new image of the enterprise. Certain trade unions even see it as a basis for questioning those forms of trade union demands which are based on the antagonism between capital and labour . . . All studies carried out on this issue (*sic*) reveal the gradual disappearance of unskilled workers, recruited solely to complete standardized, manual tasks within a Taylorist form of organization. Today it is the qualities that distinguish human beings from both animals and machines – that is, an understanding of technologies and the environment, the spirit of initiative and innovation, attention to quality, the ability to communicate, a comprehension of time and conflict management – which are everywhere (*sic*) in growing demand at all levels (*sic*) . The worker without identity . . . has been replaced by an intelligent, organized person with individualized skills, who is generally encouraged by the enterprise to develop a career strategy.

In actual fact, the above description of the new worker is not so much a reflection of reality as a 'paradigm shift', a *tendency* manifested in *one part* of industry. Kern and Schumann, who made a detailed study of this shift and are firm supporters of the theory of the 'reprofessionalization' of labour, nevertheless note that at the factory with the highest degree of robotized production in Europe (Volkswagen), there are at most only one thousand workers of this new kind in a workforce of a hundred thousand (or of three or four times this number if maintenance workers are included) and that, 'although we can expect their number to increase dramatically during the coming years, they will nevertheless remain in the minority'.[6]

The image of the enterprise as a place where employees can achieve personal fulfilment is therefore an essentially ideological invention. It conceals the real transformations that have taken place, namely that enterprises are replacing labour by machines, producing more and better with a decreasing percentage of the workforce previously employed, and offering privileges to a chosen elite of workers, which are accompanied by unemployment, precarious employment, de-skilling and lack of job security for the majority.

The advance of technology has thus resulted in the segmentation and disintegration of the working class. An elite has been won over to collaboration with capital in the name of work ethic; the great mass of workers have become marginalized or lost their job security and serve as a reserve army for industry which wishes to be able to adjust its workforce rapidly according to fluctuations in demand. Wolfgang Lecher, a researcher attached to the German trade-union research institute, analyses the situation as follows.[7]

Enterprises are adopting a strategy of flexible response on two levels simultaneously: the firm's stable core of employees must be functionally flexible; the peripheral workforce, for its part, must be numerically flexible. In other words, 'around a core of stable workers with a wide range of skills, there is a fluctuating, peripheral workforce with a more restricted range of more basic skills, who are dependent on the chance play of economic forces.'

The stable core must accept occupational mobility, both in the short term (changing their positions and acquiring new skills) and in the long term (retraining and modifying their career plans), in exchange for job security. Their skills are essentially company skills provided, enhanced and perfected by the firm by means of a process of continuous in-house training. The firm therefore relies heavily on the employees it has trained, and vice versa.

The peripheral workforce is divided into two groups: the first is employed on a permanent basis to do administrative jobs and to monitor, service and test installations but it is not highly skilled and can be renewed, enlarged or replaced at will by recruiting from the ranks of the unemployed. This source also provides a second group of peripheral workers, employed on a temporary and, as is often the case, part-time basis, as economic conditions demand. By increasing or decreasing the proportion of temporary and part-time workers at will, enterprises can optimally adjust their workforces to meet fluctuations in the market. This is made possible by the existence of a practically inexhaustible reserve of unemployed workers.

Lastly, there is the *the external workforce*, which includes extremely highly skilled professionals (such as data-processing specialists and chartered accountants), as well as workers with no particular skills (such as cleaners, transport workers and catering staff) and the large, fluctuating workforce occasionally employed by subcontractors.

In the 1990s, according to Lecher, the workforce will be divided between these three categories as follows: 25 per cent will belong to the stable core, 25 per cent will have stable jobs on the periphery and 50 per cent will be in insecure and occasional employment in unskilled external or peripheral jobs. Lecher's calculations are supported by the fact that the number of people in Britain in temporary or part-time employment, or doing 'odd jobs', rose from less than seven million in 1981 to eight million (that is, to a third of the working population) in 1985. If we add to this the people who are unemployed, the final figure is not far off the 50 per cent Lecher ultimately predicts for the third category. In Italy, where the practice of subcontracting is much more developed, and takes on both very flexible and, often, very modern forms, we would probably find comparable percentages if we had reliable statistical data.[8]

The image of the new workers, proud of their crafts, masters of their work, capable of keeping pace with technological developments, does not therefore derive from a belated concession to the humanism of labour on the part of the employers, but corresponds to a necessity produced by changes in technology. Capital has used this necessity as a lever to bring about the disintegration of the working class, the trade-union movement and what remained of social solidarity and cohesion. All it needed to do so was *to adopt the values of the utopia of work as its own*: control (that is, technical reappropriation) by the workers over the means of production; the full development within work of the abilities of the individual; and recognition of the importance of skills and the professional ethic.

This revaluation of the image of the worker rests, on the part of the employers, on a rational calculation: it is not only a question of winning the loyalty of an elite of workers they cannot do without and integrating them into the enterprise; it also means cutting this elite off from its class of origin and from class organizations, by giving it a different social identity and a different sense of social worth. In a society cut in two ('dualized'), this elite necessarily belongs to the world of 'the fighters and winners' who deserve a different status from the work-shy masses. The members of this elite of workers will therefore be encouraged to form their own independent trade unions and their own forms of social insurance, co-financed by the enterprises in which they work. At the same time, the employers will have limited the ability of this elite to bargain or fight trade-union struggles, by isolating it and stressing its privileges: its members have been chosen from among a very large number of applicants; they enjoy job security, a steady income and the kind of work and possibilities of promotion that are envied by all. And above all they owe their status to the fact that they are, professionally, the most capable; economically, the most productive; and, individually, the most hard-working.

Insofar as it corresponds in large part to the ideal of the sovereign, multi-skilled worker of the utopia of work, the employers' discourse and the strategy concealed within it, have brought about the most serious crisis in the history of the trade-union movement. If, as is the case in West Germany, trade-union organization derives its strength from its roots in the ranks of the skilled workers, the threat exists that it will rapidly degenerate into neo-corporatism. For, as Lecher says, 'the antagonism between the interests of labour and capital is overlaid by a growing antagonism between the interests of a stable core of workers on the one hand and peripheral workers and the unemployed on the other.'[9]

If, on the other hand, trade unionism is particularly strong among semi-skilled workers – as is the case in Italy where until recently there was practically no foreign workforce and where semi-skilled workers owe their job security to their trade-union organization – then the unions find themselves in the dangerous position of having strong support among a declining category of workers and weak backing from the two categories which are in rapid expansion: the mass of temporary workers, which is expanding but difficult to organize, the unemployed and 'odd jobbers'; and the new elite of 'reprofessionalized' workers, characterized by a marked tendency to defend their own specific interests by forming company unions or small craft unions.

In a situation of the Italian kind, the unions' bargaining power and political influence will thus depend on their ability to defend the particular interests and aspirations of the new labour elite, without, however, sacrificing the interests and aspirations of the other categories in order to do so. This is no easy task: it presupposes the existence of a social project transcending present divisions, appealing to the workers' cultural, moral and political motivations, and expressing itself in immediate objectives shared by all.[10]

In a situation of the German kind on the other hand, the unions, dominated by elites of privileged workers, will display a dangerous tendency to disregard peripheral workers, temporary workers and the unemployed and – consciously or unconsciously – form an ideological alliance with the employers of the 'successful' and the 'able' against the 'incapable' and the 'idle'. Here again the problem is how to 'create', in Peter Glotz's phrase, 'solidarity between the strong and the weak'.[11]

Now this creation of solidarity is only possible if we break with the work ethic and with what I have termed the utopia of work. This utopia – and, equally, its philosophy of productivity, hard work and professionalism – is devoid of all humanistic content in a situation in which *work is no longer the major productive force* and in which, therefore, *there are not enough permanent jobs to go round.* In such a situation, the glorification of hard work and the assertion that working and living can be one and the same thing, is an ideology which can only be held by a privileged elite which monopolizes the best-paid, most highly skilled and most stable jobs and justifies doing so on the grounds of its superior abilities. The ideology of work and the ethics of effort therefore become a cover for ultra-competitive egoism and careerism: the best succeed, the others have only themselves to blame; hard work should be encouraged and rewarded, which therefore means we should not subsidize the unemployed, the poor and all the other 'layabouts'.

This ideology (which in Europe finds its most overt expression in Thatcherism) is strictly rational, as far as capitalism is concerned: the aim to motivate a workforce which cannot easily be replaced (for the moment, at least) and control it ideologically for want of a means of controlling it physically. In order to do this, it must preserve the workforce's adherence to the work ethic, destroy the relations of solidarity that could bind it to the less fortunate, and persuade it that *by doing as much work as possible* it will best serve the collective interest as well as its own private interests. It will thus be necessary to conceal the fact that there is an increasing structural glut of workers and an increasing structural shortage of secure, full-time jobs; in short, that *the economy*[12] no longer needs everyone to work – and will do so less and less. And that, as a consequence, the 'society of work' is obsolete: work can no longer serve as the basis for social integration. But, to conceal these facts it is necessary to find alternative explanations for the rise in unemployment and the decrease in job security. It will thus be asserted that casual labourers and the unemployed are not serious about looking for work, do not possess adequate skills, are encouraged to be idle by over-generous dole payments and so on. And, it will be added, these people are all paid far too much for the little they are able to do, with the result that the economy, which is groaning under the weight of these excessive burdens, is no longer buoyant enough to create a growing number of jobs. And the conclusion will be reached that, 'To end unemployment, we have to work more.'

The way this ideology is functional to capitalism is by no means obvious for workers as a whole since it too effectively overlaps with the traditional ideology of the working-class movement itself in a number of respects. An appreciable section of the traditional Left and the unions thus adheres to this ideology on the basis of their own values, without perceiving (or without wishing to acknowledge) that, in a situation in which the total volume of economically necessary work is diminishing, the privileges enjoyed by the elite workers necessarily entail the social exclusion of a growing mass of unemployed people, temporary and casual workers. Working as much as possible under these conditions is not serving the collective but defending an individual privilege coveted by others. Work-based morality has here gone over into something quite opposite: possessive selfishness.

At the very point when a privileged fraction of the working class seems to be in a position to acquire multiple skills, to achieve workplace autonomy and continually widen their capacities for action – all of which are things that were ideals of the worker self-management currents within the labour movement – the meaning of this ideal is thus radically altered by the conditions in which it seems destined to be fulfilled. It is not *the working class* which is achieving these possibilities of self-organization and increasing technological power; it is a small core of privileged workers who are integrated into new-style enterprises at the expense of a mass of people who are marginalized and whose job security is destroyed – people shunted from one form of occasional, unrewarding and uninteresting employment to another, who are often reduced to competing for the privilege of selling personal services (including shoe-shining and house-cleaning) to those who retain a secure income.

Under these conditions, the values of solidarity, equity and fraternity upheld by the working-class movement no longer imply the need to work for the love of work but rather the need to share the jobs and wealth produced in an equitable way: that is, to formulate a policy for the extensive, methodical and programmed reduction of working hours (without loss of income – a point I will return to below).[13]

To reject such a policy on the grounds that it would hinder a repro-fessionalization of tasks which would allow individuals to invest themselves completely in their work, with total commitment to it, is to endorse the real dualization of the economy under cover of rejecting it. The dualization of society will be checked, and then reversed, not by the unattainable utopia of an all-absorbing, full-time job for everyone, but by formulae for redistributing work which will reduce the amount of work *everybody* does, without for all that de-skilling or compartmental-izing it. It is possible. If we are to prevent the long-term 'South-African-ization' of society, we must find another utopia.

Notes

1. William Foote Whyte et al. *Money and Motivation. An Analysis of Incentive in Industry*, New York 1955, 1970, p. 65–6. The result of collaborative research at the New York School of Industrial and Labor Relations, Cornell University, this work presents a series of monographs which shed light on the various aspects of the problem.

2. Whyte et al. p. 259 ff. The Scanlon Plan, which owes its name to a steelworker who became a management consultant, was tried out in medium-sized enterprises in the United States in the late 1940s and after. It subsequently inspired Japanese industrialists, and it was in its Japanese version that it was reimported in the late 1970s.

3. Whyte et al. p. 166 ff.

4. Since 1987, the large-scale Japanese enterprises which have finally come round to dismissing their workers have been gradually finding this to be the case.

5. 'Mort et résurrection de la pensée économique' by Danièle Blondel, a professor at the Université de Paris-Dauphine, in *Le Monde*, 1 April 1986.

6. Horst Kern and Michael Schumann, *Das Ende der Arbeitsteilung?*, Munich 1984, p. 98.

7. Wolfgang Lecher, 'Zum zukünftigen Verhältnis von Erwerbsarbeit und Eigenarbeit aus gewerkschaftlicher Sicht', *WSI Mitteilungen*, 3, 1986, p. 256 ff.

8. In the United States, the percentage of people unemployed or working less than six months a year is 25%; in addition there are 30% of casual workers in the tertiary sector who are underpaid and have no social insurance whatsoever.

9. Wolfgang Lecher, 'Überleben in einer veränderten Welt. Ein Konzept für die zukünftige Arbeit der Gewerkschaften', *Die Zeit* (Hamburg) 18, 26 April 1985, p. 44–5.

10. See Appendix.

11. Peter Glotz, *Manifest für eine neue europäische Linke*, Berlin 1985. Peter Glotz was the executive secretary for the SPD from 1981 to 1987. The problems of both the German and Italian situations are found in the French one, where they are made worse by the very low level of trade-union membership. The CGT, whose main power-base lies in declining industries and categories of workers, only retains a degree of political muscle because of its dominant position within certain public services (for example, electricity, transport, municipal services). But the actions it is able to mount, like those of the other direct or indirect employees of the state, well over half of whom belong to *Force ouvrière* and the FEN (the teachers' union), are markedly sectional and corporative in nature and do not confront the fundamental problems posed by the changes in technology, the decrease in the amount of socially necessary work available, the new differentiation between the various strata of salaried workers and the necessity of redistributing work. The CFDT, which has been more or less successful in tackling these problems, does not have a strong enough power-base to be able to confront them in practice within the framework of collective actions.

12. The fact that there is a great deal to do *which does not fall into the economic sphere* is another matter. I shall return to it later to show how such work differs from work which has an economic purpose and how its status should reflect this difference.

13. See Part III.

7

The Latest Forms of Work

Search for Meaning (1)

I now propose to examine the work of this new type of skilled worker in greater detail. For it is not sufficient merely to say that they constitute a small elite which enjoys considerable privileges. This was also true of the skilled workers of the nineteenth century, yet it did not prevent them founding the labour movement or being in the vanguard of its struggles. Could not this new elite of workers also form a new vanguard, in its own way?

This theory is held by a number of trade unionists and should not be dismissed lightly. After all, the current technological revolution will, to a large extent, be what is made of it by the workers on which it depends. It is not a purely anonymous process evolving in conformity with technological imperatives that are beyond dispute. It will be brought about by the work of the men and women involved and they are not infinitely malleable. The resistance they put up and the demands they make will shape the course of events. How quickly, how well, how completely the technological revolution advances depends on these people. What the nature of the new type of worker and the new type of human being will be, and what kind of society we are in the process of creating also depends, at least in part, on them. It will depend on the trade unions whether these men and women become the hostages and prisoners of the enterprises in which they work, united solely by their corporate spirit, or whether they become, to a greater or lesser degree, a combative and influential part of the working class. The influence which the trade-union movement will succeed in exercising over the forms and pace of these technological changes is, therefore, decisive for the future of work, of society and of the trade-union movement itself. These are all obvious facts.

The problem these new type of workers pose is of a different order:

how far can the trade union movement go in espousing their specific interests without sinking into neo-corporatism? We have already examined the question from the socio-political angle. We must now tackle it from an angle which relates specifically to their work. In actual fact a number of labour-movement theorists, in their desire not to cut themselves off from this new elite of workers, have tended to see the latter as the vanguard which will implement the Marxian utopia of work. This appears to be the position adopted by Kern and Schumann and, in certain respects, by Sabel and Piore.[1] They believe in the possibility of workers becoming 'masters over machines' and achieving autonomy through their work; and in the possibility of restructuring tasks to such a degree that the division of labour (and not just its fragmentation) can be overcome. In their view, workers should be able to identify with their work and derive from that identification an awareness of their strength and their role as liberators. This would enable them once again to follow a trade in the full sense, manufacture an entire product, achieve fulfil-ment in their work and embody the humanism of labour in a new form. In short, they could establish the unity of working and living, of the culture of work and culture in general.

It would then be possible – and there is no irony intended here – to see this new elite as a new chivalric order, a hypothesis (or thesis) outlined by Oskar Negt. Just like an order of knights, in fact, this new elite would hold the instruments of power – the entire economy, or better still, the whole of collective life – in its hands. Everything would function through this elite; it would not be possible for anything to func-tion without it. Its power, its responsibilities and its labour would all be 'structurally political'.[2] In other words, by virtue of the extent of its power and responsibilities, it would in fact have a say in, or a right of control over, political decisions – a position not dissimilar to that of the military in times of crisis. The new elite would, in theory, exercise this power to control or influence political decisions in the name of the universal values whose trustee it would have become by dint of its professional culture and the nature of its tasks. Indeed, these tasks would require the new type of worker to develop all-round intellectual capacities and manual skills and to understand the production cycle in its entirety. Work would demand of each individual both sovereignty and the ability to co-operate with other people.

This idea that individuals can regain sovereign control over the conditions governing their existence by and through their work takes on a key role in the work of Kern and Schumann. Indeed, one could conceive of sovereign individuals, whose occupation activity coincides with the exercise of sovereignty, seeing their vocation as combating everything which continues to oppress, humiliate, diminish and stunt human beings. The new elite of workers could therefore play a cultural and political role comparable to that of nineteenth-century primary-school teachers or of doctors in the heroic age when the importance of public hygiene, nutrition and living-conditions in combating epidemics came to be understood.

I have limited myself here to an explicit formulation of the hypotheses and assumptions which implicitly underlie the conclusions drawn by certain sociologists of work. I shall now compare these conclusions with analytic descriptions of the new type of work. The essential question to be clarified here is whether the members of the new elite of workers can derive from their identification with their trade a vocation to emancipate all social spheres and all aspects of the individual. Is what was true of the nineteenth-century teachers and doctors also true of this new group? Does their job have a structurally political and campaigning dimension which makes it impossible to identify with that job without at the same time committing oneself to making society develop in a direction that will result in its liberation?

We will begin with an analysis, written under the pseudonym Inox, which appeared in the (independent communist) daily, *Il Manifesto*:

> The introduction of computerization has resulted in a modification in styles of production which may be summarized as follows: the direct transformation of the product is increasingly carried out by the machine alone. It performs the operations involved directly on the raw materials; the only tasks the worker has to perform are those of feeding, setting up, supervising the process and removing the product, whether these tasks be simple or complex ones.
>
> However, it is not just the division of labour between man and machine that has altered, but also the distribution of tasks within the labour process itself: we have progressed from the fragmentation of repetitive tasks to highly integrated and interactive processes, the integration and coherence of which are ensured by the use of computerized models linking the various production processes to each other and linking production to management . . . The activities the worker performs become indirect or subsidiary, supervising and regulatory activities being the most interesting of these. The worker's abilities, knowledge and power are no longer deployed in labour as physical activity, in the skilful handling of the machines and tools used for the job and the main-tenance of the work rate, but are applied to the *system of controlling* the productive process. His work essentially involves understanding and decoding symbols and indicators. He does not handle or touch the material that is to be transformed and, more often than not, he does not even see it, except on closed-circuit television. Or sometimes only on a display screen as a series of graphic symbols, graphs or numbers. The transformation process is not immediately intelligible and can only be understood if it is related to a mental model.

The worker's skills, in large part, no longer relate to the object that is to be transformed and are concerned uniquely with controlling the relation between technology and the transformation of the product . . . Labour, which was once a succession of discrete acts, tends to become a continuous activity; it is no longer a defined task but a *sub-system*, a complete labour process.

This does not necessarily mean the activities involved become more complex; this may be the case, but it is equally possible for them to become strictly monitoring activities. What is certain is that it is no longer possible to talk of work-stations; tasks to be accomplished by completing a series of elementary jobs; or trades conceived of as a combination of skills and know-how employed in using a machine or working with raw materials.

A new type of worker, *the process worker* who is the potential key figure in the new type of factory, is becoming increasingly common. He is not, in actual fact, a new figure but what is new is that he is now to be found in all types of production. In the 1960s, there were already workers of this type in the chemical and steel industries and in industries involving continuous production where the division of labour was based on controlling the physico-chemical parameters of the product.

Integrating activities and sequencing them in real time, by using data-processing techniques applied to machinery, makes production in all branches of industry comparable to production in the process industries and thus introduces everywhere forms of organization which require new workers of this type. The interesting, and in some respects paradoxical, aspect of the phenomenon is that *the activity the worker performs is no longer connected to the object to be transformed (he no longer needs to be familiar with the raw materials and the tools used to work them); it is determined uniquely by the nature of the systems used for controlling and regulating the process.* [A.G.'s italics.]

This is interesting, since it is here that worker control, union intervention on the organization of work and the negotiated redefinition of skill levels may be brought to bear. And it is paradoxical, because it could cause the very notion of the *industrial* union to disappear altogether. For what difference is there between chemical and steel workers, workers in computer-integrated systems manufacturing Fiat engines and those manufacturing Barilla spaghetti? If the object of labour is no longer the product but the management model of a process of production, the activities of a steel roller at Italsider will probably have much in common with those of a worker controlling pasta-shell production, and bear very little resemblance to those of the worker beside him who controls the quality of the sheet metal . . . Occupational identity is no longer related to the product but to the systems of secondary technology applied to production.[3]

This analysis is interesting on a number of counts:

1. It clearly reveals the versatility of the 'process worker'. Since all industries are becoming increasingly akin to industries in continuous

production (glassworks, cement works, refineries, steelworks, chemical factories, power stations and so on), their operators have the same qualifications and have received the same basic training. Their potential mobility is therefore greater than would be the case in traditional occupations: moving from a refinery to a light-bulb factory or from a cement works to a spaghetti factory is much easier than switching trades from that of mechanic to that of electrician. The same is true for a large percentage of skilled maintenance workers (mechanics, plumbers, electricians and technicians supervising computer-integrated flexible manufacturing systems) as well as for computer programmers.

Although all skilled maintenance workers and 'process workers' must be trained in skills specific to the type of industry or unit of production in which they work, *on top of their basic training*, acquiring this specific training does not, apparently, take longer than it would to train as a semi-skilled worker in traditional industry: that is, no more than a few weeks.[4] The possibility of changing enterprise or industrial sector more easily accords workers greater existential autonomy: their skills are not merely 'in-house skills'; they have a 'trade', that is, a skill that can be taken and used elsewhere, much more so than workers trained and specialized to do narrowly defined tasks. This means they are not the prisoners of 'their' workplaces but are able to change and vary their jobs. Equally, the enterprises in which they work have no trouble in replacing them. In other words, their occupational skills can, to a large extent, be *rendered commonplace*, by which I do not mean that the work they do will become de-skilled and monotonous, but that *a much greater number of people will be able to acquire the skills it entails.* By a curious vestige of elitism, many trade unions react with great hostility to the idea that skills can and (I will return to this in a moment) must be rendered commonplace, as if the individual's aim, and source of dignity, were the possession of irreplaceable occupational skills and knowledge. Making skills more commonplace means quite simply that what I do can also be done or learnt by other people – in large numbers. In this way, a wide range of skills which were previously the sole reserve of various elites have become commonplace in the last twenty years: knowledge of foreign languages; computer literacy; an understanding of the principles of diet, contraception, the prevention of various illnesses, and so on; as well as such skills as skiing, playing tennis, horse riding and sailing.

The fact is that making skills and higher qualifications more accessible to large numbers of people is the most effective and most necessary method of combating the dualization of society described above. It is essential if there is to be a coherent policy of reducing the length of the working week by redistributing jobs, even highly skilled ones, among a much greater proportion of the active population. And, conversely, it has to be *one* of the aims of reducing the length of the working week: it must *also* be possible to use the time thus liberated for improving and broadening one's skills, occupational or otherwise. There is no alternative means of redistributing socially necessary work amongst all those able and willing to work: we should all be able to work less so that we can all earn our living by working.

2. Does the general rise in levels of qualification and the increase in autonomy at work also signify that the unity of working and living, occupational culture and culture in general will be recreated? Is it true, as the proponents of the utopia of work and a number of left-wing authors – such as Kern and Schumann in West Germany, Sabel and Piore in the United States and Mike Cooley in Britain – maintain, that the reskilling of industrial labour will eliminate its heteronomy, restore humanity's mastery over machines, promote the full development of our human faculties *within* our work and give workers back their sovereignty? The answers one gives to these questions will vary according to the dimensions one takes into account.

All work has three dimensions, and restoring its autonomy in one of these dimensions will not suffice to make it an autonomous activity, free from alienation or (which amounts to the same thing) heteronomy. These three dimensions are:

(a) the organization of the labour process;

(b) the relation with the product to be produced;

(c) the content of work, that is, the nature of the activities and the human faculties it requires.

Work only becomes an autonomous activity if

(a) it is organized by those performing it;

(b) it consists in the free pursuit of a self-appointed aim;

(c) it is fulfilling for the individual performing it.

We must now examine how things stand in relation to these three conditions.

(a) Working in autonomous groups, whose members share out their tasks, work in relays, organize their work themselves and take responsibility for keeping the machines in good running order and controlling the quality of the product, considerably *reduces* the degree of heteronomy which characterized the fragmented labour of Taylorism. However, it does not *eliminate* this heteronomy, *it displaces it*. The term 'heteronomy' in fact characterizes the specialized activities individuals must perform as functions co-ordinated from outside, by an external organization, aiming at a pre-established goal: 'The nature of tasks is predetermined in such a way as to make individuals function like the cogs of a huge machine.'[5]

This definition still holds for autonomous groups, except in one respect: the individuals involved take responsibility for organizing at group level the execution of a complex task which is seen as a group task. Within the group, these individuals enjoy a considerable degree of autonomy. But the task the group is allocated is a predetermined one, co-ordinated externally with those of other groups. The (robotized) factory still functions as if it were a huge machine: its parts are made up of automatic lines of robots operated and co-ordinated by computer and these lines of robots are linked to each other by other computers. The essential difference is that here *groups rather than individuals function as its cogs.* The members of these groups enjoy an appreciable margin of autonomy and scope for initiative but this is still autonomy *in* work, not *of* work: such work, whatever its complexity or the skill required to do it, performs a specialized task that is strictly functional vis-à-vis the material system of which it forms a part. There is no way the formal autonomy within the group's internal labour relations can be classed as existential autonomy or 'personal sovereignty' as Kern and Schumann would argue, nor as occupational sovereignty.

(b) All the comments made above by Inox concerning the lack of any kind of relation between 'process worker' and product, are equally applicable to 'reprofessionalized' workers in robotized factories. These workers do not transform or handle what they produce, any more than operators in refineries, rolling mills or pasta factories do. Worse, they only oversee the manufacture of a semi-finished product. Each autonomous multi-skilled group is only responsible for one section of the automatic line. They cannot even claim to oversee the manufacture of engine blocks or cylinder heads: all they do is ensure the robots performing some of the operations involved in their manufacture function correctly.

The alienation from what they produce is, in certain respects, even more complete here than in the Taylorized factory. The specialized skilled workers in these multi-skilled groups no longer have the producer's know-how which, in spite of everything else, unskilled workers still possessed: they never come into direct contact with the product or semi-finished product, that is, with the actual materials; their only contact is with the machines used to transform these materials. They are not specialists in the making of a particular product; they are specialists in the repairing, regulating and programming of a particular type of machine. Neither the nature nor quality of the product or semi-finished product, nor any of its parameters, depends on them: for, by contrast with traditional operators, regulators and mechanicians, they do not operate the machines or control them. They merely ensure that they follow their programme. Once they have been programmed, the machines are self-monitoring and give indications of any anomalies that occur.[6]

(c) It is not enough for a job to be interesting and varied for it to be fulfilling. Certainly, a job in which you can become fully absorbed is always better than a repetitive task. But the essential question is the extent to which the skills and faculties a job employs constitute an occupational culture, and the extent to which there is unity between occupational culture and the culture of everyday life – between work and life. The extent, in other words, to which involvement in one's work implies the enrichment or sacrificing of one's individual being. After my day's work, am I richer or poorer as a human being? If someone asks me at the height of my career, 'Is this what you wanted to be when you were fifteen?',[7] what answer will I give?

The contents of our work must be judged in the light of questions such as these. Similarly, viewing economic rationality in this light reveals how woefully inadequate its abstractions are. Working is not just the creation of economic wealth; it is also always a means of *self*-creation. Therefore, we must *also* ask apropos the contents of our work whether that work produces the kind of men and women we wish humanity to be made of. Viewed in this light, are the new type of 'reprofessionalized' workers – or, more precisely, the 'reprofessionalized' workers who derive their sense of personal identity and social dignity from their work, as Kern and Schumann, and Sabel and Piore would have it – closer to a possible ideal of humanity than the more traditional types of workers? Can the complex tasks they are allotted fill their life and *give it meaning*, without simultaneously distorting it? How, in a word, is this work *lived*? These are the three questions I now wish to examine.

1. It is impossible to equate the work done by maintenance workers or the operators of robotized systems with the practice of a trade in the full sense, on the grounds that such workers possess and employ the same skills as a master-craftsman. A trade, by its very nature, allows you to control an entire product. The trade is learnt and taught *with the aim of* achieving this product and its fully-rounded character stems from the fact that the product is both whole and complete. The product is whole and complete when it possesses its full use value for the end user. The exercise of a fully rounded trade consists, therefore, in creating entire products for the end users. Thus skilled workers, manufacturing clothes

they have designed themselves on programmable textile machines they have tinkered with and adapted to their own ends, are practising a fully rounded trade within a micro-enterprise of craftworkers. The same skilled workers, maintaining and programming a battery of such machines in a textile factory, are not practising a fully rounded trade: they employ all the same skills as before, with the exception of one: they have no control over the product and none, therefore, over the use to which the machine is put. The task they perform is not *poïetic* but *functional* in the sense defined in Chapter 3 above.[8] The fact that this task involves – formally – the same *technical* skills as the practice of a fully rounded trade does not alter its functional and alienated character. While the trade of the craftworker, who controls both product and machine, is able to realize the unity of technical culture and the culture of everyday life, the trade of the maintenance worker is limited solely to technical culture and specialized skills. Given these conditions, clinging in the name of a purely ideological, formal work ethic to the view that work is our source of personal identity and social integration, amounts to elevating identification with a specialized *function* to the status of a moral ideal, and promoting the narrow-minded and irresponsible expert – Max Weber's 'specialist without spirit' (*Fachmensch ohne Geist*) (be she or he technician or bureaucrat) – as a model for humanity.

2. The 'process worker' or computer-based systems operator is engaged in discontinuous labour, alternating between periods of intense activity and periods of inactivity, routine operations and boredom. Oskar Negt offers a noteworthy depiction of this type of labour:

> The worker who controls the uninterrupted functioning of a system of automatic machines from his control panel, does not work in the traditional sense of the word, he is not continually active: *he is on duty*. If a technical hitch should occur, he must intervene promptly or telephone his superiors, call for assistance and operate the buttons on the control panel in order to avoid more serious repercussions further up or down the production line. He acts as the *servant* of the machine, motivated by a *service ethic* that requires both his presence and his knowledge; but is this still work in the usual sense waged work in industry has given this notion? Although he only oversees the normal functioning of the limited sector for which he is responsible, he may intervene within and has to concentrate upon the production process in general and he is in no way different from the civil servant or functionary who is also only responsible within his limited sphere of competence for the execution of individual predefined tasks . . . In overseeing automatic systems in a particular enterprise, he contributes to the smooth running of sectors which, as a general rule, he knows nothing of, but which depend so closely on his activity that any error on his part would have incalculable consequences . . . The norms of the

ethic of responsibility which define the duties of the individual worker make him responsible to the whole of society.[9]

The comparison with the 'functionary who is also only responsible within his limited sphere of competence for the execution of individual predefined tasks' is particularly pertinent. In the same way as the former, the worker turned 'functionary of the machine' is indeed bound – in places such as chemical complexes, electric or nuclear power stations, aerodromes and marshalling yards – scrupulously and *unconditionally* to observe the rules and procedures to be followed in case of accident or malfunction. The 'service ethic' compels him, for example, at all costs to avoid power cuts 'which would have incalculable consequences', without a thought for the social and economic ends for which electricity is being consumed. His role is to *serve* society, regardless of its nature or the goals and priorities it has set itself.

Given these conditions, it is impossible to conclude, as Negt does, that workers can and must assume political responsibility *within* their work. Indeed, this would only be possible if the function, goal and societal consequences of a given type of production could be revealed to the workers (or collective worker) *through* the technical processes they are responsible for in their work. Now we are a long way off a situation in which all aspects of a given production process are transparent to all those involved, a fact which Negt himself acknowledges: the operator's task is predetermined, for the most part 'he does not even know' the sectors to whose smooth functioning his work contributes. Certainly, discovering the societal goals and consequences of a type of production or, better still, of a *decision* to invest in preparation for this type of production, is a political task. It is the task of the trade unions, who are best placed to undertake it, to the extent that the information to which they have – and demand – access affords them an overall view of the social process. Nevertheless, political responsibility consists not only in acquiring this overall view but also in making use of it publicly to question the goals, advisability, soundness, consequences and so forth, of a given type of production or technical decision by allowing the various arguments to be debated.

Now this sort of questioning is strictly impossible *within the context of work itself.* Technical and political responsibility cannot coincide; responsible technicians or 'functionaries' cannot act as politically active citizens *at their place of work.* They cannot question the advisability of carrying out an order to increase the power supply when they are in the control room of a nuclear power station. They cannot assume political responsibility unless they detach themselves from their work, question it and *question their own professional function and identity.* They cannot acquire and develop this capacity for political questioning *at their place of work*: such a capacity presupposes the existence of a form of culture, interests and activities which transcends a purely occupational role; it presupposes a life which is not entirely absorbed by work, in short, *the very opposite of identification with one'e work* and one's function typical of the technician/bureaucrats, 'specialists without spirit, sensualists without heart', as Max Weber called them, puffed up with their own importance and willing to serve any master as long as it furthers their career.

In these circumstances, the mission of the trade-union movement acquires a new dimension, which the CFDT in France – or more specifically the CFDT union at EDF (Éléctricité de France) and the SNPEA (Syndicat national des Personnels de l'Énergie Atomique) – assumed in exemplary fashion until the early 1980s: that of providing the 'functionaries of the machine' with a framework in which they can publicly debate, in their capacity as citizens, the societal repercussions of decisions it will be their function to implement. Can they assume responsibility for such decisions 'before the whole of society'? Is it not their moral responsibility publicly to expose the adverse repercussions on society the 'fully electric, fully nuclear' programme threatens to produce? Is it not their duty to question political, economic, cultural implications of options which the dominant politico-economic groups present as purely technical necessities?

This is a far cry from neo-corporatist conceptions of trade unionism; but a far cry also from the service ethic or occupational ethic which sees work in itself as meaningful and enriching for the individual, provided it is interesting and involves a certain degree of responsibility. Technical interest and responsibility attaching to a task are not enough to establish a humanism or a morality, or a purpose in life, in spite of what Kern and Schumann, along with may others, appear to maintain when they talk of 'the aspiration to a form of work in which one can involve oneself, where one can use one's own head'; they add, 'in short, a form of work which has a meaning'.[10]

This is the crux of the problem. *The intrinsic interest of a job does not guarantee its being meaningful, just as its humanization does not guarantee the humanization of the ultimate objectives it serves.* Humanizing a job can make even the most barbaric of enterprises attractive for the people who work in them. Work can develop individual abilities, including the capacity for autonomous action, but the individuals' professional autonomy does not necessarily lead to their moral autonomy, that is, their insistence that they will not work towards goals that have not been publicly debated and that they have not been able to examine *and assume* personally. It is to this non-coincidence of technical responsibility with moral responsibility, of professional autonomy and existential autonomy, that we must now turn.

3. The connections between occupational culture and the culture of everyday life, and even the bridges between the two have been irretrievably destroyed by the increasingly technical nature of increasingly specialized jobs.

> There is always something to do, but to a very large extent production goes on on its own and the regulation, adjustment and maintenance work we do can hardly be seen as 'real' work . . . The worker cannot even feel he has a *decisive* influence on the quality of production . . . In spite of his skills and qualifications, he sees himself as having professional *knowledge*, not *capabilities* which could be expressed in the production of something substantial: a part manufactured or a wireless repaired.

This picture of workers in the chemical industry[11] perfectly sums up the gulf between occupational training and the culture of everyday life, and between work and life. And even this picture omits to describe what the lived experience of the final stage of technological development – factories entirely controlled by computer – will be. The control room of earlier years, with its instrument panels, has disappeared. Three people are sitting in a room, each with a two-screen VDU. From a keyboard, they can relay coded instructions to a computer incorporating 1,500 parameters, 200 control circuits and 600 alarm devices, and find out from the machine how the process under way is progressing.[12] The materiality of production is bracketed off, relegated to an invisible 'beyond' with which the workers-turned-operators communicate by means of numerical symbols: tapping out the numbers on their keyboard and reading the figures off the screen.

The tangible substance of the world has been abolished. Work as a physical activity has been abolished. All that is left is a purely intellectual, or rather, mental activity. This is the ultimate, the absolute triumph of what Husserl defined as 'mathematized nature': reality as we perceive it has been stripped of all its tangible qualities, the lived experience of original thought has been 'switched off'.[13] Work has disappeared because life has withdrawn from the universe. There is no one left; only numbers silently chasing numbers, numbers which cannot be questioned because they are insensible and mute. At the end of the day, the operators get up. They have nothing to show for their day's work, no physical, visible, measurable achievement: *they have created nothing.* Yet this nothing has drained them: during their day's (or night's) work they have imposed upon themselves that self-denial which consists in repressing their sensory existence: existing as pure intellect, eliminating and suppressing all living contacts with the lifeworld in and through their bodies, as so many potential disruptions of the function they must fulfil. The world as conceived by Hobbes is finally embodied in these people: only mathematical properties are held to be 'real' and really to exist in the natural world, just as, on another level, the 'reality' of all things is, in economic thought, their price (exchange value) as commodities. Only what can be calculated, quantified and expressed in figures is 'real'. Everything else has only a 'subjective' existence, that is, it is in a sense added on to the world by subjectivity and must be relegated to the margins of thought.[14] The repression of all that does not stem from the intellect and from mathematical calculations is deemed to give access to 'truth'; only *homo œconomicus* and his twin brother and shadow: the computerized worker, inhabit the region of the true.

Hence the pertinence of the question posed by Husserl, which will also be the starting point for the proponents of Critical Theory: *does the domination of Nature bear upon the abstract–universal mathematized nature of the physical sciences ('wissenschaftliche Natur') or on the experienced nature of the lifeworld ('lebensweltliche Natur')*?[15] Or, put another way: what relation to oneself as a sensory, corporeal existence, inherent in the world through the body, governs the methodical application of a technique?

Significantly this question, which was fundamental to Critical Theory, especially in its early stages, has practically disappeared from the work of Habermas. The 'lifeworld' (*Lebenswelt*), in Husserl's work, is primarily the sensible, three-dimensional world we *know* through our bodies, as certainly and unmistakeably as our bodies themselves. The world is ours, and we belong to it – *are part of* it – through our bodies. The meaning of this relationship of mutual inherence is perpetually informed and reworked by a cultural matrix which we learn at the same time as we learn to see, walk, talk, exist in our bodies as a relation to others and to the humanized world of culture we are born into. It is nevertheless the substance of the world experienced through our bodily inherence in it which is the ground of our lived certainties, the matter which will be given shape, form, style and pattern by culture[16] or denied by barbarism.

Given all this, the question now – dismissed by sociological/cultural and functional approaches alike – is whether a type of activity or a culture makes use of the possibilities of bodily existence by allowing these freely to develop and shaping the surrounding environment in a way which encourages them to flourish within it; or whether, by contrast, the surrounding environment, created of activities through which individuals do violence to themselves, does violence to bodily existence by its very configuration, its materials, and the demands it makes. The lifeworld is not, as in Habermas, primarily the world of traditions and norms which we adhere to as being 'only natural', for all norms, traditions and convictions can be called into question in a crisis situation, or undermined by doubts (for example, after an illness, the death of a close relative, the break-up of a relationship or a failure of some kind). On the other hand, nothing can shake the certainty with which we experience the sensory qualities and the material values ('good', 'agreeable') or counter-values ('sticky', 'stinking') of the world.[17] In light of this, we have to ask at what cost have we come to accept as our lifeworld, this world which is moulded by the instruments of our civilization. To what extent have we, by adapting to it, become maladapted to our own selves?[18] Does our civilization produce a life-world to which we belong through *our culture of living*, or does it leave the entire domain of sensory values adrift, in a state of barbarism?

The inability of our dominant culture to think reality as it is lived is in itself a reply to these questions. *Technical culture is lack of culture in all things non-technical.* Learning to work means unlearning how to find, or even to look for, a meaning to non-instrumental relations with the surrounding environment and with other people. This environment itself bears the imprint of technical violence. It is lived as an atmosphere of everyday violence. Violence is, essentially, a relationship with the body. This becomes immediately obvious when we identify the opposite of violence: that is, tenderness. Tenderness is a relationship with another person's body, which we treat as sensitive with the aim of heightening its sensitivity and enabling it to enjoy being itself; this relationship with another person's body necessarily implies heightening our own sensitivity. Violence, by contrast, is a relationship of technological instrumentalization of the things of this world whose sensory qualities have been denied and it is, as a result, a form of repression which devalues our own sensitivity. The dominance of instrumental rationality is to be seen in the functionality both of our everyday tools and of the objects and spaces we have designed to support and contain our bodies: chairs, tables, furniture, streets, means of transport, urban landscapes, industrial architecture, noises, lights, materials and so on. This all stems from, and in turn promotes, the practice of treating the environment in which we live in an instrumental way, doing violence to Nature, and to our own and other people's bodies. The culture of everyday life is – with all the disturbing ambiguity this antinomic creation contains – a *culture of violence* or, in its most extreme form, a systematic, thought-out, sub-limated, aggravated *culture of barbarism*, denying itself in its very asser-tion by the punks, or exhibiting a proto-fascist anti-aesthetic of insensitivity, cruelty and ugliness with the skinheads.

To a work culture which cuts itself off from the sensory substance of the lifeworld, corresponds the production of a world without sensory values and a hardened sensibility, which hardens thought in its turn. This is admirably expressed by Horkheimer and Adorno, who observe that the technicism of the machine age has as its corollary:

> . . . the self-dominant intellect, which separates from sensuous experience in order to subjugate it. The unification of intellectual functions by means of which domination over the senses is achieved, the resignation of thought to the rise of unanimity, means the impoverishment of thought and of experience: the separation of both areas leaves both impaired. The restriction of thought to organization and administration, practised by rules from the cunning Odysseus to the naive managing directors of today, necessarily implies the restriction which comes upon the great as soon as it is no longer merely a question of manipulating the small. . . . The more complicated and precise the social, economic and scientific apparatus with whose service the production system has long harmonized the body, the more impoverished the experiences which it can offer. The elimination of qualities, their conversion into functions, is translated from science by means of rationalized modes of labor to the experiental world of nations, and tends to approximate it once more to that of the amphibians.[19]

Herein lies the root for accepting barbarism, that is, the a-critical submission to the technological imperatives of any kind of machinery whatsoever, even if it were in the service of genocide or leading to it. For the basis of criticism is not in theory but in the taste a lived experience of the world has for the person experiencing it. The task of theory (or rather philosophy) and literature, each in its own way and at its own level, will be to unravel the web of the dominant discourse which reduces lived experience to silence.

It is now easier to see what we can and cannot ask of technology. We can use it to increase the efficiency of labour, and reduce the toil involved and the number of working hours. But we must remember that the superior power of technology has a price: it divorces work from life, and occupational culture from the culture of everyday life; it demands a despotic domination of oneself in exchange for an increased domination of Nature; it reduces the field of lived experience and existential autonomy; it separates the producer from the product to the point where she or he no longer knows the purpose of what she or he is doing.

The price we have to pay for technicization is only acceptable if the latter saves work and time. This is its declared aim and it can have no other. It is to allow us to produce more and better in less time and with less effort. Each hour of labour the new type of worker performs saves ten hours of traditional labour, or thirty hours, or five – the amount is immaterial. If their objective is not to save working time, then their occupation is meaningless. If their ambition or ideal is for work to fill the life of each individual and be its principal source of meaning, then these aims are in complete contradiction with what they are doing. If they believe in what they are doing, they must also believe that individuals do not find fulfilment in their profession alone. If they enjoy *their* work, they must be convinced that work is not everything, that there are other things which are equally, or even more, important. Things for which they, personally, need more time, things people never have enough time to do. Things which 'the technicism of the machine age' will, and must, give them time to do, thus giving them back a hundredfold what 'the impoverishment of thought and sensory experience' has made them lose.

I cannot emphasize this too strongly: *a job whose effect and aim are to save work cannot, at the same time, glorify work as the essential source of personal identity and fulfilment.* The meaning of the current technological revolution cannot be to rehabilitate the work ethic and identification with one's work. It only has meaning if it broadens the field of non-work activities in which we can all, the new type of worker included, develop that dimension of our humanity which finds no outlet in technicized work.

Notes

1. See Michael J. Piore and Charles F. Sabel, *The Second Industrial Divide*, New York 1984.
2. 'The worker's responsibility is a *political responsibility* . . . The production of social wealth results more from an activity of conscious regulation, aware of its responsibility, than from an immediate manual–intellectual work activity. *Work has become structurally political*,' Oskar Negt, *Lebendige Arbeit, enteignete Zeit*, Frankfurt am Main 1984, pp. 191–2.
Negt, a former pupil of Habermas, was one of the most outstanding theorists and leaders in the student movement of the 1960s. He now teaches sociology at the University of Hanover and is still regarded as an important theorist among the Left in the trade unions.
3. Inox, 'L'operaio di Processo', *Il Manifesto*, Rome, 12 November 1986.
4. Horst Kern and Michael Schumann, *Das Ende der Arbeitsteilung*? Munich 1984, p. 77. The authors give details of training courses for maintenance workers during the robotization of a production line in the car industry: out of a total of eighty-two days, sixty-two are devoted to the acquisition of *basic skills* in computing and electronics and twenty-five to the installation and equipment specific to that particular factory. It can be concluded that *a professional maintenance worker who switches factory or industry can adapt to his or her new job in less than a month.*
5. Chapter 3, p. 32.
6. 'For the engine-block machining line, for example, any variation in the order of a thousandth of a millimetre is registered and indicated at the control station. When there is

excessive variation, the engine block is automatically removed from the transfer line. The worker cannot ignore the fact that one of his/her tools needs changing.' Thomas Adler, 'Zur Bedeutung der neuen Produktionsfarcharbeiter', *Express*, Offenbach, 4 March 1986. pp. 14–16. The author is a politically active worker at Daimler-Benz in Stuttgart.

7. That is, before being completely socialized. It will be evident that the answer to these questions cannot be determined exclusively by cultural norms. In other words, it cannot derive from sociology alone. In my opinion, the thinking of Habermas – amongst others – shows a fundamental inadequacy in this respect. In Part II I shall return to the subject of the gap which necessarily exists between the individual subject and his or her social being. It is only by dint of this original gap that the individual *can* make an autonomous judgement of social reality and refuse to conform to its norms.

8. See p. 32.

9. Negt, pp. 188–9.

10. Kern and Schumann, p. 105.

11. Kern and Schumann, p. 272-7.

12. Kern and Schumann, p. 260.

13. Edmund Husserl, *The Crisis of European Sciences and Transcendental Phenomenology. An Introduction to Phenomenological Philosophy*, trans. and with an Introduction by David Carr, Evanston 1970, §§ 9g and h, p. 46 ff.

14. Edmund Husserl, *The Crisis of European Sciences and Transcendental Phenomenology* §§ 9i, p. 54.

15. William Leiss, *The Domination of Nature*, Boston 1974, p. 135 ff.

16. Cf. André Gorz, *Fondements pour une morale*, Paris 1977, p. 165 ff: 'Nature, valeurs vitales, valeurs du corps'.

17. Cf. A. Gorz, p. 146 ff.

18. This type of question in no way refers us back to a 'human nature' or to a 'human essence'. I shall return to this point later.

19. Max Horkheimer and Theodor W. Adorno, *The Dialectic of Enlightenment*, trans. John Cumming, New York 1972, London 1979, p. 36.

8

The Condition of Post-Marxist Man

Search for Meaning (2)

With the specialization of jobs, the division of labour has made it possible for vast amounts of knowledge to be employed across the whole of society. The speed with which technology has advanced, the power of the productive machinery and the wealth of the industrialized nations are all a product of this process.

But each individual is master of only a minute fraction of the expanding wealth of knowledge employed. The culture of work has fragmented into thousands of tiny areas of specialized know-how and has thus been cut off from the culture of everyday life. Occupational skills provide neither the references nor the criteria which would enable people to give meaning to the world, direct its course of events and find their own direction within it. De-centred from themselves by the one-dimensional nature of their jobs and know-how, their physical existences subjected to violence, they are forced to live in an environment which is becoming steadily more dislocated and fragmented, victims of mega-technological aggression. This world, which cannot be integrated by lived experience, has nothing of a lifeworld; rather, it is experienced as the lifeworld's painful absence. Everyday life has splintered into isolated pockets of time and space, a succession of excessive, aggressive demands, dead periods and periods of routine activity. This fragmentation, which is so resistant to a lived experience of integration, is reflected in a (non-)culture of everyday life, made up of thrills, transitory fashions, spectacular entertainment and fragments of news.

History has thus dismembered what Marx's vision made whole. Marx predicted that the domination of Nature by science would enable individuals to develop a totality of capabilities *within* their work, and that thanks to this '*richest development of the individual*', '*the free self-realization of individuality*' would become a need whose satisfaction

91

would be sought and found outside work, thanks to the 'general reduction of the necessary labour of society to a minimum'.[1]

This reduction to a minimum is already in progress: industrial
societies produce increasing amounts of wealth with decreasing amounts
of labour.[2] Yet they have not created a culture of work which having
'fully' expanded the individuals' abilities, would allow them to develop
'freely' during their disposable time – through voluntary co-operation,
scientific, artistic, educational and political activities, and so on. There is
no 'social subject' culturally or politically capable of forcing through a
redistribution of labour which would allow everyone to earn their living
by working, yet allow them to work less and less and at the same time
receive an increasing income representing their share of the increasing
socially produced wealth.

Such a redistribution is, however, the only way of giving meaning to
the decrease in the volume of socially necessary work. It is the only way
to prevent the disintegration of society and the division of the working
population itself into a number of occupational elites on the one hand, a
mass of unemployed or casually employed people on the other, and an
even greater number of indefinitely interchangeable and replaceable
workers in industry and, more especially, industrialized and computerized services, sandwiched between the two.[3] It is the only way, by
reducing the amount everyone works, to make skilled jobs accessible to
a greater number of people; to enable those who so desire to acquire
new skills and qualifications at any stage in their lives; to reduce the
polarizing effect work has on the way of life, compensatory needs and
personality (or depersonalization) of each individual.

Indeed, as the periods of disposable time become longer, non-
working time can become something other than the obverse of working
time: something other than time for rest, relaxation and recuperation; or
for activities secondary and complementary to working life; or idleness –
which is but the obverse of compulsory hetero-determined wage slavery;
or entertainment – the counterpart of a work which, by its monotony, is
anaesthetizing and exhausting. As disposable time increases, it becomes
both possible and necessary to find other activities and relations to
structure it, in which individuals develop their faculties in other ways,
acquire other skills and lead a different sort of life. It is then possible for
our jobs and workplaces to cease to be our only sources of identity and
the only spaces in which socialization is possible; and for the sphere of
non-work to cease to be the sphere of private life and consumerism. It
becomes possible for new relations of co-operation, communication and
exchange to be forged in this free time and for a new societal and
cultural space, composed of autonomous activities with freely chosen
aims, to be opened up. There is, then, a possible evolution towards a

new relation between working time and disposable time finally reversing the present situation: it allows for autonomous activities to become more important than working life, the sphere of freedom more important than the sphere of necessity. The way we organize the time we spend living need no longer be dictated by the time we spend working; on the contrary, work must come to occupy a subordinate place within the life plan of the individual.[4]

Individuals will, then, be much more exacting about the nature, content, goals and organization of their work. They will no longer accept stupefying work or subjection to oppressive surveillance and hierarchical structures. Liberation *from* work will have produced liberation *within* work, without as much as transforming work (as Marx predicted) into free self-activity with goals of its own. In a complex society, heteronomy cannot be abolished completely to be replaced by autonomy. It is possible, however, for tasks performed within the sphere of heteronomy itself to be reskilled, restructured and diversified – notably (though not exclusively) by allowing individuals to *self-manage their working time* – in such a way as to increase the degree of *autonomy within heteronomy*. It would be wrong, therefore, to imagine there is a clear-cut separation between autonomous activities and heteronomous work, the realm of freedom and the realm of necessity. The former does indeed have repercussions on the latter but can never subsume it entirely.[5]

This vision of a society of liberated time, or what the German Left refers to as a 'society of culture' (*Kulturgesellschaft*) by comparison with the 'work-based society' (*Arbeitgesellschaft*), is consonant with the *ethical content* (the 'free self-realization of individuality') of the Marxian utopia. Yet there are nevertheless a number of important philosophical and political differences between the two.

Marx believed the full development of individual capacities would accompany the full development of productive forces and lead necessarily to a *revolution* (in the philosophical sense) on two levels simultaneously:

1. Individuals who were fully developed *within* their work would take control of the latter in order to assert themselves as *de jure* subjects of what they already possessed *de facto*. In other words, the freedom historical development had *given* them, in the form of a set of capacities, would take possession of itself by means of *reflexive revolution*, that is, by the subject positing itself as such. This is the meaning of the distinction Marx makes between the *full* development of *individuals* and the *free* self-realization of *individualities* in what he terms 'higher activities', activities he locates in 'disposable time'.

2. Marx sees this reflexive – and strictly speaking existential – revolution, through which freedom (individual existence endowed with the means of achieving autonomy) becomes an end in itself, as one side of a historical dialectic whose other side is the necessity for economic revolution. As the amount of necessary labour diminishes, 'labour in the direct form [ceases] to be the great well-spring of wealth, labour time ceases and must cease to be its measure, and hence exchange value [must cease to be the measure of] use value . . . With that, production based on exchange value breaks down' and the 'free development of individualities', and the 'reduction of the necessary labour of society to a minimum' become the goal.[6]

In other words, economic rationality (and not just capitalist rationality) has gone as far as it can. It has never had any end-goal other than the most efficient possible use of available means and the most efficient possible organization of systems of means. It is an essentially instrumental form of rationality, whose end-goal is the rational functioning of systems of means, for the purpose of accumulating means (by profit-making) which will provide for even more efficient systems of resources. Its means are thus its ends and its ends are means towards other means. Economic rationality economizes the 'factors of production' – essentially time and labour – in order to re-employ them 'elsewhere in the economy', with the aim of saving time and labour, which are, in their turn, to be re-employed elsewhere. Economic rationality saves labour in pursuit of an ever-vanishing end-goal which is always out of reach and this end-goal is never the liberation of time itself, that is, the extension of the time we have for living. The function of leisure itself is to 'create jobs', to be useful for commodity production and profitable investment.

Now, with the full development of the productive forces, this dynamic of accumulation ceases to be workable. Instrumental rationality is thrown into crisis and its fundamental irrationality becomes patent. The crisis can only be resolved by applying a new form of rationality to savings in labour, a form of rationality consistent with the only objective which can give these savings any meaning: that of making time available for these 'higher activities' which are their own ends unto themselves, at one with the movement of life itself. Such activities are no longer ones which must be rationalized so they take up less time. On the contrary, spending time doing them, not saving time, becomes the objective. The activity is its own end; it *serves* no other purpose.

It is thus as if the crisis of economic rationality were the vacant site of another form of rationality *which will give meaning to the whole of the development that precedes it.* And this other rationality is, in Marx, none other than the rationality of fully developed individuals generated by the full development of the forces of production, who take reflexive possession of themselves in order to become the subjects of what they are, that is, in order to adopt as their goal the free self-realization of their individuality. According to Marx, material development thus engenders at once its own crisis and the historical subject who will be capable of overcoming it by revealing the meaning of the contradiction concealed within this development.

Liberation *within* work is, for Marx and Marxists, particularly those in workers' organizations, the necessary prerequisite for liberation *from* work; for it is through liberation *within* work that the subject capable of desiring liberation·*from* work and of giving it a meaning will be born. Hence the supreme importance Marxist authors attribute to reprofessionalized multi-skilled workers, responsible for 'sovereign' and complex tasks. They have a tendency to view these workers as the historical subjects of a potential reappropriation both of the productive forces *and* of the development of the individual by the individual her- or himself.

Now this is obviously an unsustainable utopia. Even Marx's own works reveal a gross contradiction between his theory and his exceptionally astute phenomenological descriptions of the relation of worker to machinery: the alienation of the worker from the means of labour, from the product and from the knowledge embodied in the machine. Nothing in this description justifies the theory of 'attractive labour' or the appropriation (appropriability) of the totality of productive forces as a result of workers developing a totality of capabilties; and this is true for his early writings as much as for *Grundrisse* and *Capital.*

Curiously enough the same is true, as we have seen, of Kern and Schumann. Their research indicates a tendency towards restructuring and reprofessionalizing the tasks of a small minority of industrial workers but this reprofessionalization does not justify the authors' theory of 'sovereign' workers with fully developed faculties. On the contrary, Kern and Schumann's monographs reveal that *the degree of autonomy within heteronomy* enjoyed by the workers *is what they have to struggle for,* just as the recognition of skills – the source of workers' power in production – has always been something workers had to fight for.[7]

However, if this is the case, if liberation *within* work (which is always partial and relative) is at stake in the workers' struggle, this means *the development of the forces of production does not of itself bring about either this liberation or its historical and social subject.* In other words individuals do not struggle for this liberation, and the full development of their faculties associated with it, because of what they are already *but because of what they aspire to be and have not become* or not yet become. And the question of why they aspire to achieve free, autonomous self-realization will not be answered as long as it is seen from the perspective adopted by Marx. For him, this question simply did not arise because his philosophy (or anti-philosophy) took the form of an inverse Hegelianism: he saw history as the process through which meaning took possession of the real, this meaning being not spirit, as it was for Hegel, but the fully developed individual becoming the master of Nature and of the process by which Nature was mastered – this individual being none other than the Universal Proletarian.[8]

This utopia is dead: whether we take Kronstadt 1920, Moscow 1928, 1930, 1935 or 1937, Berlin 1933, Treblinka 1943, Hiroshima 1945, Paris 1968, or any other date as the signal of its demise. History might end in nuclear winter, or a global Chernobyl or Bhopal; it might unfold by continually reinforcing the domination of individuals by increasingly powerful means of dominating Nature; or by developing increasingly barbaric forms of violence against the growing mass of those who have been excluded, both within the industrialized world and outside it. If we avoid all this, it will not be because history *has* a different meaning but because we will have succeeded in investing it with one. If, thanks to the liberation of time, the full development of productive forces leads to economic rationality (and its crisis) being transcended and individualities being freely developed, it will not be because this is the meaning of history but because we will have made history take on this meaning.

Everything about our freedom hangs in the balance, including that freedom itself. The condition of post-Marxist Man is that the meaning Marx read in historical development remains for us the only meaning that development can have, yet we must pursue this meaning *independently of the existence of a social class capable of realizing it.* In other words, the only non-economic, post-economic goals capable of giving meaning and value to savings in time and labour are ones individuals must discover within themselves. No historical necessity imposes on us the reflexive revolution which the defining of these goals implies. The political will capable of realizing them has no pre-existent social base and cannot rest on any particular class interest or any past, present or future tradition or norm. This political will and the moral aspirations that inform it can only draw upon themselves: their existence presupposes and will have to demonstrate *the autonomy of ethics* and *the autonomy of politics.*

It is in this sense that I propose to read the programme for the reconstruction of a European Left set out in Peter Glotz's *Manifest.*[9] The analysis which serves as his point of departure appears to be a kind of counterpoint to the *Communist Manifesto*: the third industrial revolution destroys traditional bonds of solidarity, blurs the dividing lines between classes, breaks down social and family ties and keeps propelling society towards individualization (*Individualisierungsschub*). This may imply 'a new social mobility or isolation, a growth of opportunities or the destruction of any possibility of community, a possible liberation from the many constraints that derive from work or the family or every-day culture, but also the danger of a withdrawal from social life, the destruction of solidarity.'

> The electronic civilization will eliminate millions of jobs . . . but at the same time, it could bring savings not only in work but also in raw materials, energy and capital. It offers us an opportunity to go beyond a system which produces for the sake of producing, to consign to machines the unpleasant, low-status jobs and to obtain for individuals growing amounts of *disposable time*. The workers, whose lives today are determined by the rhythm of work and for whom free time is hardly more than time for 'reproduction' of their labour power, for recuperation and for entertainment, could become to an unprece-dented degree sovereign masters of their own lives (and time) without having first to go through a bloody process of revolution and counter-revolution, which would give rise to such hatred that constraints would necessarily have to be maintained.[10]

However, political action cannot count on any homogeneous social base to 'force technology to give birth to such a utopia', nor, more import-antly, on any large and powerful social base such as the working class represented in the age of mass production and mass workers. Those sectors in which the great size of the workforce corresponded to the economic, or even strategic, importance of the production – the political and union bastions of the traditional Left – are all in decline: mining, the steel industry, shipbuilding and the heavy industries associated with it. The key sectors in the third industrial revolution employ relatively small workforces, with a high percentage of technical and clerical staff, with no tradition of trade-union association or affiliation to a particular political party. 'The new technologies and their intelligent application do not lead to the revolutionary union of the pauperized working masses but to the segmentation and division of the workers into quasi-classes which, in accordance with the diversity of their interests, act in a highly differentiated fashion.'

Political action can only be successful if it is able to

> create 'majorities' by bringing together groups which have no definite social anchorage . . . Admittedly, work will remain an important field of activity exerting its influence on the formation of individual identities. But increas-ingly powerful influences are suddenly emerging from other quarters . . . The question arises: will the European labour movement be able to maintain its

influence in the centres of production and will it be able to extend this to the spheres of reproduction and the world of 'leisure'? Will there be a European Left capable of *assigning social goals* to the innovation process?[11]

The task is clear but 'the situation is not rosy: the Left will have to put together a coalition which brings the greatest possible number of the strong [that is, chiefly members of what I have called the 'elite of workers'] together in solidarity with the weak, against their own interests. For strict materialists who see interests as more determining than ideals, the task is a paradoxical one and yet it is our task today.'[12] It presupposes a 'highly convincing project and unshakeable audacity'.[13] It requires, in other words, a cultural project, a vision of the future, which – as the socialist project did – transforms moral demands and the *need to give meaning to the future* into political energy.

This amounts to saying that the autonomy of the political is the necessary condition for political action. The latter can no longer be based on the interests of electoral clienteles, if we are to avoid a 'Balkanization' of political life which will further accelerate the decomposition of society. It calls for a project of society which transcends the sectionalization of interests because it is borne by a vision – a 'utopia' – capable of giving *meaning* to the third industrial revolution, that is, a purpose and an orientation born of hope. Now a political project which transcends conflicting interests by setting societal goals (and not just social ones), necessarily carries a high degree of moral content. This is not to say that politics and morality coincide here, but that the necessary autonomy of the political presupposes the autonomy of the ethical imperative if it is to call upon it.

As it will have become clear, this ethical imperative – the free self-realization of individualities through activities which have no economic rationality – does not coincide with any form of work or trade pursuing an economic end. The subjects embodying this imperative are not created by socially necessary production or the peripheral activities essential to material production. Almost all trades and forms of labour presuppose a form of specialization which, while not necessarily being either narrow or stupefying, thwarts rather than fosters the full intellectual, physical, aesthetic, emotional, relational and moral development of the individual.

Nevertheless, the element of autonomy within heteronomy which a growing percentage of occupations entail is sufficient for existential autonomy to be seen as a *possibility that is thwarted* by the way society is organized. The limited autonomy work and modes of socialization offer individuals is sufficient to make a growing number of them aware of their potential and *of the limits of the autonomy conceded them.*

These limits have lost their legitimacy: they cannot be justified by the urgency of our material needs nor by the cohesion of our disintegrating society. On the contrary, lived forms of community relations, solidarity, mutual aid and voluntary co-operation only exist on the margins of this social system and its type of rationality, thanks to the autonomous and disinterested initiatives of freely associating individuals. Similarly, many of our vital needs – unpolluted air and water, areas preserved from industrial development, foodstuffs free from chemical adulteration, non-violent care and so on – can only assert themselves by opposing the rationality of the system, in an unequal and often violent struggle against the 'functionaries' of the state/industrial megamachine.

Both limited autonomy within work on the one hand, and on the other the disintegration of society, which makes us look for alternative modes of socialization and community integration, lead to individualization and the withdrawal of individuals into the sphere of non-work activities and life outside the system. The withdrawal from political parties, trade unions and the other cumbersome organizations which seek to monopolize 'public affairs', is one aspect of this movement towards individualization. The other is the growth in popularity of religious, charitable, associative and alternative – in short, disinterested – activities.

> The desire for autonomy finds its expression in criticism of and opposition to all forms of non-legitimized hetero-determination and, at the same time, in a willingness to participate in self-organized forms of life and labour; in forms of behaviour in which other people are treated as partners, not subordinates; in the priority given to quality of life over material success and a career; and in a growing awareness of the fragility of the natural foundation of life on Earth.

Thus concludes a report by the SPD's Commission on Fundamental Values.[14]

The commission bases its findings on the results of surveys which have put the same questions to representative samples of waged workers over the past twenty years. These surveys reveal that a rapidly growing percentage of employees (about half the present number, as opposed to 29 per cent in 1962), especially those under thirty (nearly two-thirds, as opposed to 39 per cent in 1962) attach greater importance to their non-working activities than to their paid jobs. However, 80 per cent of them think their working conditions have improved in the last ten years; nearly half (but more than half the young people interviewed) consider their work 'interesting' but do not think it should dominate their lives.

Surveys in Scandinavia and Britain have made similar findings, in particular those conducted by R.E. Lane, who observes that, 'One life-satisfaction study reveals that satisfaction with non-working activities contributes more to variables in the Index of Well-Being than any other item in the Account',[15] and F. Block and L. Hirschhorn, who note that, 'The more time people spend outside of the paid labour force, before, after and during a work career, the more they find that work is no longer a sufficient focus for organizing their lives'.[16] Consumption and the money which makes it possible, Lane goes on to say, only have a tenuous link with the things that make people happy: autonomy, self-esteem, a happy family life, the absence of conflicts in life outside work, friendship. In other words, quality of life depends on the intensity of human bonds and cultural exchanges, relations built on friendship, love, brother- and sisterhood and mutual aid, and not on the intensity of commodity relations.[17] But this also implies that *sociological categories can no longer explain individual behaviour and motivations.* Sociology – and this is the implication of the British studies quoted above – has reached its limits. It is the autonomy of individuals which sets these limits. This nascent, as yet insecure autonomy, coveted and threatened by the cultural industries and leisure moguls constitutes the empty space in which a renewed Left's societal project will have to be rooted, if the Left wants to remain in existence.[18]

In brief, the functionalization and technicization of work have shattered the unity of life and work. Even before the present crisis worsened, work had ceased to ensure a sufficient degree of social integration. The progressive reduction in the amount of socially necessary work available has accentuated this process and aggravated the disintegration of society. Whether it takes the form of unemployment, marginalization and lack of job security, or of a general reduction in working hours, the crisis of the work-based society (that is, based on work in the economic sense of the word) forces individuals to look outside work for sources of identity and social belonging, possibilities of achieving personal fulfilment, and activities with a purpose which enable them to acquire self-esteem and the esteem of others.

Work is set to become one activity among a number of others, of equal or greater importance. The ethic of the free self-realization of individualities, which Marx believed would be the result of a decreasingly exacting, increasingly stimulating working life, today requires individuals not to identify themselves with their work but to become more detached from it; to develop other interests and situate their paid work, their occupation, within a multi-dimensional vision of their existence and of society. Activities performed for economic ends are to constitute only one dimension of existence and to become less and less important.

This is precisely the direction in which the aspirations of a significant number of people are moving. The crisis of the political parties – and the rise in popularity the churches and humanitarian associations are currently enjoying – stem initially from the former's inability to offer a practical and cultural outlet for these aspirations in which their political expression could be anchored. The crisis facing political parties is not primarily a crisis *of* the political but an indication that *the political space has been left vacant* by the organizations and apparatuses that behave primarily as machines for governing through a state apparatus which it is their ambition to control. By contrast, the political is primarily located where all nascent political forces placed it in periods of on-going change: the labour movement itself, its trade unions and political parties, grew out of cultural and mutual aid associations, that is, out of study and self-education aimed at countering the dominant ideas and culture; out of forms of life and self-organization which foreshadowed possible alternatives to the dominant way of life and social organization: a 'concrete utopia'.

Peter Glotz formulates this pre-eminence of the cultural in times of social upheaval well when he writes, 'How is the Left to achieve cultural hegemony as a preliminary to achieving political power? How is it to form from the initially growing diversity of individual political critiques a small number of ideas which people will accept, retain and assimilate as personal convictions?'[19]

A new utopia[20] is needed if we are to safeguard what the ethical content of the socialist utopia provided; the utopia of a society of free time. The emancipation of individuals, their full development, the restructuring of society, are all to be achieved through the liberation *from* work. A reduction in working hours will allow individuals to discover a new sense of security, a new distancing from the 'necessities of life' and a form of existential autonomy which will encourage them to demand more autonomy *within* their work, political control of its objectives and a social space in which they can engage in voluntary and self-organized activities.

I will attempt to sketch out below what a society of free time might be like, how different types of activity could fit into this framework and what transitional policies could produce it. But before we deal with the nature and feasibility of a concrete utopia such as this, it is important to identify its ontological foundations more precisely. Why, indeed, opt for a reduction in working hours? Why use at least parts of our liberated time to take over certain service activities currently provided by public or commercial bodies, on a voluntary, self-organized, co-operative basis? Why not instead turn the activities people somehow or other traditionally did for themselves into professional, paid ones? Why not get professional specialists in childminding and mothering to look after our children right from the moment they are born; professional employees in the tourist, culture and leisure industries to look after our ever-younger pensioners; professional home-helps to look after the aged; professional comforters and consolers to look after the dying? Why not adopt Alfred Sauvy's proposal and draw up an inventory of all our needs and potential demands, give them cash value and create jobs capable of satisfying them? Would this not provide virtually inexhaustible 'sources of employment'? Are not the possibilities of increasing our needs and, consequently, the potential growth of commercial exchanges and employment, unlimited? Why not admit that work done in the domestic sphere (the so-called sphere of reproduction) is socially useful, provide a wage for it and, as Barry Jones has proposed, view housewives as part of the labour force and housework as employment in the 'quinary sector', essentially concerned with the endless satisfaction of endlessly recurring needs (for example, the provision of food and amusement, tasks related to sexual activity, etc.)?[21]

The answer to these questions is not to be found purely in political decisions or social and economic expediency; no more than in the values of the pre-modern tradition from which Reason was to liberate us by making us adopt those solutions which were most rational and most expedient. Rational in respect of what ends? Are there not, above and beyond inherited values and practical expediency, other types of rationality – indeed, limits to all possible types of rationalization and socialization – consonant with the ontological multi-dimensionality of existence? This is the perspective from which I now propose to examine the extent to which the concept of work is relevant to the various forms of activity whose distinctive characteristics will become clear as we proceed.

Notes

1. Karl Marx, *Grundrisse*, Harmondsworth 1973, pp. 541, 611, 706.

2. See above, p. 8 n. 3, for more details.

3. See W. Lecher's analysis above, Chapter 6, for more details.

4. On this topic, see Oskar Negt, *Lebendige Arbeit, enteignete Zeit*, Frankfurt am main 1984, pp. 167 and 178, and Peter Glotz, *Manifest für eine neue europäische Linke*. Berlin 1985, pp. 54 and 92.

5. Cf. André Gorz, *Farewell to the Working Class*, London 1982, pp. 94, 102–4 and 107–9, where I follow Adret (*Travailler deux heures par jour*, Paris 1977) and, more especially, Charly Boyadjian, in emphasizing this fact – which runs counter to the argument certain hasty readers have attributed to me, according to which there would be a clear-cut opposition between the two spheres.

6. Marx, pp. 705–6.

7. On this topic, see the excellent and still relevant article by Antonio Lettieri, secretary of the CGIL, 'Factory and School', in André Gorz, ed., *The Division of Labour*, Hassocks 1976.

8. Cf. Gorz, *Farewell to the Working Class*, ch. 1, in which this analysis is set out in detail.

9. Glotz, *Manifest . . ., passim.*

10. Glotz, *Manifest . . .*, p. 34–5.

11. Glotz, *Manifest . . .*, p. 35–6.

12. Glotz, *Manifest . . .*, p. 37.

13. Glotz, *Manifest . . .*, p. 44.

14. Erhard Eppler, ed., *Grundwerte für ein neues Godesberger Programm*, Reinbek bei Hamburg 1984, ch. 5, particularly pp. 111–26.

15. R.E. Lane, 'Market and the Satisfaction of Human Wants', *Journal of Economic Issues*, no. 12, 1977, p. 815.

16. F. Block and L. Hirschhorn, 'New Productive Forces and the Contradictions of Contemporary Capitalism: a Post-Industrial Perspective', *Theory and Society*, no. 7, 1979, p. 373. These quotations are taken from the remarkable essay by Claus Offe 'Arbeit als soziologische Schlüsselkategorie?', *'Arbeitsgesellschaft': Strukturprobleme und Zukunfts-perspektiven*, Frankfurt/New York 1984.

17. All this of course runs counter to the idea that the corresponding activities must be professionalized and commercialized in order to 'create jobs'. I shall return to this in Part II.

18. This is the essence of Alain Touraine's research and the reason why this research is located at the frontiers of sociology, in an area ignored by political parties.

19. Glotz, *Die Arbeit der Zuspitzung*, Berlin 1984, p. 7.

20. In the sense defined above, p. 8.

21. Barry Jones, *Sleepers, Wake! Technology and the Future of Work*, Melbourne and Oxford 1983, pp. 51–2.

PART II
Critique of Economic Reason

Men, therefore, may prefer to use money as a yardstick even in efforts which do not have the aim of making additions to a society's stock of utility. Even where the aim is to add to solidarity, collective effectiveness, or societal authenticity, men, once committed to rationalization, deployed a variety of cost-benefit analyses to measure their performance . . . A whole host of social problems from urban renewal to delinquency-prevention projects remain a mess in part because of the use of money for ends that money alone cannot serve.[1]

Habermas, from whom I have taken this quotation by R.C. Baum, brings a more complex analysis to bear. According to him it is not simply the unequal development of the criteria and means of regulation which is involved, but, 'capitalist modernization follows a pattern such that cognitive-instrumental rationality surges beyond the bounds of the economy and State into other, communicatively structured areas of life . . . and this produces disturbances in the symbolic reproduction of the lifeworld'.[2]

To put it another way, economic rationality, which is a particular form of 'cognitive instrumental' rationality,[3] is not only wrongly extended to cover institutional actions to which it is not applicable, it 'colonizes', reifies and mutilates the very relational fabric on which social integration, education and individual socialization depend.[4] Habermas sees the reason for this 'colonization' in 'the irresistible dynamic' developed by 'economic and administrative sub-systems'[5], that is hetero-regulation by money and state power.

The autonomization of these sub-systems leads to the split between specialized professional cultures (*Expertenkultur*) and the culture of everyday life. This no longer possesses the criteria and the obvious reference points which allow individuals to find their bearings in the world and regulate their relationships for themselves. The decline and growing lack of relevance of the culture of everyday life exposes it to penetration by 'expertocracies' and to the 'colonization of the lifeworld' by specialist professional bodies of knowledge. The 'communicational infrastructure' disintegrates and the reproduction of the lifeworld of self-regulated social relations, based on understanding arrived at through free debate, communication and the development of common norms, is thrown into crisis.

Habermas's analysis, which I here summarize very schematically, is obviously superior to previous attempts to interpret and render intelligible the current crisis of the industrialized societies. But his outlining of the area in which economic rationality is applicable is summary and essentially sociological. He claims that neither administrative regulation, nor regulation by money, can be applied to the domain of the 'symbolic reproduction of the lifeworld'. Or, to put it another way, administrative regulation or monetarization (that is, transformation into paid jobs) of activities which have as their aim *the giving or transmitting of meaning* inevitably throws them into crisis.

Later, we will try to differentiate these activities, to explore their meaning, and situate them in relation to those which lend themselves to economic rationalization. But, first, it remains for us to understand what economic rationality consists of, and what is the internal, driving force behind the imperialism which it manifests in relation to other types of rationality. Why did 'the colonization of the lifeworld' not encounter stronger resistance sooner? Why has 'the model of capitalist modernization' been able to gain a foothold and develop 'the irresistible dynamic of economic and administrative sub-systems'? What is there in economic rationality which has allowed it to gain ground in the lives of individuals, to the detriment of spontaneous relationships of solidarity?

Notes

1. R.C. Baum, 'On Social Media Dynamics' quoted by Jürgen Habermas, *Theory of Communicative Action* (TCA), Cambridge 1987, vol. 2, p. 293.

2. TCA, vol. 2, p. 304–5.

3. Max Horkheimer had coined the concept of instrumental rationality to replace Max Weber's '*Zweckrationalität*' (rational choice of means and strategies for achieving an end, or 'purposive rationality'). In implicit agreement with Theodor Adorno, Habermas uses the concept of 'cognitive-instrumental' rationality to denote the unity of techno-scientific, economic and administrative approaches.

4. TCA, vol. 2, p. 332 ff.

5. It constitutes almost all of ch. 8 of TCA, vol. 2.

9

From 'Enough is Enough' to 'The More the Better'

Economic rationalization begins with counting and calculating. So long as they are not subjected to it, human activities are free from economic rationality: they are at one with the time, movement, and rhythm of life. For as long as I grow all I need to feed my family, my donkey and my two goats on my patch of land; for as long as I cut wood for the kitchen and for heating because there is wood to be had from the hedges or in the neighbouring forest, economic rationality is absent from my work: it takes the time that it takes to do what there is to do, and when the necessary work has been done, work can give way to leisure.

But from the moment when I am no longer producing for my own consumption but for the market, everything changes. Then I need to learn to calculate: given the quality of my soil, would it be better to grow more green vegetables or potatoes? Would a motorized cultivator pay for itself in less than two seasons thanks to the increased production it would make possible? Instead of cutting my wood by hand, would it not be better to buy a circular saw which would save me time and which I could make pay for itself by cutting my neighbours' wood too?

All this can be calculated, must be calculated, if I want to earn the wherewithal to enable my family to live and live 'adequately'. So, I must calculate the productivity of the soil, the amount of work necessary for different crops, the cost of tools, seeds, fuel and so on, and the productivity, that is the income which I can achieve in one hour of work depending on which crop I produce. So I will calculate, and organize my life according to this calculation on homogeneous, linear time schedules, which are insensitive to the natural rhythms of life.

Counting and calculating is then the quintessential form of reifying rationalization. It posits the *quantity of work* per unit of product *in itself*, regardless of the lived experience of that work: the pleasure or displeasure which it brings me, the quality of the effort it demands, my affective and aesthetic relationship to what is produced. I will grow more onions, cabbages, salads or flowers according to the profit I can count on. My activities will be decided as a function of a calculation, without my preferences or tastes being taken into account. I will welcome technical innovations which increase the productivity of my work even if they technicize it, subjecting it to rigid requirements, turning it into jobbing work. But I have no choice: unless I follow or even run ahead of technological development, I will soon no longer be able to live off the sale of my products: I will no longer be 'competitive'.

The conditions which must be fulfilled for economic rationality to prevail may be set out as follows:

1. Work must have commodity exchange and not personal consumption as its end. As long as this latter prevails, the producers will decide between several variables: between the level of satisfaction and the additional effort needed to raise this level; between the attraction of saving time and the trouble caused by the intensification of labour that makes it possible, and so on. In practice, in work done for oneself (work in the private sphere) we never seek for maximum productivity and therefore do not count our time; we do not quantify the result obtained per unit of time. The pursuit of productivity and the measurement of time do not appear in the sphere of *work for oneself* (in, for example, housework) except insofar as this is contaminated by the economic rationality which dominates the rest of our lives: in other words to the extent that housework is a subordinate activity which must be done as quickly as possible in the time left by paid work which is itself the main activity. By itself, work done for oneself remains resistant to economic rationalization. It does not – and cannot – have any exchange value; it has only a use value and has this only in the private sphere where it is carried out.[1] Thus, as Barry Jones rightly notes:

> In subsistence economies, agriculture is not regarded as an 'industry' for the farmers – it is their way of life. They produce essentially to meet their own needs, with a small surplus to be stored or traded; they are not concerned with economic profitability, export potential, return on capital or concentrating on a single crop; they are not racing the clock or competing with their neighbours. The rotation of the crops matches the rotation of the seasons; the work takes a lifetime to carry out and is never completed. The concepts of wages, hours or holidays are not relevant.[2]

2. To be guided by economic rationality, production must not only be intended for commodity exchange; it must be intended for exchange

on a free *market* where unconnected producers find themselves in competition facing similarly unconnected purchasers. This condition is not fulfilled so long as producers can, in the manner of guilds, corporations and producers' syndicates, set the price of each sort of product and, especially, lay down the permissible processes and techniques of production. These, as is well known, were minutely regulated until the eighteenth century. Agreement on price and techniques not only constitutes a contractual self-limitation of competition; it also involves a self-limitation of the possibilities of profit and, hence, a *self-limitation of needs*. Economic rationality is thus held back at its roots through the limited nature of needs and through a consensus on their limits. In short, production intended for commodity exchange is regulated in these instances by the same principle of 'sufficiency' as production for one's own domestic consumption; there is no point in working more than is required to satisfy one's *felt needs*. Nor is there any point in seeking maximum productivity, in counting one's time, in rationalizing work when one can meet one's needs by working according to one's natural rhythm. Counting and calculating itself is useless from this perspective. *The limited nature of needs constitutes an obstacle to economic rationality.*

Hence the extreme difficulty experienced by the first industrialists in obtaining continuous full-time working. The idea that homeworkers could be induced to continuous effort by offering them attractive wages geared to productivity proved false at the beginning of the industrial era (and continues to be so even in modern industry, in both East and West).

A man, for instance, who at the rate of 1 mark per acre mowed 2½ acres per day and earned 2½ marks, when the rate was raised to 1.25 marks per acre mowed, not 3 acres, as he might easily have done, thus earning 3.75 marks, but only 2 acres, so that he could still earn the 2½ marks to which he was accustomed. *The opportunity of earning more was less attractive than that of working less.* He did not ask: how much can I earn in a day if I do as much work as possible? but: how much must I work in order to earn the wage, 2½ marks, which I earned before and which takes care of my traditional needs? . . . [An] obvious possibility . . . [was] to try the opposite policy, to force the worker by *reduction* of his wage-rates to work harder to earn the same amount than he did before.[3]

Economic rationality is not applied when people are free to decide their own level of need and their own level of effort. They tend then spontaneously to limit their needs in order to be able to limit their efforts, to match these efforts to a level of satisfaction which seems to them *sufficient*. This level may clearly vary over time; but nonetheless it is the

category of *the sufficient* which regulates the balance between the level
of satisfaction and the volume of work for oneself.

But the category of *the sufficient* is not an economic category: it is a
cultural or existential category. To say that what is enough is enough is
to imply that no good would be served by having more, that more would
not be better. 'Enough is as good as a feast' as the English say.

The category of *the sufficient*, as a cultural category, was central in
traditional society. The world was ruled by an immutable order,
everyone occupied the place assigned to them by birth, had what was
due to them and did not expect more. The desire for more was in itself a
rebellion against the order of the world: it was laden with 'covetousness',
'envy', 'pride', so many sins against the 'natural order' and against God.
Usury was essentially diabolic: as a practice it had its usefulness and thus
was tolerated but what was intolerable was the usurer himself, this
Midas, for whom wealth was money and who never had enough of it,
whatever his fortune, for the simple reason that once you begin to
measure wealth *in cash, enough* doesn't exist. Whatever the sum, it
could always be larger. Accountancy is familiar with the categories of
'more' and of 'less' but doesn't know that of 'enough'.

We know that the break-up of the traditional order and the development of mercantile and financial capitalism, and subsequently of
industrial capitalism, were mutually engendered, each being at once the
cause and the consequence of the other. However, what matters here is
that counting and calculating will have gradually substituted an
absolutely constricting formal order for the traditional order. When
religious or moral normative certainties were shattered by the corruption
of religious institutions, calculation emerged as a privileged source of
unquestionable certainties; what was demonstrable, susceptible to
organization, predictable by virtue of a calculation, had no need of the
guarantee of any authority to be true and universally valid.

Calculation allowed an emancipation from all external tutelage while
at the same time generating an order against whose objective laws there
was no appeal. This order provided a rigid, reassuring, imperious,
incontestable framework, independent of all human will. The organization of activities and of life itself in terms of an accountancy calculation
was *quintessentially* an *ordering* through which man, on the scale of his
own life, came nearer to the work which God (the 'great watchmaker')
accomplished on a cosmic scale. Economic rationality functioned as a
substitute for religious morality: through it man attempted to apply the
eternal laws which governed the universe to the predictive organization
of his own affairs. Its aim, beyond the material ends it gave itself, was to
render the laws of human activity as rigorously calculable and predictable as those of the cosmic clock's workings.

The meaning of economic activity was thus that activity itself, in so far as irrespective of any goal, it produced order and signified submission to laws independent of human will. As discipline, ascesis, penitence and organizing passion, it was its own *raison d'être*, material ends serving only as contingent supports or means to an end. The accumulation of wealth was only the proof of the accuracy of the calculations and this accuracy required indefinite confirmation through the reinvestment of the profits.

What is important here is that the 'spirit of capitalism' severed the link between work and need. The goal of work was no longer the satisfaction of felt needs, and effort was no longer matched to the level of satisfaction to be attained. The rationalizing passion became autonomous with respect to all determinate goals. In place of the certainty of experience that 'enough is enough' it gave rise to an *objective measure of the efficiency of effort and of its success: the size of profits. Success was no longer therefore a matter for personal assessment and a question of the 'quality of life', it was measureable by the amount of money earned, by accumulated wealth. Quantification gave rise to an indisputable criterion and a hierarchical scale which had no need of validation by any authority, any norm, any scale of values. Efficiency was measurable and, through it, an individual's ability and virtue: more was better than less, those who succeed in earning more are better than those who earn less.*

Quantitative measure inherently admits of no principle of self-limitation. The category of 'the sufficient', and the category of 'too much' are equally alien to the spirit of capitalism. No quantity, when serving to measure a performance, can be *too* great; no enterprise can earn too much money nor any worker be too productive. By quantifying to make calculable, economic rationalization therefore eliminates all criteria which would allow people to be satisfied with what they have, or what they have done or plan to do. No quantity is the greatest possible, no success is so great that a greater success cannot be imagined. Henceforth, the rank that everyone occupied in the hierarchy of skills and merits would be an essentially relative rank: it would be determined by comparison with others; it was against them that everyone had to measure themselves; it was in out-performing the others in perpetual competition that everyone had to earn their rank. No authority, no statute could guarantee anyone their rank.

To this logic of each person's *unlimited* effort to surpass the others, the labour movement opposed, from its very beginning, an opposite logic: the rejection of competition between individual workers, solidarity between them with the aim of achieving both *the self-limitation of the efforts of each* and the *limitation* of the amount of work which could be demanded of all. To the economic rationality of unlimited maximization and boundless excess, the labour movement thus opposed a rationality based on the humanism of need and the defence of life. The *humanism of need* was expressed in the claim for a wage *sufficient* to meet the needs of the worker and his family; *the defence of life* was expressed in the demand for a reduction of working hours, in the demand for the right to 'time for living'.

Economic rationality has never, therefore, in essence, been *in the service* of any *determinate* goal. Its object is (we will come back to this shortly) the maximization of the type of efficiency that it knows how to measure arithmetically. The main indicator of this efficiency is the rate of profit. And the rate of profit depends, in the last analysis, on the productivity of labour. The pursuit of an unlimited maximum of efficiency and profit would therefore demand the greatest possible growth of the productivity of labour and, as a result, of production. Increasing quantities of capital must be accumulated in machines that are both increasingly efficient and more numerous and this capital has to produce a return enabling the capitalist to install even more efficient machines, and so on.

To make it worth investing increasing amounts of capital, it was clearly necessary that increasing production should find purchasers, and therefore that consumption should continue to expand well beyond the satisfaction of actually *felt* needs. Economic rationality therefore had gradually to lose the 'natural base' that had been provided for it by the existence of needs that only increased production could meet. Civilization and society were coming to a crossroads: *either* a rationality other than economic rationality would have to restrain production and therefore limit the expansion of the economic sphere to the benefit of other spheres, governed by other criteria: *or else* economic rationality would have to make the needs of consumers grow at least as quickly as the production of commodities and commodified services. But in this latter eventuality – the one which has in fact materialized – *consumption would have to be in the service of production*. Production would no longer have the function of satisfying existing needs in the most efficient way possible; on the contrary, it was needs, which would increasingly have the function of enabling production to keep growing.

Unlimited maximum efficiency in the valorization of capital thus demanded *unlimited* maximum *in*efficiency in meeting needs, and *unlimited* maximum wastage in consumption. The frontiers between needs, wishes and desires needed to be broken down; the desire for dearer products of an equal or even inferior use value to those previously employed had to be created; what had merely been desirable had to be made necessary; wishes had to be given the imperious urgency of need.[4] In short, a demand had to be created, consumers had to be created for the goods that were the most profitable to produce and, to this end, new forms of scarcity had unceasingly to be reproduced in the heart of opulence, through accelerated innovation and obsolescence, through that reproduction of inequalities on an increasingly higher level, which Ivan Illich[5] called 'the modernization of poverty'.

Thus, on pain of becoming a type of rationality subordinate to societal ends defined elsewhere, economic rationality needed continually to raise the level of consumption without raising the rate of satisfaction; to push back the frontier of the *sufficient*; to maintain the impression that there could not be enough for everyone. To put it another way, the principle of unlimited maximization needed to supersede all principles of self-limitation whether of effort or of the level of satisfaction, and to do so right down to the working class itself. What in the spirit of capitalism was an expression of the passion for organization and for quantification had, among the consumers of the 'affluent society', to be an expression of 'mimesis', that is, of a craving – methodically orchestrated through commercial advertising – to have what 'others' had which was more or better or different from what you yourself possessed. It was therefore essential that a substantial gap should always exist between the mass of the population and the privileged elite whose conspicuous consumption had to raise the desires of the other social strata to a higher level and shape their tastes according to the whims of changing fashion.

This hetero-determination of the level of needs would have been much more difficult *if individuals had been free to adjust their hours of work to the income which they felt they needed.* As productivity and real wages rose during a period of growth, an increasing proportion of the population would have chosen to work less. But workers were never allowed to adjust the hours they put in to the amount of money they felt would take care of their needs. Economic rationality has no room for authentically free time which neither produces nor consumes commercial wealth. It demands the *full-time employment of those who are employed* by virtue not of an objective necessity but of its originating logic: wages must be fixed in such a way as to induce the worker to maximum effort.[6]

The unions, for their part, have never been keen to challenge the principle of the full-time employment of individual employees. To admit that people might actually prefer to work less, although this might mean earning less, and that ultimately everyone might choose their own level of consumption and duration of work, was to admit that the wages for full-time work exceeded the level of felt needs for at least part of the working population. Wage claims would thus have lost their legitimacy and, worse, employers might well have wanted to reduce wages if a growing proportion of workers was happy with earning less than what they would be paid for working full-time.

Thus employers and unions objectively came to collude on this matter: for both, people were to be defined as being above all *workers*, everything else being subsidiary and a matter of private life. On the employers' side, wage earners *were* nothing more than labour power; once they had crossed the threshold of the enterprise, they ceased being people and became functions. Accepting the employment as part-timers of more people than were needed, was for employers to run the risk of finding themselves no longer in the presence of labour power but of *people* all of whom had their own individuality and lives, and who would therefore be hard to discipline, co-ordinate and command.

Equally, on the union side, it was only as labour power that individuals were to be defended and represented. Their interests might be defined extensively: the 'reproduction of labour power' not only depends on individual purchasing power but also on the housing conditions, transport, training and rest requirements and so on, that the unions had good grounds to include in the scope of their negotiations. But the demand for free time has often only been voiced by unions when reluctant union machines faced the threat of being outflanked by rank-and-file rebellion. The point is that in their free time individuals cease to be workers; the desire for free time is precisely the desire for self-definition through other activities, values and relationships than those of work.

In short, individuals might well escape both the control of the employer and that of the union through the growth of free time (unless the unions extend the scope of their activities in new directions, as Italian and German trade unionists have begun to press them to do[7]). *In particular they might even escape the grip of economic rationality* by discovering that more is not necessarily better, that earning and consuming more do not necessarily lead to a better life, and that there can, therefore, *be more important demands than wage demands.* Demands which are more important, but also more dangerous for the employer, for the social system, for capitalist relations of production to which they imply a radical challenge. Wage demands are, in fact, the only demands which do not undermine the rationality of the economic system. They remain consonant with the principle that 'more is better', with the quantifying of values. Demands bearing on working hours, the intensity of work, its organization and nature, are, on the other hand, pregnant with subversive radicalism: they cannot be satisfied by money, they strike at economic rationality in its substance, and through it at the power of capital. 'The market-based order' is fundamentally challenged when people find out that not all values are quantifiable, that money cannot buy everything and that what it cannot buy is something essential, or is even *the* essential thing.

But workers will not discover the limits of economic rationality until their lives cease to be wholly occupied and their minds preoccupied by work: until, in other words, a sufficiently large area of free time is open to them for them to discover a sphere of non-quantifiable values, those of 'time for living', of existential sovereignty. Conversely, the more constricting work is in its intensity and hours, the less workers are able to conceive of life as an end in itself, the source of all values; and the more as a result they are induced to regard it in economic terms; in other words to conceive of it as a means towards something quite other which would, objectively, be valuable in itself: money.

Charly Boyadjian has given us a remarkable description of this destruction of workers' personalities through the compulsion to work, to the point where they know nothing beyond the wish for more work so that they can earn more; and the rediscovery of non-economic, unquantifiable values, with all the radical challenge this implies, when the compulsion to work is slackened.

The author worked in a shoe factory where split-shift working was in operation, forty-eight hours and six days a week and

it was easy to find volunteers for Sundays as well. I'm sure that there were times when you could have asked them to work seven days out of seven for a whole year; they'd have done it, if they'd been pushed . . . And there were people who worked after hours as well, cash in hand, as well as their split shift, either through alienation, or sometimes from necessity. You see, when you were working forty-eight hours a week, cash really became the thing you were after . . . A friend said to me, jokingly (but jokes always have a serious, side): 'Me, when I'm not working, I don't know what to do, I'm bored stiff, I'm better off at work.' Your factory is your life. *When you're at work, it's kind of secure, you've nothing else to do, it's all set up for you, you don't have to use your initiative.* You have a bit more money, you'll buy as much electrical gadgetry as you can. You'll chase after money, but it won't do you much good in the end. It won't buy you any time. In fact, you just lose quantities of it: to gain, let's say, ten minutes on something or other that you do every day, you'll lose an hour a day at work to pay for it. It's quite mad. But you even get to like it in the end. *It's real security, you have no more responsibility, it's almost like going back to childhood.* This applies to everyone: before I came to this factory, I was an activist, politically 'advanced', but I was sucked into these same ways of carrying on.

The author tells how physical and nervous exhaustion stifles the life of a couple, erodes sexual relations ('you end up so exhausted that you completely forget the other person, you really haven't got time'), and destroys the ability to think:

Even I, during these periods, though I was on an anti-racist committee, I was a hell of a lot more racist . . . Intellectually, you're hopeless, for the very good reason that you can't make the physical effort of listening to someone else and arguing with them; so you become really authoritarian. After a while you get to be so exhausted that it's not your brain that's in charge but advertising slogans.

When the crisis came, working hours were reduced to forty a week and then, a month later, to thirty-two, spread over four days:

Then, bit by bit, there was an unbelievable phenomenon of physical recuperation. The idea of money really lost its intensity. I don't mean it had disappeared but eventually even the blokes with families to look after said, 'It's better now than before.' It's true that we lost a good deal of money, £40 to £50 compared with before [or 25 per cent of former income] but, quite soon, only one or two of the blokes minded.

It was about now that the blokes become increasingly radical because we had begun to have a lot of discussions . . . It was now, too, that friendships began: we were now able to go beyond political conversation, and we managed to talk about love, impotence, jealousy, family life . . . What's odd is that *during this period of short-time working, work on the black economy lessened* . . . It was also at this time that we realized the full horror of working in the factory on Saturday afternoons or evenings. Before, the blokes had put up with it, but now we were once again learning the meaning of the word living, working Saturdays came to seem an enormous grind . . . Similarly, for Sundays or Bank Holidays, which were paid at triple time, management admitted to us that they had difficulty finding people . . . There had been a change of attitude, they weren't able to buy workers as easily as before.[8]

Charly Boyadjian brings out perfectly the dual irrational driving force behind the 'the more the better' passion. In the passages I have italicized he observes that for the worker the obsession with work and earnings has the same meaning as the passion for economic calculation had at the birth of capitalism: work disciplines and orders life, it protects individuals against the collapse of normative certainties and against the responsibility of taking charge of their own lives. Their lives are all mapped out. Work is a protective shell, 'It's all set up for you.' Questions about the meaning and goal of life are resolved in advance: since there is no room in the worker's life for anything other than working for money, money is the only possible goal. In the absence of time for living, money is the only compensation for lost time, for a life spoiled by work. Money symbolizes everything that the worker has not, is not, and cannot be because of the constraints of work. This is why work will never pay *enough*; but also why money earned by working was originally perceived as *being worth more* than the life one had to sacrifice to it.

The worker will therefore look for this something which *gives its value to the money earned,* which symbolizes a better life than the one he has sacrificed by working nights and weekends. This something could be pushing children towards studying but might also be, to start with, owning a car, a symbol of freedom and escape; buying your own house, a symbol of sovereignty sheltered from the outside world; domestic appliances, symbols of a comfortable way of life which, as Boyadjian notes, is practically never achieved, partly because of time, partly because the symbolic value of appliances often fails to correspond to a real use value. Thus, 90 per cent of chairmen of large companies questioned by the *Harvard Business Review* reckon that it is impossible to sell a new product without an advertising campaign, 85 per cent that advertising 'often' leads to the purchase of products for which the purchasers have no use and 51 per cent that advertising leads people to buy things they don't really want.[9]

Full-time employment of employed individuals responds then not only to a desire for domination on the part of the employers but also, more deeply – and very consciously in the 'Fordist' model – to a concern to shape individual ways of life and the model of individual consumption as functions of economic rationality, that is, of the need to obtain a return on growing quantities of capital. The principle of the quantification of all values prevails to the extent that it succeeds in regulating conduct and preferences in all spheres: *more is better,* whether this applies to speed, power, income, turnover, capitalization, life expectancy, levels of consumption and so on, whatever the concrete content or the use value of these increasing quantities might be. *People must be prevented from choosing to limit their working hours so as to prevent them choosing to limit their desire to consume.* A growing number of wage earners must work and earn *beyond their felt needs,* so that a growing proportion of income may be spent on consumption determined by no need. For it is such optional, superfluous consumption, which can be directed, shaped, manipulated according to the 'needs' of capital more than to individuals' needs. *It is to the extent that consumption frees itself from felt needs and exceeds them that it can serve production, that is, serve the 'needs' of capital.*

This is the secret of the 'irresistible dynamic' with which the 'economic sub-system' extends its grasp. And this, too, is where the contradiction of a system, in which economic rationality is not made to serve any other rationality which imposes limits on it, becomes glaringly obvious. Such a system demands meeting felt needs *at the lowest cost* but, at the same time, *maximum expenditure* on consumption exceeding felt needs. It has nothing to gain from eliminating poverty and reducing inequality; for needs are limited and cannot assure an indefinite growth of production. Wants and the desire for the superfluous are, by contrast, potentially unlimited. Meeting unsatisfied needs by transferring revenue from the rich to the poor thus runs counter to economic rationality as it expresses itself, totally unfettered, in capitalist rationality. For such a transfer would come down to increasing need-determined demand which seeks satisfaction *at the lowest cost*, at the expense of fashion- and fancy-led demand which lends itself to any and every extravagance.

To maintain economic activity it thus makes more sense to provide for the rich rather than the poor (for example by reducing taxes on higher incomes) and, as a result, to innovate continuously in 'top of the range' products, with considerable symbolic value, rather than in the area of products bought for their use value.

'I see advertising as an educational and activating force capable of producing the changes in demand which we need. By educating people into higher living standards, it ensures that consumption will rise to a level justified by our production and resources.' This reflection of the chairman of J. Walter Thomson, one of the largest American advertising agencies, dates from the beginning of the 1950s. It has the merit of clearly defining the meaning of 'creativity, inventiveness and initiative' which, according to our latter-day Saint-Simonians, should 'change the face of the earth and totally renew it' (the phrase is Serge July's). It is concerned with nothing less than creating in the minds of people needs of which 'they haven't got the faintest idea' (the words are those of the chairman of J. Walter Thomson) in order to make them consume and manufacture wholly new products which are supposed to initiate a new cycle of accumulation, a new period of economic growth.

It will have been evident that the preceding analyses have continually and imperceptibly shifted levels: growth appearing to be required by individuals, sometimes by partial capital, sometimes by the macro-economic (capitalist) system. For the demands which express themselves at these different levels have between them an almost perfect coherence. Once quantification has been adopted as a method of evaluation and guide to decision-making, unlimited growth is required at all levels: as dissatisfaction, envy and desire for 'more' on an individual level; as a demand for unlimited maximization on the level of partial capitals; as a demand for perpetual growth at the systemic level; as an ideological valorization of increased performance (speed, machine power, size of plant, height of buildings, agricultural productivity and so on) at the level of civilization. This can be clearly felt in the way the word 'growth' is pronounced: it is loaded with value judgement, designating the best and highest of goals. Its content is totally immaterial, only the rate matters, which, in its turn, whatever it might be, can reflect either an acceleration or a slowing-down of growth, an advance or a retreat in the order of the Good. The emotional, quasi-religious value with which the word is charged is not the product of reasoning but of an a priori, normative judgement. Reasoning would, in fact, allow for controversy over the advantages and disadvantages of continuous, accelerated, slowed or negative growth. Normative judgement, on the contrary, prejudges the outcome of any possible debate: it does not assert that the economic system such as it is, in the current international situation, needs growth – which would leave open the question of foreseeable changes in either that system or situation – but that growth is good in itself: the more the better.

Growth of the economy as a system, growth of consumption, growth of individual incomes, of the nation's wealth, of national power, of milk yields, of airspeed or the speeds of runners, swimmers or skiers, the same quantifying undifferentiated value judgement applies on all levels and excludes in principle all idea of limitation or self-limitation. Quantitative measurement as a substitute for rational value judgement confers supreme moral security and intellectual comfort: the Good becomes measurable and calculable; decisions and moral judgements can follow from the implementation of a procedure of impersonal, objective, quantifying calculation and individual subjects do not have to shoulder the burden anxiously and uncertainly: 'It is virtuous to earn money', declared a great French Protestant financier in 1987.

The 'irresistible dynamic' with which the 'economic sub-system' swallows up all areas of social activity and life shows up now in a new light: it is not inherent in *this* economic system; it is inherent in economic rationality itself. It would be vain to seek to distinguish capitalist rationality from economic rationality, by asserting that everything we have just said concerns the former but not necessarily the latter. Economic rationality could never, in fact, express itself fully before the advent of capitalism: before then its existence in great trading companies and in money-lending was hemmed in, restricted, decried. Accountancy was erratic and uncertain, arithmetic a mysterious art, the search for profit a sin, competition a crime; and it is a well-known fact that when Anton Fugger, the greatest banker of the sixteenth century, died none of his possible heirs accepted the succession: they reckoned that they had more important or more rewarding things to do than earn money. Economic rationality could not begin to express itself until the traditional order had decayed to such an extent that economic reasoning could free itself from the externally and internally imposed limitations of the customs and commandments of religion. Until then, in so far as it did exist, it was enslaved: forced to cope with alien or even contrary requirements and to serve ends assigned to it by political or religious authorities.

Capitalism has been the expression of economic rationality finally set free of all restraint. It was the art of calculation, as developed by science, applied to the definition of the rules of conduct. It raised the quest for efficiency to the level of an 'exact science' and thus cleared the factors of moral or aesthetic criteria from the field of decision-making. Thus rationalized, economic activity could henceforth organize human behaviour and relationships 'objectively', leaving the subjectivity of decision-makers out of account and making it impossible to raise a moral challenge on them. It was no longer a question of good or evil but only of correct calculation. 'Economic science', insofar as it guided decision-making and behaviour, relieved people of responsibility for their acts. They became 'servants of capital' in which economic rationality was embodied. *They no longer had to accept responsibility for their own decisions* since these were no longer attributable to them in person but were the result of a rigorously impersonal calculation procedure in which individual intentions had (apparently) no place.

What Husserl said of mathematized 'natural sciences' is equally applicable here. Mathematization renders a certain type of lived relationship with the world into formalizations which 'represent and disguise' (*vertreten und verkleiden*) this relationship and free us from the need to maintain it through our own intentions. The procedures of calculation acting as a sort of surrogate intentionality functioning in a quasi-automatic and autonomous way, 'it is because of the disguise of ideas that *the true meaning of the methods, the formulae, the "theories", remained unintelligible* and, in the naive formation of the method, was *never* understood.' To put it another way, what is really at stake and the meaning of 'economically rational' decision-making are removed from all possibility of rational examination and criticism by the fact that economic rationality itself is formalized into calculation procedures and formulae *inaccessible either to debate or to reflection.* We are left with debates between experts, quibbling over technicalities of method not with the substance of the debate, or at least only concerned with the substance in so far as it is the unspoken hidden agenda of a technical debate on method.

Through mathematization, a specific project has been incorporated into a particular method guaranteeing conformity to the original intention, and this method, formalized and autonomous, has definitively insulated the project against any reflexive self-examination. Subjects no longer think of themselves and lead their lives as the subjects of a certain intentional relationship to reality but as if they are *operators* putting a set of mathematical procedures to work. They no longer experience their knowledge as a relationship to 'truth' nor their actions as a transformation of data towards a goal, but as a relationship with a body of formalized procedures and as an ideal technical know-how, a *technē*: 'a mere art of achieving, through a calculating technique according to technical rules, results' *over the meaning and value of which the operator has no judgement*: 'A technicization takes over all other methods belonging to natural science . . .'[11] The *original* thinking that genuinely gives meaning to this technical process and truth to the correct results . . . is excluded.'[12]

Technicization allows subjects to be absent from the operations they themselves carry out. It guarantees the rigour of their action and thought by removing thought from the sphere of subjectivity *but also from examination.and criticism.* The claim to absolute objectivity implies the absolute naiveté of operational behaviour, which is incapable of accounting for itself. This road naturally leads to the 'philosophy of the death of man', the theory of the subject as 'non-existence into the emptiness of which discourse pours indefinitely' (the phrase is Michel Foucault's). What is true of the operator setting to work techniques of calculation carrying a petrified meaning which lacks any nourishing intentionality is elevated to the level of a universal truth in the 'philosophy of the death of man': the subject is spoken by the language, there are only speaking, desiring machines, and so on. The self-denial of the subject proper to calculation techniques becomes the paradigm of all thought; philosophers, in the wake of technical operators, assert their absence from their philosophical constructions with a ferocity and bellicosity which precisely belie the content of their self-denial. Structuralism will have been the ideology of triumphant technicism.

So again we find, on the level of thought, what was described in the first part of this work as the split between work and life. Mathematical formalization allows us to think what can neither be experienced nor understood. It turns thinking into a technique. With it is born the possibility of thinking Being in its indifferent exteriority and as exteriority. As Husserl never failed to emphasize in relation to Galileo, what is involved here is one of the greatest conquests of the mind, *provided that the abstraction from the self which mathematical operations allow remains a conscious operation of the subject, a conscious method.*

But it is precisely this condition which will no longer be satisfied or even capable of satisfaction as mathematical techniques become widespread. These are learned and applied as if they are recipes '. . . reliable in accomplishing obviously very useful things, a machine everyone can learn to operate correctly without in the least understanding the inner possibility and necessity of this sort of accomplishment.'[13] They allow actions which can neither be thought nor willed and whose effectiveness results from the application of formulae which are themselves impenetrable to thought. Exteriority thought as such settles into thinking itself in the guise of formulae which form a screen between the formalized operation and the operating subject. Thanks to these formulae subjects can become absent from and innocent of their operations; they can function like automata, mathematically formalizing any process which can be reduced to its exteriority – that is which can be reduced to a mechanism governed by laws – and conceive their own operations – therefore conceive of themselves – *on a machine model,* finally giving birth to that thinking machine which replaces the thinking of exteriority by the exteriority of thinking itself and which henceforth serves as a reference for explaining the human mind: the computer, calculating machine and 'artificial intelligence', machine for composing music, writing poems, diagnosing illnesses, translating, speaking, all in one . . . The capacity to conceive these machines finally comes to conceive of itself as a machine; the mind which has become capable of functioning as a machine recognizes itself in the machine which is capable of functioning like itself – without realizing that in reality the machine does not function like the mind but only like mind when it has learned to function as a machine.

These remarks do not claim to *explain* but to describe. I wanted to demonstrate the common roots of economic rationality and of 'cognitive-instrumental reason'; these roots being a (mathematical) formalization of thinking which, codifying the latter into technical procedures, *insulates it against any possibility of reflexive self-examination* and against the certainties of lived experience. Technicization, reification, monetarization of relationships have their cultural anchorage in this technique of thinking whose operations function without the involvement of the subject and whose absent subjects are unable to account for themselves. This is how this cold civilization is able to organize itself, its cold, functional, calculated, formalized relationships, making living individuals strangers to the reified world which is nonetheless their product, and its formidable technical inventiveness going hand in hand with a decline of the arts of living, of communication and of spontaneity. Because lived experience is virtually forbidden to speak, a technicist and quantifying culture has as its pendant that *unculture of living* which we described at the end of chapter 7.

Notes

1. This is a principle already established by Adam Smith when, in book 3 of *The Wealth of Nations*, he excluded from the field of economic evaluation *work which is not exchangeable against any other* or, as he wrote 'which produces nothing which might then buy an equal amount of work'. Adam Smith (and not Marx who simply followed him on this point) defined this non-exchangeable work as economically 'unproductive', in order to conclude 'Unproductive workers and those who do not work at all are all supported by revenue', a remark referring to the aristocracy and land-owning middle classes as much as to their servants and to the bureaucracy.

2. Barry Jones, *Sleepers, Wake! Technology and the Future of Work*, Melbourne and Oxford 1983. p. 82.

3. Max Weber, *The Protestant Ethic and the Spirit of Capitalism*, London/Sydney 1985, p. 59 (my emphasis). Many similar examples can be found in *Capital* Volume 1 and in David S. Landes's *The Unbound Prometheus*, but relating to British textile manufactures in the eighteenth century. This was alluded to at the end of Chapter 1 in connection with J. Smith's *Memoirs of Wool*.

4. I have developed these aspects in *Strategy for Labour*, Boston 1967, ch. 3.

5. Ivan Illich, *Tools for Conviviality*, London 1976. On this topic see also 'Affluence Dooms Itself' in André Gorz, *Ecology as Politics*, London and Boston 1980.

6. One of the very rare works to have shown the break with the capitalist developmental model which the right of the workers to decide for themselves the extent of their working hours would involve is the excellent *La révolution du temps choisi*, largely written by Laurence Cossé and Jean-Baptiste de Foucauld for the 'Echanges et Projets' group under whose signature the work appears (Paris, 1980).

7. On this point see the Appendix.

8. Taken from Adret, *Travailler deux heures par jour*, Paris 1977 (my emphasis).

9. Quoted by the Swedish economist Gunnar Adler-Karlsson in his 'Gedanken zur Vollbeschäftigung' in *Mitteilungen zur Arbeits- und Berufsforschung*, 4, 1979.

10. Edmund Husserl, *The crisis of European Sciences and Transcendental Phenomenology. An Introduction to Phenomenological Philosophy*, trans. and with an introduction by David Carr, Evanston 1970, §9h, p. 52.

11. Ibid, §9g, p. 48.

12. Ibid, §9g, p. 46.

13. Ibid, §9h, p. 52.

10

Market and Society, Capitalism and Socialism

The imperialism of 'cognitive-instrumental' reason and particularly of economic rationality, in its capacity as a guide to decision-making, draws its force, at the individual level, from the apparent objectivity of the criteria of judgement provided by calculation. Calculating is a technique which dispenses the subject from giving meaning to decisions and from accepting responsibility for them: it is the calculation alone which will decide. But this means that economic calculation is incapable of providing a meaning whenever subjects rely on it completely and that it is incapable of deciding whether it is relevant to a given issue. As a substitute for value judgement and by dispensing with such judgement, it cannot, by its very nature, define the limits of its own applicability. These limits can only be imposed on it from outside, precisely through value judgements which, by presenting themselves as such, deliberately deny the relevance of economic calculation when certain ethical principles are at stake.

The history of capitalist societies can thus be read as being *first* the history of the gradual abolition of the limits impeding the deployment of economic rationality, and then the history of the reimposition of new limits: from the abolition of slavery, of the sale of women, of the sale of children and of child labour, and so on, up to the regulation of the working day and the price of labour, the setting of standards for housing density, hygiene, pollution control, and the like. To put it another way, *the central problem of capitalist society, and the central issue in its political conflicts, has been, since the beginning, that of the limits inside which economic rationality is to operate.*

The industrial and commercial bourgeoisie has constantly fought against any limitation of the rights of individuals to pursue their own interests. It has led this fight in the name of what it is customary to call economic liberalism, employing two separate lines of argument, whose internal consistency is far from being obvious: an economic line of argument in favour of the free play of 'market forces', and an ideological line of argument in favour of freedom of enterprise which is said to 'mobilize the creative energies of individuals for society.'

From a philosophical point of view, the argument in favour of the free play of 'market forces' took on a particularly elaborate form in the work of Friedrich A. Hayek. Modernizing and rationalizing the theory of the 'invisible hand', Hayek maintains that the market is the totalizing of a great quantity of data and, especially, of information and initiatives, which far exceeds human understanding or the data-collecting ability of even the most refined statistical apparatus. In other words, the collective resultant (as reflected in the market) of initiatives undertaken by individuals who are free optimally to adjust their actions to the changing situation, is in principle unpredictable and unknowable. Consequently, the results of laissez-faire will always be of a superior efficiency and rationality, to those of attempted intervention, of regulation and of planning which, however well informed they may be, cannot but distort the market's tendency to perform optimally.

Society, in other words, must bow to the market; it must accept the resultant of the myriads of independent initiatives that economic agents undertake, on the basis of their direct and limited knowledge of a limited segment of the social field. No one, not even (indeed, especially not) a state endowed with a powerful apparatus for forecasting and information gathering, can collect as much knowledge as that fragmented knowledge held by scattered economic agents. All attempts to intervene, to direct or regulate economic activity by general measures, will therefore be risky and largely blind, thus preventing the optimal adjustments.

Hayek, like all liberal economists, therefore claims that economic calculation is neither possible nor rational on a social scale or on the scale of the system. The overall resultant of individual economic calculations must be left to chance, that is to the free play of the market. But this also means that the society which will result from these individual economic activities must be left to chance: it will have to be a sort of by-product of economic activity. Politics must abdicate in favour of the market; *it must recognize that the definition of the optimum lies outside its competence.* The only interest common to all individuals, and thus their only social bond, is that of being protected from any constraints hindering their freedom to act in their own interests.

It would be vain to search for any value judgement concerning the societal function of entrepreneurs and free enterprise in economic argument. On the contrary, neither enterprise nor entrepreneurs pursue societal goals; neither is a producer of society. This is the least of their worries. Society, they tell us, will be at its best if, left to chance, no one shows concern for anything but their own good. Let everyone freely pursue their own interests; the rest, that is, the good society, will come to everyone on top of this. No one has to be responsible for it, it does not need anyone to will it, which means that *it must be beyond the power of each and of all.*

And this is precisely the essential point for supporters of economic liberalism: the freedom of individuals to pursue their own interests implies an absence of responsibility towards the collective. This absence of responsibility, in liberal theory, is justified by the fact that 'people are not good'; they do not and cannot wish for the good. A society dependent on their will would therefore be the worst of all. On the other hand, a society which is the unanticipated result of scattered individual initiatives will always be better than the goals set by individuals: it will be precisely the best possible. In the end people never do what they wish: *they do good without wishing to*; better still: *they do good provided that they do not wish to*; they are traduced into doing good by the chance resultant of their scattered initiatives. The moral categories of 'evil' and 'good', of equity and justice have no relevance on this level.

It is here that we can gauge the abyss which divides liberal *thought* from liberal *ideology*, more particularly from entrepreneurial ideology, such as that propagated chiefly by the new Saint-Simonians. In liberal *thought*, each entrepreneur pursues his own interests, that is, the greatest possible profit. Their initiatives are the result of economic calculations. These calculations guide their decision-making, evaluate the risks involved, situate the alternatives and are free of all moral or social concern: you must win either by carving out a place for yourself or by fighting off those who covet the place you occupy. In liberal *ideology*, on the contrary, entrepreneurs are creators of society and of culture: they have 'the genius of discovering in their contemporaries the "latent need" for an object or a service that, in our everyday round, we would not have imagined'; their enterprise 'represents and fulfils a cardinal value which we perceive as materializing freedom itself, namely innovation'; they are among those who 'mobilize what is best in themselves for society' and who, in giving society 'creative impulses', acquire power over it. Therefore it would be more appropriate, they tell us, to reverse the terms of the problem: one should no longer seek to integrate the economy into society but, on the contrary, to 'develop policies which integrate society into the economy', that is, as we have seen, to make society conform to the requirements of economic rationality. No goals which run counter to the latter should be given legitimacy.[1]

The intellectual regression by comparison with the political debates of the last one hundred and fifty years is spectacular. The new ideologists of the entrepreneurial bourgeoisie throw overboard the liberal theorists who, from Adam Smith to our own time, were concerned with removing society from the control of men who, as industrialists, merchants or bankers, are not, and cannot be, concerned with the social good by the very nature of their activities. Even Hayek holds that the field in which economic rationality is allowed to operate without hindrance should be limited by an upper chamber whose members, elected by reason of their moral authority, stand outside and above parties. Not to assign limits to the play of economic rationality (and to competition and to the laws of the market which result) is, in fact, to move towards the complete disintegration of society and the irreversible destruction of the biosphere.

Therefore, logically enough, the first groups to oppose the unlimited play of economic rationality were the aristocracy and land-owners. As Karl Polanyi[2] has shown, there was a 'Tory socialism' well before the birth of working-class socialism. Indeed, Polanyi very pertinently defines socialism as the *subordination of the economy to society* and of economic goals to the societal goals which encompass them and assign them their subordinate place as means to an end. Economic activity must be put to the service of ends which go beyond it and which establish its usefulness, its meaning. Thus there may be a 'Tory socialism' endeavouring to restrain economic activity so that it neither abolishes pre-capitalist social bonds in the countryside, destroys social cohesion, causes the decline of agriculture, makes towns uninhabitable, or the air unbreathable, and so on, nor gives rise to a wretched proletarian mass, reduced to beggary, theft, prostitution, 'ducking and diving', and the like.

'Tory socialism' assumes, however, that a society exists which can, by virtue of its intact cohesion and stability, allow economically rational activities and at the same time *contain their dynamic within the limits it assigns to them.* This might have seemed possible in Disraeli's time. It is not possible in our day. So when Hayek and others – German Christian Democrats, French and Dutch centrists, the majority of British Conservatives, many American Democrats, and so on – declare that they support the idea of a guaranteed basic income paid by society to all those citizens deprived of the possibility of earning their living through work, there are no grounds for calling this socialism. Such a guaranteed basic income in no way integrates the mass of those excluded into an *intact society.* It cannot even be said that *society* grants them this income so as to make them feel secure and accepted. Quite the reverse, it is *society* which marginalizes and excludes them and sentences them to idleness; and it is *the state* which, by an administrative instrument, pays them enough to subsist after a fashion, without in any way including or reintegrating them into the web of social exchanges and relationships (except in the most temporary or marginalized way). In short, while a guaranteed basic income runs counter to economic rationality, it does not make it serve the goals of a superior rationality. On the contrary, the guaranteed basic income presents itself as an enclave in the heart of economic rationality *whose domination over society it seeks to render socially acceptable.*

This example illuminates the weakness of past social-democratic policies and the ease with which social-democratic ideology was superseded, in the name of economic rationalization, by the ideology of the market and of free enterprise. Social-democratic policy has never, in fact, been the sort of socialism defined by Karl Polanyi: it does its utmost to create *enclaves* in the heart of economic rationality but without in any way limiting its domination over society. These enclaves, on the contrary, were themselves dependent on the good working of capitalism and intended to promote it. Their continual extension did not come from a political desire to put economic rationality in the service of a comprehensive vision of what society should be; it rather derived from the obvious fact that capitalist development gives rise to collective needs which cannot be expressed by effective demand and which are therefore unable to be supplied by the market: the need for space, air, clean water, light, silence, public transport, accident and sickness prevention, public hygiene, education, services compensating for the breakdown of family and communal solidarity, and so on.

In short, the criterion of economic rationality, as perceived by 'economic agents', including the most 'brilliant' entrepreneurs, is not enough to exhaust the functional and structural requirements of the economic system and life in society. Left to itself, the market economy always evolves inexorably towards collapse, according to the 'Tragedy of the Commons' scenario mentioned earlier.[3] To be viable, it must be contained by regulations, prohibitions, subsidies, taxes, public interventions and initiatives which distort the working of the market: by regulating agricultural prices through policies of export subsidies and stockpiling; by subsidizing housing and rents; by socializing the cost of health care, education, old age pensions; by placing high taxes on fuel, tobacco and alcohol; by financing research and development; by enacting laws governing town planning and public health; by banning some drugs and monitoring the price of others, and so on; that is, in general, by redistributing an increasingly substantial part of the available resources in such a way as to limit, direct or generate supply by virtue of *political* criteria, or by wholly substituting public initiatives where no private initiatives are forthcoming.

Yet these political criteria have never had the coherence of an overall plan, of a social project. The redistribution of 40, 50 or even 60 per cent of the gross national product has not been enough to give birth to a *society* which is in control of economic activity and which can submit it to its ends. This redistribution has remained an aggregate of *correctives*, auxiliaries and complements, framing economic activity without either dominating it, encompassing it or making it serve a different rationality. Activity directed towards economic goals has remained the driving force. It is this which has continued to determine the social relations, modes of socialization and functional integration of individuals; and the collective needs which it could neither apprehend nor satisfy were dealt with not by society itself but according to procedures codified by the state bureaucracies. Thus, far from helping to submit the economy to its ends, the state has filled in for the decay of social bonds and solidarity and has brought about a growing demand for it to take charge of such matters.

The condemnation of the welfare state in the name of economic liberalism is thus a piece of mindless ideology. State provision does not stifle society and limit the spontaneous deployment of economic rationality; it is born of this very deployment, as a substitute for the societal and familial solidarity that the extension of commodity relations has dissolved, and as a necessary framework preventing the market economy finishing up in a collective disaster.

What is true, however, is that the welfare state has not been and never will be a creator of society; but neither is the market and nor will it ever be either. It is this fact which explains the feeble resistance to the progressive dismantling of the welfare state; this dismantling does not strike at society, nor does it alter social relationships; it strikes at the interests of individuals who are not united by any lived social solidarity nor by any conception of what society should be.

The problem of socialism remains then, if one fully understands by socialism the subordination of economic rationality to societal ends, that is to the ends that everyone pursues and can only pursue with the participation of others and which create their common sense of belonging.[4] We have said enough about this in all that has gone before not to have to show here that these ends cannot be economic ends once the productive forces are highly developed and differentiated. They can only be political and ethical ends, delimiting the place that activity performed for economic ends must have in the life of the city and extending indefinitely the public spaces in which individual and collective autonomous activities can be deployed.

The question remains open, however, of determining which activities can be subordinated to economic rationality without losing their meaning and for which activities economic rationalization would be a perversion or a negation of the meaning inherent in them. It is this question that I will now seek to clarify.

Notes

1. The quotations are taken from Paul Thibaud's 'Le triomphe de l'entrepreneur' in *Esprit*, December 1984.

2. Karl Polanyi, *The Great Transformation*, Boston, Mass. 1957, p. 166 ff.

3. See above, Part 1, Chapter 4, p. 47.

4. Nationalism is an even more misleading substitute for this sense of belonging, in that it substitutes for common societal aims statist goals of power and 'grandeur', defined and pursued by *raison d'État*, outside of and, if necessary, against society.

The Limits of Economic Rationality

Search for Meaning (3)

The problem I shall be discussing here is not of recent provenance. Marx himself used the notion of 'work' in an undifferentiated fashion, regarding the work of an industrial labourer and that of a composer or a scientist as activities of the same type. Given that view, it was quite simple for him to argue that when work had ceased to be a necessity, it would then become a human need.

However, in their efforts to demonstrate that the 'work-based society' is not on its last legs and that work is going to continue to be at the centre of our lives, the current ideologues press this view of work as an undifferentiated entity even further. The activities of the technician, the police officer, the odd-job man, the deliverer of hot croissants, the home-help, the mother, the shoe-shiner, the priest and the prostitute are all treated as 'work'. All of it, they argue, is socially useful and it all deserves remuneration in one way or another.

A text by a Finnish feminist (which is in other respects extremely interesting and opposed to the current all-pervading economism) is instructive in this regard. She writes:

A survey carried out in Finland in 1980 showed that the average family performs 7.2 hours of unpaid work per day, seven days a week, or in other words 50.4 hours per week. Women do more than five hours of this work per day and men less than two; daughters do 1.2 hours and sons 0.7. The *monetary* value of this unpaid work is equal to 42 per cent of GNP (and 160 per cent of the national budget), a figure arrived at by taking the wages of local authority home-helps as a base . . . Economists have generally shown little interest in this invisible economy. They consider it a necessary *secondary economy*, an auxiliary to the *primary economy*, serving to reproduce labour power and to consume what has been produced.[1]

And since everything done within the framework of the family is, in the end, indispensable and socially useful, what could be more legitimate than to claim a 'decent wage' for '*all* the work' done, mainly by women, in the domestic sphere?

But where does all this work begin, and where does it end? Is domestic labour (the author uses this term and not 'domestic work' to show that she really is talking about 'production') work in the same sense as that of an industrial worker? Do people really 'work' five hours in their homes after having worked seven or eight hours outside the home? This is what Pietilä implies when she writes: 'The *monetary* value of unpaid work is equal to 42 per cent of GNP. . . . It would be much greater if it were assessed at the rate for providing the corresponding goods and services if these were bought on the market.' In other words, equity and economic logic appear to demand that everything people do be evaluated according to its *exchange value* on the market: the night the mother spends at the bedside of her sick child should then be paid at night-nurse rates; the birthday cake Grandma baked charged at the price it would cost in a confectioner's; sexual relations paid for at the rate each of the partners might get at an Eros Centre, maternity at the price charged by the surrogate mother.

And why not admit that all these unpaid bits of 'work' would deserve to be transformed into specialized, paid jobs, since this would surely solve a lot of problems? Would their social usefulness not justify such a move? The idea of 'wages for motherhood' and 'wages for housework' is becoming a fashionable one (I shall return to this later), since society could not exist without children and households. It could not exist if people stopped washing, dressing and feeding themselves properly. Are people therefore being useful to society when they do these things? Have I a right to payment if I brush my teeth three times a day and, as a result, the health service makes savings? Can we and should we regulate monetarily and administratively – in terms of demographic, economic and social optima – the 'work' of 'producing' children, of keeping clean, of looking after ourselves and our environment? Is sexual activity to be seen as part of our work because orgasms stimulate creativity in our jobs? Are the sports we play part of our work because the dynamism they give us can be of profit to the economy? And if not, then why not?

Might it be because there are things one does that are not done for the purpose of exchange, activities which, as a result, have no price, no exchange value, 'work' that has no 'utility' and which consequently merges with the satisfaction its performance procures, even if that work demands effort and fatigue? Who is to say, if these activities exist, what they might be?

Certainly not economists and sociologists. Because they start out from the functioning of the social system, they can only apprehend the functionality of individual activities, not the meaning they have for the individual subjects who perform them. They inevitably posit *the system as subject* (this is the defining characteristic of instrumental thinking) and see the living, thinking subjects as the instruments it employs. Everything, then, seems useful to the system since, in fact, it is the totalization of everything that happens. Objective thought will naively conclude that men and women (along with children, and Nature) 'work' for the system, whatever they do and that their reality resides in this 'function'. Therein lies one of the roots of totalitarianism and barbarism.

We have, then, to learn to think what we are by starting out from ourselves; we have to re-learn that we are the subjects, to learn that sociology and economics have limits, and socialization too; re-learn to *make distinctions within the notion of work* in order to avoid the error of remunerating activities that have no commercial objective and subjecting to the logic of productivity acts which are only properly consonant with their meaning if the time they take is left out of account.

It is not therefore enough merely to define the criteria on which economic rationality is based. We have to define the criteria by which we judge them to be applicable. If we are to do this, we must examine our activities more closely and ask what meaning the relations they allow us to establish with other people contain and whether these relations are compatible with economic rationality.

Economically Rational Work

Work as modern economics understands it is an activity deployed *for the purpose of commodity exchange*, an activity necessarily subject to an *accounting calculation.*[2] Workers work 'to earn a living' – that is, to obtain in exchange for work whose products have no *direct* utility *for themselves* the means to buy all the things they need that are produced by people other than themselves. This work which they sell must be performed *as efficiently as possible*, so that it can be exchanged against equal and, if possible, greater amounts of work embodied in goods and services themselves produced as efficiently as possible.

This primary objective of work in no way excludes the possibility of workers *also* taking an interest in their work or deriving pleasure or personal satisfaction from it. But these are merely secondary goals. However interesting it may be, work done for exchange on the market cannot be regarded as being of the same type as the activity of the painter, the writer, the missionary, the researcher or the revolutionary, who accept a life of privation because *the activity itself, not its exchange value, is their primary goal.*

In order to pursue economic efficiency, it has to be possible to measure the *productivity* of labour (that is the quantity of labour per unit of product). The quantitative measurement of productivity is the only possible means of comparing performance levels and defining methods and research techniques capable of increasing productivity, in other words, the only means of *saving labour* and *gaining time.* All this is evident in the classical way in which work is carried out in industrial production. However, since the workers are wage labourers, they themselves have no interest in achieving maximum economic efficiency and do not seek to fulfil that aim. Rather it is their employer who seeks it, in *his* own interest and the interest of the enterprise, and who must then contend with the ensuing difficulties of inciting the workers to achieve higher productivity.[3]

Achieving maximum economic efficiency of labour is only in the interest of the actual workers when they are self-employed, for example, in craftwork or in the provision of services. Their labour will only be rational in economic terms if the services they provide *are qualitatively and quantitatively superior to those which people are able to provide for themselves using an equal amount of their own labour.* It will then be possible for them to charge their clients for a greater amount of labour time than they actually spend and their clients will still benefit from the exchange. This is the case where plumbers or hairdressers who provide a home service are concerned. They do what their clients would not have been able to do for themselves. Their labour enables their clients to save time and improve their quality of life. In this way, these tradespeople increase the amount of wealth society has, without valorizing any capital, by increasing the quantity and quality of skills and knowledge in circulation within it. This would be impossible were it not for the existence of a *market* which permits specialized labour, which has no use value for the person providing it, to be exchanged for money – the 'universal equivalent' of the wealth produced by the labour of society as a whole.

These remarks are all the more valid in the case of activities which combine professional know-how with highly efficient equipment which ordinary individuals cannot afford to own: with capital, in other words. Cleaning and repair services and collective catering services, amongst others, come into this category, as does mechanized and automated material production.

In short, economic rationality seems properly applicable to activities which:

(a) create use value;

(b) for exchange as commodities;

(c) in the public sphere;

(d) in a measurable amount of time, at as high a level of productivity as possible.

Contrary to what is widely held to be the case, *it is not enough for an activity to be performed for exchange on the market* (with a view to receiving remuneration) *for it to be work in the economic sense of the word.* It is essential to understand this if we are to define the limits of the economic sphere. In order to underline this point, I will now examine a number of different types of activity which are characterized by their lack of one or other of the four parameters mentioned above. These activities can be divided into two main groups:

A. activities performed for the purpose of remuneration or *commodity activities*;

B. *non-commodity activities*, for which remuneration is not – or cannot be – the primary goal.

A. COMMODITY ACTIVITIES

1. Work in the Economic Sense as Emancipation

$$[(a) + (b) + (c) + (d)]$$

I do not intend to repeat the definition of economically rational work here. Instead I will concentrate on underlining the importance of parameters (b) (commodity exchange) and (c) (in the public sphere). The fact that an activity is the object of a commodity exchange *in the public sphere* immediately denotes it as being a socially useful activity, which creates a use value that is *socially accepted* as such. In other words, this activity corresponds to a 'trade': it has a public price and a public status, and I can get an indefinite number of clients or employers to give me money for it without having to enter into a *personal* and *private* relationship with them. In any case, these people themselves do not ask me to work for them as private individuals (as, for example, a domestic servant would be required to do) but to do a specific job under specific conditions, for a specific price.

The existence of a public contract for the sale of my labour thus designates it as being *labour in general* which is incorporated – and incorporates me – into the system of economic and social exchange. It designates me as being a *generally* social, generally useful individual, as capable as anyone else and entitled to the same rights as they are. In other words, it designates me a *citizen*. Paid work in the public sphere therefore constitutes a factor of social insertion.

It is already possible to see here that different types of work will not bestow the same degree of dignity on those who do them, nor will they afford them the same possibilities of social insertion. The 'housewife' who gets a job in a school canteen or the farmer's daughter who goes to work in a canning factory are not simply exchanging unpaid work for similar work for a wage. They are acquiring a different social status. Previously, they 'worked' in the private sphere and their work was directed towards particular individuals by virtue of the *private*, personal bond that existed between them. Their work had no *direct* or *tangible* social utility. The unwritten family code dictated that its members should have a duty to one another, in the interests of the domestic community as a whole, and there therefore existed no space in which they ceased to belong to one another. There was, then, no question of calculating one's time and saying, 'That's my work done for now. I'm off.' Allocating 'wages for housework' to 'housewives' would change nothing in this regard.

To these women, getting a job in a canteen or factory thus meant finally being able to break free of their confinement within the private sphere and *gain access to the public sphere*. Their duties were no longer dictated by the intangible obligations of love and family membership but by the rule of law. This granted them a legal existence as *citizens*, a socially determined and codified existence which was to be matched by a private sphere sheltered from all social rules and obligations, in which each individual had sovereign possession of her or his own self.

The consequences of the social codification, regulation and determination of work are consequently far from being entirely negative. These processes mark out the limits of the private and the public spheres, confer a public, social reality on individuals (what sociologists would call an 'identity'), *define their obligations and hence consider them to be freed from them once these obligations have been fulfilled.* I am freed from my obligation to my boss or client once I have 'finished my day's work' or honoured my contract; my boss or client are free of their obligations to me once I have been paid. The commodity relations characteristic of the public sphere are exempt from private bonds and obligations. If private bonds do exist, then they preclude the existence of commodity relations.

We come here to a point we shall have to tackle from a number of different angles: commodity relations cannot exist between members of a family or a community – or that community will be dissolved; nor can affection, tenderness and sympathy be bought or sold except when they are reduced to mere simulacra.

What is important to bear in mind here is that the existence of a public, economic sphere has enabled personal relations to develop in their own right and become independent of that sphere: the *oikos*, that is, the sphere of private life and personal relations, now only marginally constitutes a sphere of economic production. *The right to accede to the public, economic sphere through one's work is a necessary part of the right to citizenship.*

2. Servants' Work

$$[(b) + (c) + (d)]^4$$

Services which do not *create* any use value, whilst still being the subjects of public commodity exchanges, are essentially servile jobs or servants' jobs. The job of a shoeshiner falls into this category as it entails selling a service which the client could have quite easily provided for himself in less than the amount of time he spends sitting watching the person crouching at his feet. He is not paying for the usefulness of the service provided but for the pleasure of having someone serve him.

The same goes for people paid by others – either directly or through service companies – to do their housework, even though the latter lack neither the time nor the physical ability to do it themselves. The work cleaners do does not, therefore, produce more free time across the whole of society nor is it an improvement on the result their clients could obtain if the latter did such work themselves. These servants merely enable their clients to gain a couple of hours by doing a couple of hours' work in their place.

There can be an *indirect* economic rationality for such work if the time these servants save for their employers is used by the latter to perform activities which are much more socially or economically useful than the activities the servants would be capable of performing. *But this is never entirely the case.*

For one thing, the work of a servant prevents the person doing it from demonstrating, acquiring or developing more advanced skills. The humble social status to which such people are confined conceals this fact and serves as a pretext for attributing the humble nature of their work to their inherent inferiority. There was no problem in doing this in times when servants were recruited from the ranks of oppressed classes or races; it becomes rather more difficult when they have A-levels or a degree.

For another thing, servants never serve their master or client in his or her purely public capacity (as a head of state's chauffeur does, for example). They also serve their master in her or his private life, for his or her own private comfort. They are paid, in part at least, to please a particular individual and not merely because they are economically useful. In other words, their work *does not fall entirely within the public sphere*: it consists not just in supplying a certain amount of labour at a certain price as stated in their contract, but also in giving pleasure, in giving of themselves. This relationship of servility remains concealed whilst there exists a work contract regulated by law or whilst the work is done in public (as in the case of shoeshiners or those who work providing pleasurable services). It is exposed when servants are paid for the pleasure they procure for their masters in private. I shall return to this in connection with prostitution.

3. Functions, Care, Assistance

$$[(a) + (b) + (c)]^5$$

Under this heading I shall group those activities which create use value, for the purpose of commodity exchange, in the public sphere, but whose productivity is impossible to measure and hence impossible to maximize.

We are obviously dealing here primarily with the monitoring, controlling and maintenance jobs described in Chapter 7. They are comparable, as Oskar Negt has so accurately observed, to the 'work' of police officers, firemen, tax officials, fraud-squad officers, and so on: these are people who are *on duty* but are not *working*: their task is to intervene should the need arise but it would be better if it did not, and ultimately they perform their function best when they have nothing to do. These activities are therefore not jobs but functions for which 'functionaries' are paid for the hours they are present. Better to have too many employees with relatively little to do than a small workforce which would be unable to cope in the case of an emergency or a serious difficulty. One could undoubtedly argue that the size of this workforce is determined all the same by a calculation and therefore corresponds to a form of economic rationality. However, this argument is not relevant to our concern here, which is the applicability of economic rationality to a determinate *activity* (or type of work). The paradox, in so far as these functions are concerned, is that *economic rationality at the level of the system requires that economic rationalization should not be applied to the activities of its agents.* They have to be paid independently of their productivity.

The reason for this is not simply that the amount of effective work cannot be planned and does not therefore depend on the agents themselves: *these agents must not have an interest in there being work for them to do.* The fireman should not have an interest in there being a fire, nor the police officer in there being public disorder, nor the inspector in there being frauds, nor the doctor on night duty in there being an emergency. They should be incorruptible, disinterested, loyal and just – like the idealized cop of American cinema – and act 'out of a sense of duty', in the interest of the system or the general public, not in their own interest or that of their professional body.

The same also holds, *mutatis mutandis,* for all those activities which meet a need for care, assistance or help. The efficiency of such activities is impossible to quantify. Not only because the nature and number of demands for assistance are independent of the people providing care or assistance but because the reasons for these demands are impossible to plan. A doctor's productivity cannot be measured in terms of the number of patients she or he sees per day; nor that of a home-help in terms of the number of disabled people's houses he or she cleans; nor that of a childminder in terms of the number of children in her or his care, and so on. It is possible for the efficiency of 'carers' to be in inverse proportion to their visible quantitative output.

The service they provide cannot be defined *in itself* independently of the people whose individual needs they cater for. The point is not, as in manufacturing work, to produce predetermined acts or objects, which can be separated from the actual person producing them but to define the acts or objects to be produced according to other people's needs. Adjusting supply to suit demand, in other words, depends on a person-to-person relationship, not on the execution of predetermined, quantifiable actions.

The perverse effects produced by the quantification of caring activities are particularly striking in the case of the French or German health systems. By introducing a system of productivity-related remuneration for GPs, the French system of 'payment by treatment'[6] has created a double barrier between doctors and patients:

(i) If the treatments doctors provide are to be made quantifiable they must be made to correspond to a standard definition. This a priori definition (what medical insurance schemes call 'nomenclature') pre-supposes a standard definition of needs and, therefore, the standard-ization of patients. Patients have to correspond to predictable 'cases' that slot readily into a classification table. The GP's first task will thus be to classify the patient: individual consultations and examinations are

abandoned in favour or radiography and laboratory tests, advice and explanations are replaced by prescriptions, and so forth. The doctor–patient relationship gives way to a purely technical relationship. The consumption of medical services and pharmaceutical products increases and so does the patients' frustration.

(ii) 'Payment by treatment' acts as an incentive for the doctor to maximize his or her gains by maximizing productivity (that is, the number of patients treated per hour). Now, the slightest suspicion that the primary objective of the persons administering care is to maximize their gains has the effect of undermining the relationship between doctors and patients (or between teachers and pupils or between carers and those in their care) and casts doubt on the quality of the assistance they are providing. This assistance should, in fact, be provided *in the patient's interest, not the GP's.* This is the very essence of the doctor–patient relationship (or teacher–pupil relationship, etc.), and is a condition of its effectiveness. Persons administering care must not have a personal interest in people needing their care. The money they earn should be a *means* of exercising their profession and not its end. Somehow, earning their living should not, so to speak, come into the bargain.

The same goes for all the other caring and educational professions. These jobs are only done well when they are performed out of a 'sense of vocation', that is, an *unconditional* desire to help other people. Receiving remuneration for the help she or he gives should not be the doctor's basic motivation; such a motivation is in competition with a strictly professional motivation which could or indeed must take precedence in case of need. In the occupations in question, the relationship between doctors and patients (or between teachers and pupils or between carers and those in their care) is *distinct from their commercial relationship and is presented as quite independent of it*: 'I'm here to help you. Of course, I also intend to earn a living. But money is what enables me to do my job and not vice versa. What I do and what I earn have no real relation to one other.'[7]

The patients (or pupils, and so on) recognize this incommensurability by the fact that they still feel indebted to their doctor (or teacher, etc.) even after they have paid them. They have received from the latter something greater than, and different from, what money can buy: the service provided, even when it is well remunerated, *also* is of the nature of a *gift*, more precisely, a giving *of him or herself* on the part of the doctor (or teacher, etc.). She or he has been involved in the service he or she has provided in a manner that can be neither *produced* at will, nor bought, learned or codified. She or he has shown an interest in the other person as a human being and not just in their money; he or she has established a relationship with the other that cannot be expressed in terms of a predefined technical procedure or a computer programme. This relationship will have a tendency to extend beyond the public sphere into the private, that is, into relationships governed not by social conventions, rules and norms that are generally held to be valid, but by a personal understanding gradually built up between two individuals and valid for them alone.

Because they demand that one give of oneself, only people who have chosen to perform helping and caring activities do them well. Such activities are best carried out by volunteers. In a society in which time and skills are no longer in short supply, these activities can be developed, then, in ways that are totally different from current conceptions. The current conception of such activities is still based on the idea that work for economic ends has to take up the most important part of our lives and that, in consequence, the so-called 'convivial' activities such as the provision of home help and home care (for the handicapped, the aged, the sick, and mothers with young children) constitute a 'sector' apart which can serve to provide unemployed young people with low-paid, part-time jobs, until something better comes along. It is thus that the 'convivial sector' – a phrase coined by a certain French minister for social affairs – came into being; and that a new dividing line was established in that process of compartmentalization of the spheres of life which Max Weber warned us against: on the one side specialists in heartless professions, on the other specialists in soulless conviviality. 'Conviviality' would be turned into a low-grade occupation and those who had 'proper' jobs would be all the less obliged to engage in it.

Now in a society in which time and producible resources are no longer scarce, the opposite of the above is to be expected: convivial activities could be gradually de-professionalized and, as the number of working hours diminishes, done on a voluntary basis within the framework of mutual aid networks. These voluntary activities would become *one* of the focuses of a multi-faceted life, alongside paid work (twenty to thirty hours per week) and other non-economic activities, such as cultural and educational activities, maintaining and renovating our surroundings, and so on.

We must rethink all the activities which require us to give of ourselves with a view to developing self-organized, voluntary services. The impasses with which the welfare state has to contend originate in part in the absurd conception of society which requires one sector of the population (people who have retired or been pensioned off early) to be paid to be inactive; another sector to be paid to work long hours; and a third to be paid to perform, on a temporary basis and for want of something better, what the first have no right, and the second no time, to do. If we continue in this manner, in the twenty-first century (by about 2030) there will be approximately the same number of pensioners as people in employment. By the time they retire, they will have done about thirty years' paid work and will still have about twenty to twenty-five years ahead of them in which they will be able to carry on working, and will in general wish to do so. The entire social organization of non-economic activities (such as helping, caring, cultural and development activities) should be redefined on the basis of these facts, by creating a kind of *synergy* within a two-tiered system supported on the one hand by centralized services provided by institutions, and on the other by self-organized, co-operative services staffed by volunteers.[8]

Having analysed those activities which allow people to give of themselves, we can now turn our attention to activities in which, paradoxically, it is precisely this giving of oneself which is the object of a commodity exchange. I give myself or give of myself so that I can earn money; I give this act a monetary value and thus negate it, yet I am nevertheless still bound to perform it as a gift. Such commodity exchanges, which bear upon what I *am* and cannot possibly produce at will, are forms of prostitution. They establish a commodity relationship between private persons relating to each other as unique individuals, and are performed in the *private* sphere.

4. Prostitution

$$[(a) + (b) + (d)]^9$$

The prostitute undertakes to provide a determinate form of pleasure within a determinate period of time. The client cannot obtain an equivalent, in terms of quality and quantity, of the service the prostitute sells from unpaid partners in so short a time. There is, therefore, a use value created. However, there is an obvious contradiction between the sale of such a service and its nature.

In commodity exchange, buyer and seller enter into a contractual relationship for a set period of time; they are free from their obligations to each other once payment has been made; the offer made by the seller determines the buyer as an anonymous individual, interchangeable with any other: having the requisite amount of money is the necessary and sufficient condition for receiving the service. Now, in the case of prostitution, the client presents himself as a buyer whose money is sufficient to give him the right to request and obtain from the prostitute a service which he expects to *define himself*, for the sole reason that he wants that service.

Of course, the commodity exchange is conducted at an agreed price but this price depends on the personality of the client and on the nature of the service he asks for. The commercial transaction thus takes place entirely in the private sphere and relates to the provision of a personal service which is adapted to meet a demand that is made on a personal, private basis.

We are dealing here with a servant–master relationship in its purest form: *one person's 'work' IS another person's pleasure.* Work, here, has no object other than to produce this pleasure. The client's pleasure consists in consuming the work done on his or her private person. This consumption is immediate and direct. It is not mediated by any product whatsoever. It is this immediacy which distinguishes pleasure procured through servile labour from, for example, the pleasure a head chef procures for those who consume his 'sublime creations'.

But there is more to it than that. There *is no reason* behind the client's desire for this pleasure. This is one of the major differences between the 'work' of a prostitute and, for example, that of physio-therapist. The latter also attends to the physical well-being of her clients, but the clients have to have a motive for demanding her services. This motive will then become the subject of a diagnosis, after which the therapist will use her sovereign judgement to determine a form of treatment which, though personalized, employs well-defined techniques according to a predetermined procedure.

Whilst the 'carer' is, then, in the client's service, this in no way makes her the latter's instrument of pleasure. On the contrary, the 'carer' is in a position of dominance: she decides what the nature of the operations carried out will be and does not give of herself except *within the limits of a codified procedure which she controls from start to finish.* The technical nature of the procedure acts as an insurmountable barrier: it prevents the therapist's personal implication in the task from developing into complete complicity or intimacy.

The situation is exactly the reverse in the 'work' of the prostitute: her technical know-how must be deployed in the way the client desires (without having to give a reason). What the client hopes to buy is the prostitute's complete implication in the acts he demands: she must submit to his demands *by putting herself into her work* and not by performing these tasks mechanically. She must be both subject and freedom, but a freedom which can do no other than to make itself the instrument of another person's will. In other words, she must be that contradicatory, impossible, phantasmatic being, the 'beautiful slave' (whom the young prince receives as a present in *The Arabian Nights,* riding naked on a white horse); the slave who uses all her intelligence and sensibility freely to carry out her master's desires and who is *free to do only this*; the slave who, in reality, is never anything but someone playing at being the phantasmatic being who haunts her master's thoughts.

'Pay your money and you can do what you like with me.' This short phrase says it all: the prostitute posits herself as a sovereign subject in order to demand payment and as soon as this demand is met, she renounces her sovereignty and changes into the instrument of the payer. She thus asserts herself as a free subject who is going to play the role of a slave. Her service will be a simulation; she makes no secret of this. In any case, the client is well aware of it. He knows he cannot buy true feelings, real involvement. He buys simulated versions of them. And in the end what he demands is that the simulation should be more real than the real thing, that it should allow him to experience a venal relationship in his imagination as if it were a real one.

Technicity is thus reintroduced into this venal relationship under another guise and in another manner: in the prostitute's mastery of the art of simulation. The acts she proposes are divorced from their implied intention: their function is to give the illusion of an intention or implication that do not actually exist. They are *gestures* – gestures performed with masterful skill which simulate a *giving of oneself.* The technical practices of simulation thus enable the prostitute to refrain from implicating herself in a relationship which signifies total involvement: she effectively absents herself from this relationship; she ceases to inhabit her body, her gestures, her words at the moment of offering them. She offers her body as if it were not her own self, as an instrument from which she is detached.

She convinces the client she is selling *herself* and convinces herself it is *not* herself *she* is selling. The 'I' of the proposition, 'I sell myself', posits itself as someone other than the 'myself'.[10]

Now, unlike all the other servants whose jobs entail professionally simulating deep concern, good humour, sincerity, sympathy and so on, the prostitute cannot reduce the services she provides to the ritual play of gestures and set phrases which characterize the commercial forms of servility, friendliness and devotion. Over and above offering of herself the gestures and words which she is able to *perform* without involving herself in them, she offers of herself what she *is* beyond all simulation: her body, that is, that through which the subject is given to itself, and which, without any possible dissociation, constitutes the ground of all its lived experiences. You cannot surrender your body without surrendering *yourself* or let it be used by other people without being humiliated.

For 'sexual services' to become a commercial service like any other, they would have to be reduced to a sequence of technicized and standardized acts which anyone could perform on anyone else, according to a predetermined procedure, without having to surrender *themselves* physically. Only then could 'sex' become the rationalized 'work' someone would do to give someone else an orgasm, following a codifiable technique comparable to a form of medical 'treatment', without there being a (real or simulated) giving of themselves or intimacy.

This is more or less what one feminist writer proposed in a long article published in Germany in 1987. According to her, there is a positive side to AIDS in the sense that it has revealed the merits of those orgasms obtained by other means than sexual penetration, which would justify women refusing 'coital men' and establishing sexual relationships based on the much more rational and hygienic act of masturbation, whose technical subtleties have, according to the author, been mistakenly ignored until now.

The logical development of this process of technization would seem to be the introduction of mechanical masturbation using copulating machines. It would permit 'sex' to be rationalized by entirely abolishing the sphere of intimacy. Individuals would no longer need to belong to each other: mechanized humans would be mirrored by humanized machines; orgasms could be bought and sold in the public sphere in the same way as live, hard porn shows.[11]

Two points emerge from the preceding analysis:

(i) There are acts we cannot *perform* at will or on demand and which can only be sold as simulations. These are the necessarily private relational acts through which one person participates in another's feelings – for example, sympathy, understanding, affection or tenderness – and causes the latter to exist as an absolutely unique subject. Such relationships are by nature private and, moreover, resistant to all measures designed to improve their productivity.

(ii) There is an inalienable dimension of our existence, the enjoyment of which we cannot sell to anyone else without *giving of ourselves* into the bargain, and the sale of which devalues the act of giving without relieving us of the obligation to perform it as a gift. This is the essential paradox of prostitution, that is, of all forms of selling *oneself* and renting *oneself* out.

Obviously, prostitution is not limited to 'sexual services'. Every time we let someone buy for their own use what we *are* and could not possibly *produce* at will using technical skill – the renown and talent of the venal writer or the surrogate mother's womb, for instance – we are engaging in acts of prostitution.

The case of the surrogate mother merits closer study. It should enable us to clarify the possible implications of a specific public allowance paid to mothers *in recognition of the social and economic utility* of their 'maternal function'.

4a. Maternity, the Maternal Function, Surrogate Mothers

There is no possible comparison between the social function of mother-hood and its lived meaning. For every woman, pregnancy freely consented to or freely chosen is the absolutely unique experience of a life from within herself desiring to become other while continuing to be part of herself. Once born of her, that life which has become other will still need to be *given to itself*. For this is what bringing up a child means: assisting a life, which is at first still intimately linked to the body of its mother, to detach itself from that body; to take control of itself; to become an autonomous subject.

The relation of a mother to *her* child is therefore not a social relation, no more than the life of the small child is something social. To be a mother is to protect, cherish and raise not just *a* baby, but precisely that baby which is not interchangeable with any other, not merely because it came from her body, but because being its mother means experiencing the absolute certainty that it is *for itself* that incomparably and ineffably unique centre of reference we call a subject. To wish that a subject be itself, to grant it the right to be itself is the essence of the love relation. Maternal love is one of its forms.

It is, however, true that, from the point of view of the social system, maternity is also a 'function' which women absolutely must perform if society is to perpetuate itself. The conflict between these two things is, therefore, radical. The mother's body initially shields the baby from the clutches of society. And, to the extent that maternal love reveals the child to itself as an absolutely unique subject *with a right to its own uniqueness*, it is not merely the maternal body but the maternal relation to the child that threatens the survival of society.[12]

Indeed, from the point of view of the social system, mothers possess an exorbitant power which challenges society's rights over its (future) citizens. Society therefore does everything it can to limit and restrain women's power over their children, and also to appropriate and subjugate women themselves by depriving them of rights over their own bodies, their lives, their very selves. This is the fundamental cause of women's oppression. The 'socialization of the maternal function' will only resolve the radical conflict between society and women if the former manages to produce children without need to have recourse to the bodies of the latter; or if women accept having the childbearing function detached from their persons and allow society to use their wombs for its own ends and pay them for the privilege.[13]

It is, therefore, upon the relation of women to their bodies and their relation to motherhood and their children that the possibility or otherwise of a monetary and/or administrative regulation of procreation depends; that is to say, the possibility or impossibility of commercial and/or social and political eugenics. The issue of how we conceive the remuneration of the maternal function raises, then, the more fundamental question of what kind of civilization we want to live in.

A specific social allowance paid to mothers has a fundamentally different meaning depending on whether it is conceived in the interests of the mother or in the interests of society.

(i) In the former case, the allowance sets the seal upon a woman's sovereign right to be a mother and to raise her child in complete independence, without being accountable to anyone. The question in that case is not what use the mother is to society, but what use society is to the mother and her child. Motherhood is understood as an autonomous undertaking whose possible outcome will be the child's acquisition of autonomy: the mother is allowed to make the child a sovereign subject; its upbringing can be a process of *giving the child to itself.*

(ii) In the latter case, the allowance is granted to the woman by virtue of the socially useful function she performs by *giving society* the children it needs. The mother may then be rewarded, honoured and decorated for the accomplishment of her duty as childbearer, which in this case is regarded virtually as a form of work (in most countries, she has also been honoured as a 'heroic mother' if all her children are killed in a war). It is no longer her personal self-fulfilment, nor the personal self-realization of the child that counts, but the service rendered to the nation.

In this latter case, the mother therefore loses both her sovereign rights over her children and her rights over her own self. If she fails to fulfil the obligations society prescribes for her, she may be deprived of her rights as a mother. She is socialized and colonized to the depths of her very being and remains what patriarchal societies have always wanted her to be: a humble body which societies use for their own ends.

A 'wage for motherhood' instituted in the name of 'the social useful-ness of the maternal function' therefore introduces the idea that a woman may become the equivalent of a surrogate mother for society. The state may rent her womb in order to get its supply of children. And once it is social usefulness that counts, the socialization of the repro-ductive function can be taken a very long way. In effect, the surrogate mother rents herself out to bear a child which is not, genetically, her own. If one accepts this principle, there is nothing scandalous about envisaging the same service being provided not to individuals but to the state; in other words, in envisaging that the childbearing function may become specialized and professionalized along eugenic lines. Women with sturdy constitutions would then be paid for developing within their bodies embryos provided by genetic banks, and for giving birth to children bearing the genetic characteristics that were most useful to the system.

This resembles Aldous Huxley's *Brave New World,* but it also resembles the practices of the Third Reich: women whose progeniture would not fit in with the eugenic norms were there prevented (by steril-ization) from becoming mothers; by contrast, procreation was encour-aged in the *Lebensborne* ('fountains of life') where young women of Nordic type were impregnated by young SS men so as to provide the Reich and the Führer with the future racial elite. The children born in these procreation centres never knew their parents.

We have to choose, then, on what basis we demand a specific social allowance for mothers. If this is done in the name of the emancipation of women, we cannot *also* invoke the social usefulness of the maternal function (and vice versa). Rather than providing the feminist cause with a more solid foundation, the social usefulness argument only serves to weaken it unnecessarily. A woman's right to be (or not to be) a mother has no need, in fact, of any supplementary justification: it derives its legitimacy from the inalienable rights of the human person to dispose of itself in a sovereign manner. The granting of a specific and sufficient social income to mothers derives from the same principles as the *unconditional* social protection of the integrity of persons and their health and freedom. It has nothing to do with their economic profit-ability or their social utility.

The same goes for the creation of day nurseries and nursery schools. The fact that they are necessary for women's emancipation is a sufficient reason for having them: they make women's personal growth as mothers compatible with their personal growth as citizens (and vice versa). They do not require any economic justification.

B. NON-COMMODITY ACTIVITIES

The preceding analyses are concerned exclusively with activities performed for commodity exchange. They demonstrate that not all paid activities are 'work' in the same sense of the word. And they cannot all meet the same criteria of rationality, nor can they all be equally included, *a fortiori*, in the economic sphere.

The female worker does not work in the same sense as the maid, nor the 'carer', the prostitute or the fireman in the same sense as the worker. There can be no society, no life, without 'work', but not all societies and lives are based on work. Work and the work-based society are not in crisis because there is not enough *to do*, but because *work in a very precise sense* has become scarce, and the work that is to done now falls less and less into that particular category.

The crisis of work and of the work-based society will not be overcome by an increase in the number of shoeshiners, as George Gilder[14] believes, nor by a rise in the number of domestic servants, hostesses and service-station attendants as Philippe Séguin[15] maintains, nor by an increase in the number of prostitutes, housewives/husbands, tourist guides or theme-park personnel. Not that all these people do not 'work'; but what they do does not have the same meaning as work in the economic sense and there are certain dangers in putting their activities in the same category as the latter.

It is true that 'work' has not always had the meaning it has assumed in work-based societies. In particular, it has not always been an activity performed for commodity exchange, in the public sphere. Nor has it always been a source of citizenship for the 'workers'. On the contrary, in ancient Greece it was considered incompatible with citizenship. This was because the greater part of the production of life's necessities was performed in the private domestic sphere (the *oikos*). Until the birth of capitalism, there was no public economic sphere in today's sense. The members of the household produced their food, their thread, their cloth, their clothing and their fuel. They did not count their time. Indeed, they did not know how to calculate, and they lived by two clear and obvious precepts: 'it takes as long as it takes' and 'enough is sufficient'.

The production of that use value of which we are ourselves both the originators and the sole beneficiaries I shall term *work-for-oneself*. It is one of the two principal forms of non-commodity activity. I shall examine the ambivalent meaning it still has today, and then go on to deal with *autonomous activities*, activities which are neither necessary nor useful and which constitute an end in themselves.

1. Work-for-oneself

In the industrialized societies today, all that subsists of such work-for-oneself are activities of self-maintenance: washing, dressing, doing the washing and the washing-up, housework, shopping, washing and feeding children and putting them to bed. Work-for-oneself has been reduced to 'chores', that is, to those activities which are not only not *destined* for commodity exchange, but which are not even *exchangeable*. The results of these activities are ephemeral, being consumed as soon as they are produced; they cannot be stocked; they have to be begun again day after day; they are of no use to anyone else. The whole of domestic production, on the other hand, that work-for-oneself that is '*poietic*', has been transferred from the private sphere to the public, industrial, market-oriented economic sphere. The question facing us, then, is the following: can this transfer continue, must it continue until work-for-oneself is completely eliminated?

I will examine this question from a number of angles, firstly dealing with the household as an indivisible unit and then returning to the relations between the individuals of whom it may consist.

The tendency for work done for oneself to be transferred to industrialized production and external services is regarded in the dominant economic thinking as still having a long way to go before it has fully exhausted its potential. You can replace shopping by ordering goods on Prestel and having them delivered to your door, while the need to cook can be replaced by a hot-meals delivery service. Housework can be done by teams of professional cleaners, going from house to house while the occupants are out, until such time as they themselves are replaced by programmable domestic robots. Children can be looked after from a very early age by professional childminders in nurseries which also operate at night. Hygiene and bodily care can also, in large part, be provided by professional services available in each block, run on the lines of gymnasiums, health and fitness centres or beauty parlours: each resident would submit their body to the attention of these services in the morning or evening – or both. And so on and so forth. According to the economists of the employers' organizations, there are very considerable 'untapped residues of employment' in these areas.[16]

The sense of unease this type of projection generates results from its confusion about the objective being pursued. That objective is not at all the same as it was in the heroic age of capitalist or socialist industrialization. The point then was to try to reduce the time women and men devoted to domestic tasks, in order to employ that time, at a far higher rate of productivity, in industry and collective undertakings. Hence, in

Israeli kibbutzim or in Chinese popular communes, the whole range of household tasks was socialized: communal cooking, meals eaten together in the refectory; children looked after night and day in the 'Children's Block' (except in the evenings, when they could spend an hour or two with their parents); washing and mending done in the communal wash-house/linen-room. The general object was to have people 'work' less at home for themselves, so that they could work more for the collectivity (or, in capitalist society, for their employers). The socialization and industrialization (of the production of bread, cloth and clothing, of washing and mothering/child-rearing) were intended to save time *across the whole of society* and allow that time to be redeployed in the economic sphere.

Now, in the present conditions, the externalisation of domestic tasks is directed towards the opposite goal. The point is no longer to socialize household tasks so that they absorb less time *across the whole of society*. It is now the quite contrary object that is being pursued. The idea is that these tasks *should occupy the greatest number of people and absorb as much working time as possible, but in the form, in this instance, of commercial services.* This is because it is no longer labour that is scarce, but paid jobs. Now more hours of paid work are to be devoted to domestic tasks than they would actually take up if everyone did them for themselves. 'Making work', 'creating jobs': these are the goals of the new tertiary anti-economy.

The army of cleaners, waitresses, waiters, cooks, kitchen-hands and delivery men and women called upon to do our housework, cooking and shopping and to deliver hot meals to our homes take no less time (if we take into account the working hours accumulated in the installations and equipment involved) than we ourselves would if we were to do the things they do for us. The time they gain for us is not productive time, but time for consumption and comfort. They are not working to serve collective interests, but to serve us as individuals, and to give us private pleasure. Their work is our pleasure. Our pleasure 'gives them work' which we consume directly; this is the defining characteristic (as we have seen in the case of prostitution) of servile labour.

Philippe Séguin openly acknowledged this fact when he wrote, 'In the future, quality of service will be more sought after than mere productivity. I am convinced that, as styles of consumption develop, the consumer will be prepared to pay a higher price to obtain a better service.'[17] And we find a similar argument in a pamphlet published by the CFDT:

> Providing services that are intended to substitute for those forms of self-production which households are often forced into for want of the supply

of appropriate services is also a plus for employment. We might cite as an example the services which enable those women who wish to (sic) to be relieved of a part of the domestic tasks which still fall most heavily on them.[18]

It seems, in this model, to be merely a question of supply. If 'consumers' do not buy more services, and services of a better quality, it is because these are not being supplied. If households 'are forced into' doing their own cooking, shopping and housework, this comes about because of a 'want of the supply of appropriate services'. If only this supply existed, women 'who wish to' could be relieved of their drudgery and a plethora of 'jobs' would be created. But *who are* the women who might 'wish' to be relieved of this drudgery? *On to whom* might they unload these tasks? In what conditions are people prepared to do other people's housework? *Who* pays them, and *with what* and how much?

The abstract categories of macro-economic reasoning make it possible to evade this kind of question, and with it the question of whether the cleaners, hot-pizza delivery boys, messengers and service-station attendants are also 'prepared to pay a higher price' for these services, whether they too can afford to transfer their domestic tasks to yet other service workers, to have themselves served hot meals at home after work. The ideology of jobs for jobs' sake produces the same kinds of nonsense as neo-liberal 'supply-side economics'.

We must therefore restate an obvious point: to pay someone else to do two hours 'housework' in my stead, work which I could just as easily do myself, it has to be the case that two hours of *my* work earn me more than two hours of *her or his* work earn for the worker. Otherwise, I will find myself in the same position as the two mothers who pay one another to look after each other's children and I will be better off working two hours less (unpaid) and doing my housework myself. *The development of personal services is therefore only possible in a context of growing social inequality, in which one part of the population monopolizes the well-paid activities and forces the other part into the role of servants.* We can see here a South-Africanisation of society, that is, the realization of the colonial model within the metropolitan heartland. We can also see what a German sociologist has called 'house-wifization',[19] that is, the transferring of what was traditionally regarded as 'housewife's work' to an economically and socially marginalized mass of people.

The professionalization of domestic tasks is therefore the very antithesis of a liberation. It relieves a privileged minority of all or part of their work-for-themselves and makes that work the sole source of liveli-hood for a new class of underpaid servants, who are *forced to take on other peoples' domestic tasks alongside their own.*[20]

Thus a completely absurd social division of labour is established. One section of the population is so fully occupied in the economic sphere that it does not have time for its domestic chores; the other is forced to take on the domestic chores of those people who, by their devotion to work, prevent them from finding a more interesting job. Only an obstinate clinging to the ideology of work prevents the advocates of this model from seeing that *if everyone worked less, everyone could do their own domestic tasks AND earn their living by working.* I am not suggesting that the length of the working day can be reduced overnight, by two hours a day for example. What I am saying is that a staged reduction, without loss of real income, could eventually go much further than two hours a day as the productivity of the economy increased, and that this is essentially a political question.[21] That question concerns the kind of society we wish to create: one in which everyone performs for themselves, in their own time, the tasks that lie within their private sphere, or one in which, in the name of the ideology of jobs for jobs' sake, a pattern of life is promoted in which those who work in the economic sphere are dissuaded from doing anything whatever by and for themselves.

This latter option would have the effect of creating a dominant pattern of life (proposed by the cultural and leisure industries and directed, to the envy of all the rest, at the richest 20 per cent of the population) in which only two types of activity remained, those which were performed only to earn money and those (games, shows, tourism, therapies, sports requiring expensive equipment) to which money alone could give access. In this model, the majority of the population would be professionally specialized in handling a particular aspect of other people's lives and would in turn have most of the aspects of their own lives taken care of professionally. The economy (or, rather, anti-economy) founded on the proliferation of personal services would thus bring about universal dependence and heteronomy and define as 'poor' those people who were 'forced', at least to some extent, to take care of their own needs for themselves.

Now, this model is fundamentally out of step with the aspirations individuals actually develop when time and resources cease to be scarce. Developments within the kibbutzim are instructive in this regard. As a relative degree of abundance was achieved, families developed a tendency to take back themselves an increasing share of the 'chores' of which they had been relieved by the collective services. Work-for-oneself ceased to be regarded solely as an imposition; in certain respects, it became a need and a means of winning back a greater degree of personal sovereignty in the form of a greater sense of self-belonging within the private sphere. Parents demanded the right to spend more time with their children, insisted on keeping them with them all night, and criticized the staff who looked after them. The boundary line between the time domestic tasks *took* from one and the time one *gave* to them became blurred. People began to *prefer* taking on certain tasks themselves – and not only such jobs as looking after babies, in which it is impossible to distinguish the element of 'chore' (washing, changing, feeding) from the emotional relationship and from play, but also such things as looking after personal objects, which only really belong to you if you maintain, use and tinker with them yourself.

The fact is that work-for-oneself plays an essential role in the creation and demarcation of a private sphere. The latter cannot exist without the former. You can see this very clearly when all the jobs in the domestic sphere are taken over by external services: you cease to be 'at home' in your own house. The spatial organization of the dwelling, the nature, form and arrangement of familiar objects have to be adapted to the routine attentions of service staff or robots, as they are in hotels, barracks and boarding schools. Your immediate environment ceases to belong to you, in much the same way as the chauffeur-driven car comes to belong more to the chauffeur than to the owner.

Every act of appropriation – even the appropriation of one's own body – requires 'work' (in the sense of *'ergon'*, the expenditure of energy) and time. Work-for-oneself is, basically, *what we have to do to take possession of ourselves* and of that arrangement of objects which, as both extension of ourselves and mirror of our bodily existence, forms our niche within the sensory world, our private sphere.

The problem which faces those societies where time has ceased to be scarce is therefore quite the opposite of the one to which the model of the 'electronic dwelling' and the total transfer of work to professional services provides an answer. The important thing there – and this runs quite counter to that model – is to extend the scope of the work-for-oneself through which persons come to belong to themselves, through which they come to belong to one another in their communities or families and through which each person comes to be rooted in the sensory materiality of the world and to share that world with others.

'Work-for-oneself' does not have to be limited to what you do for yourself, nor the 'private sphere' to the intimate space that belongs to you alone. I am 'at home' not only in the room or corner I inhabit, the place where I keep my personal possessions, but also in the familiar space (house, courtyard, street, neighbourhood or village) that I share with other persons or private communities. Or rather I am at home in this common convivial space so long as I participate in its development, its organization and its maintenance in voluntary co-operation with other users. Work 'for oneself' then finds its natural extension in work 'for ourselves', just as the community of the family finds an extension in the informal co-operative that provides immediate services and in the informal associations of mutual aid between neighbours.

All this clearly presupposes styles of architecture and town planning which make it easy to meet and interact, and which encourage shared use and common initiatives and lend themselves generally to the reappropriation of the immediate environment by those who live in it; these are all things which are more highly developed in Scandinavia than in other countries, on account of the existence there of co-operatives for the self-management of apartment blocks. The trend there is for each building to be equipped with a sauna, a workshop/repair-shop, a cafeteria, a games room for children, a crèche, a room for the handi-capped and so on. For the aged, a dispensary, a communal kitchen, a refectory and a meals-on-wheels service are provided by volunteers (most of whom are also old) from among their fellow tenants and/or by social workers whom the local authority places at the disposal of the residents where this is requested.

If a general meeting so decides, co-operative activities may also extend to the creation by the residents of an organic kitchen garden alongside the building or to the construction of a playground or adventure playground, to the setting up of a consumer co-operative and a barter market for clothing, household implements and toys, to mutual aid in case of illness, bereavement or personal problems and to the organization of evening classes or parties.

Each tenant may choose either to use the self-organized services or the more anonymous ones provided by the local authority. The former are not designed to compensate for the shortcomings of the latter, but to shape them and orient them in a decentralized manner, towards needs defined by the residents themselves.[22]

What we have here is the synergy of voluntary activities and insti-tutional services which I mentioned above with reference to helping and caring activities.

The grassroots community can thus become the intermediate micro-social space between the private and the public, macro-social spaces. It can protect individuals from becoming isolated, lonely and withdrawn. It can *open up* the private sphere on to a space of *common sovereignty*, shielded from commodity relations, where individuals *together* determine for themselves their common needs, and decide the most appropriate actions for satisfying them. It is at this level that individuals can (once again) become masters of their own destinies, their own way of life, the content and scope of their desires or needs and the extent of the efforts they are prepared to put in to meet them. It is in this practical experience of micro-social activities that a critique of the capitalist consumption model and of social relations dominated by economic objectives and commodity exchange can be anchored.[23] It is at this level, in fact, that social bonds of solidarity and living co-operation can be formed and that we can have direct experience of that perfect reciprocity of rights and duties that is entailed in *belonging* to a collective: the rights it accords me are the duties it accepts towards me as a member, but being a member also means that I have duties towards it which are the rights it claims over me.

Co-operation on the basis of solidarity within voluntary communities and associations is the basis *par excellence* for social integration and the production of social bonds. It is by starting from that basis and building upon it that we can regain a society and set limits to the economic sphere.[24] A fundamental precondition for this is a reduction of the time spent in paid work.

Up to this point, I have treated work-for-oneself as if it were performed by the whole community. I have therefore left out of account here the division of tasks and the relations of domination which may exist among the various members within the domestic community. In this, I have followed the *modern* conception of the family, according to which a man and a woman (or women, or men) who choose to live together are to be regarded in law as one person. Their union is assumed to be a *voluntary union of equals* and, unless they themselves stipulate otherwise, they are supposed *to share everything* and lead a 'common life'.

This complete sharing (or 'union') implies that *they make no distinction between what each person does for themself and what they do for the other.* Their common life takes place within the common private sphere and that sphere is, in its essence, outside society's gaze and protected from any external interference. What the members of the community do or do not do there and the nature of their relations and their activities is their own private business. Their union, in other words, is assumed to be a union of sovereign persons, who are able to, and have decided to, auto-determine their relations in forms which are their own concern alone. The idea of domination imposed by one member of the community over another (or others) is therefore theoretically excluded from this conception of their union. The well-being and fulfilment of the community is supposed to be the goal of each of its members and the well-being and fulfilment of each of its members the goal of all the others.

Now this conception of the domestic community is a late achievement of modernity and, moreover, one which is still largely incomplete. Women, who in most cases are still expected to shoulder the burden of household chores in fact do more 'work for them' than work for themselves.

When women become aware of this situation and refuse to accept it, the question arises as to whether we are to get beyond this situation by (a) the dissolution of the family as a 'union'; or (b) the completion of its unity?

(a) Since its rebirth during the 1950s, the women's liberation movement has always had a radical wing, which has campaigned for the dissolution of the nuclear family. They argue that women must no longer be expected to do all the 'work of reproduction for free'. They must no longer 'serve' men and the patriarchal family and, through it, a social system which oppresses and exploits them. Their 'housework', which makes work in the economic sense and the physical reproduction of society possible, has to be recognized for its economic utility and accorded social dignity. This recognition must take the form of a 'decent remuneration of *all* the work of *all* women.' By virtue of this remuneration, women would be freed of their economic dependence on men. They would no longer be condemned to remain with men in spite of themselves in the interests of their children. They would not have to share 'everything' with them, including their lives. They would be paid for doing their domestic work just as man is paid for his work. 'Housewife' or 'mother' would be a socially recognized occupation. Thus husband and wife would each work in their own spheres and these respective spheres would interpenetrate only very partially. Their respective tasks and obligations would be clearly defined. The domestic sphere would be the exclusive preserve of women and they would be its sovereign, undisputed rulers. There could be no question of men taking on part of the work there. Wages for housework would, moveover, have the effect and the secondary function of dissuading them from doing so.

This conception deliberately breaks with the ideal of the total emancipation of women to meet up again with the pre-capitalist form of the family. Ivan Illich – who defends this conception, supporting it with anthropological arguments, alongside a relatively influential tendency within the women's movement, particularly in the German Federal Republic – argues that the desire to put women on the same footing as men, considering them as part of the labourforce', has the effect of rendering them inferior.[25] Wherever they are in competition with men, their work is always less valued and less well paid. Now, this economic inferiority has not always existed: it appeared with the invention, by capitalism, of *work* (in the modern economic sense) as a quantifiable performance, that can be regarded in isolation from the person who supplies it. Before the invention of work, which, says Illich, is *unisex* by definition, man and woman developed in quite distinct spheres of activity where they each exercised undisputed power. Their occupations were gendered, incommensurable and complementary. What each of them did was neither shared nor appropriated by the other. The family as indivisible unit was only invented in Europe, quite late in the day, at the beginning of the modern era to provide a legal basis for the rural, and later for the urban, family enterprise.

Now the recognition of the family as a unit has the effect, argues Illich, of making the unisex conception of work penetrate into the domestic sphere where 'under the guise of shouldering some of the housework, they [men] open a new field for competition and resentment between the sexes.' As jobs become more scarce and men tend to invade what was the women's sphere of power, competing with them on their own terrain, 'discrimination against women, in their own homes, will become more pronounced.'[26]

The idea, then, in this conception, is to restore women's power over the domestic sphere by excluding male 'work' from that sphere. This is the (generally hidden) meaning of the demand for wages for housework. This would, it is argued, guarantee women independence in the home while at the same time bringing social recognition for the usefulness of their domestic labour.

The other side of the coin, obviously, is that women will tend to be confined to the private sphere: society will pay them to stay at home. This is where, in the context of fewer and fewer jobs, she will be considered most useful socially and politically. This social utility will, however, be purely *functional*. Women will *serve* the established order by remaining outside the economic activity which has given them access to the public sphere and citizenship. They therefore run the risk of once again being excluded from that sphere. They will only escape that risk on a permanent basis if women form themselves into an autonomous political force with a permanent organization, capable of engaging in continuous political activity.

We arrive then at a segmentation of society that is more complex and radical than the forms of 'dualization' mentioned in Chapter 6. It is true that this division of society into 'gendered' spheres, which are themselves further subdivided, is the goal pursued by this current within feminism.

(b) Against the position advocated by Illich, I shall now argue for a contrary conception, by suggesting a different interpretation of the materials used in *gender*. My thesis will be as follows: it is not the conjugal union, appearing at the beginnings of the modern era, but the incomplete nature of that union which explains women's exploitation within the family. And the remedy for this situation cannot be the separation of the respective spheres of women and men, but the emancipation of women extending right into relations within the domestic sphere.

If the conjugal union was a late invention of modernity, this is not because it was an anthropological nonsense[27] ('unnatural' as they might have said in days gone by); it is because the family can only establish itself as an autonomous indivisible unit if husband and wife belong mutually to one another and, in their private sphere, have duties only towards each other in perfect reciprocity. So long as husband and wife belonged principally to the feudal lord or to the clan or the village community, their extra-conjugal obligations, which were specific to the respective genders, were an insurmountable obstacle which *power* raised against their mutual belonging one to another. What they had to do in the interests of the collectivity or the lord took precedence by a long way over what they could do in their common interest. Customary or legal rules defining their respective tasks made themselves felt in the home itself and *socially* determined their obligations to one another. The idea that they could throw themselves into a common enterprise was inconceivable. They were not free sovereignly to define their activities and relations as their personal desires and circumstances allowed.[28] Their domestic sphere was not, properly speaking, a private sphere.

It was, therefore, only with their emancipation from feudal domination (and from the traditions which perpetuated it) that a man and a woman could form a union and engage in activities for their own common good within a sphere of shared sovereignty, the private sphere. This was not an invention of capitalism. It emerged through the struggles of the peasantry and laid the ground for the autonomy of the family and the family enterprise: the fruits of labour must belong to those who produce them; the members of a domestic community owe each other loyalty, care and assistance and, within the private sphere, only have to answer for their actions to each other; their relations are private, not legal relations; the domestic sphere lies outside social control and the scope of political power; once one has crossed the threshold of the home, relations between persons are based on understanding, mutual consent and voluntary co-operation, not on obligations formalized in law.

This is the *essence* of the family community. It only conforms to that essence if everything its members do is considered *by each of them* as done by and for the whole community. But this obviously supposes that all the members consider the interest of the community to be their own interest, and vice versa. This can only be the case if the conjugal union of man and wife is a voluntary one and the co-operation between the partners is a *voluntary co-operation between equals*, freely choosing common goals for themselves and freely agreeing about how tasks are to be divided.

Family unity does not therefore exist when one of the partners is required by law to submit themselves to the will of the other. It actually ceases to exist when one of the partners calls on the legal system to regulate their relations with the other: their union is then dissolved *de facto* even before it is dissolved *de jure* through lack of mutual consent and voluntary co-operation. *So long as the woman owes obedience and faithfulness to the man or can be constrained by him, she is the servant of a community of which he is the head and the conjugal union between the two is a legal fiction.*

The family as a sphere of private sovereignty in which a woman and a man voluntarily share everything is therefore not a hangover from the pre-modern era but an *incomplete achievement of modernity.* It will only be completely accomplished when the emancipation of women has been finally achieved, which, in practical terms, means when man and woman voluntarily share the tasks of the private sphere as well as those in the public sphere and belong *equally* to one another. It is only at that moment that the conjugal union will achieve conformity with its essence. It is only at that moment that women, finding themselves in a relation of co-operation between equals with men, will be able to experience the activities in which they engage for the good of the family community as activities of which they are the artisans as well as the beneficiaries, as work-for-oneself.

It is remarkable that this *idea* of a union between equals also corresponds to men's and women's spontaneous aspirations. When they are asked to define the life pattern they would wish to be able to create, most of them choose, as their ideal, the model in which 'the man and the woman both work part time and have a second activity, which they engage in *together* in their free time.'[29] In this model, 'wages for housework' clearly become redundant, since the gradual, programmed reduction in working hours does not entail a loss of revenue. By contrast, the payment of 'wages for housework' tends to exclude women from work in the economic sphere and *perpetuates the obligation for men to work full time.* A fundamental choice about the kind of society we want to live in is involved here.

2. Autonomous Activities

In Greek philosophy, freedom and necessity were opposites. The individual became free when he was relieved of the burden of daily necessities. In so far as the extent of these necessities grew as his needs grew, self-limitation and frugality were indispensable virtues for a free man. These virtues were not, however, enough. To free the individual from the grip of necessities, these had also to be assumed for free men by a group of people who, by definition, were not free: slaves and women. There was therefore, on the one hand, a sphere of liberty and, on the other, a sphere of necessity. People operated in one or the other. They belonged either to the one or the other. It was not usual for them to divide their time between the two.

In the celebrated passage in *Capital* in which Marx reintroduces the theory of the 'two realms', the Aristotelian conception becomes more flexible, but is not transcended; there is still a sphere of necessity and a sphere of freedom. This latter 'begins only where labour which is determined by necessity and mundane considerations ceases.' Just like Aristotle, Marx therefore regards 'necessity', 'need' and 'external purposes' (*äußere Zweckmäßigkeit*) as being of the same order: they are determinations which the subject does not sovereignly derive from his own being and therefore negations of his sovereignty. The realm of freedom only begins 'beyond the realm of necessity' and merges with 'that development of human energy which is an end in itself' ('*der Kraftentfaltung die sich als Selbstzweck gilt*'): with the pursuit of the Good, the Beautiful and the True. The only important difference from Aristotle is that the unfolding of freedom in Marx – or, in other words, in communist society, where the forces of production are fully developed – no longer presupposes that the burden of necessity should be shouldered by unfree social strata. The machine has taken the place of the slaves and the 'associated producers' organize themselves so as to reduce the necessary labour time 'to a minimum', so that everyone can work, though only a little, and that everyone, *alongside* their work, can engage in activities which are themselves their own end. Everyone can divide their time between the two spheres.

I refer to those activities which are themselves their own end as autonomous activities. They are valued for and in themselves not because they have no other objective than the satisfaction and pleasure they procure, but because *the action which achieves the goal is as much a source of satisfaction as the achievement of the goal itself*: the end is reflected in the means and vice versa; I may will the end by virtue of the intrinsic value of the activity which achieves it and the activity by virtue of the value of the end it is pursuing.

If, in Marx's day, the chief opposite of freedom was necessity, this was because work for economic ends and work-for-oneself in the domestic sphere both served essentially to produce what was necessary and allowed practically no time for anything else. Because of the lack of time, work-for-oneself was to be rationalized: time would have to be counted and saved even in the private sphere. This was, so to speak, sucked into and colonized by the economic sphere and tasks there became, as Illich has shown, 'shadow work' predetermined by the manufacturers of household appliances.[30]

Now, the sphere of necessity today is neither so extensive as it was in Marx's day, nor does it have the same characteristics. Almost all of the production and jobs necessary for life are industrialized; the principal part of our needs is supplied by heteronomous work, that is, by work that is subject to a social division of labour, specialized and professionalized and performed with a view to commodity exchange. Neither the exchange value of such work, nor its length, nature, goal or meaning can be determined by us as sovereign individuals. Morever, this heteronomous work,[31] through the sale of which we procure almost all we need, also serves to produce superfluous goods or to incorporate in necessary goods useless elements whose real or supposed symbolic value merely serves, in modifying the image of the product, to increase its exchange value (its price). We are therefore less in thrall to the 'necessities' of existence than to the external determination of our lives and our activity by the imperatives of a social apparatus of production and organization which provides willy-nilly both the essential and the superfluous, the economic and the anti-economic, the productive and the destructive.

This is why, in our daily experience, it is no longer so much the freedom/necessity distinction which is decisive, but the autonomy/heteronomy opposition. Freedom consists less (or rather consists less and less) in freeing ourselves from the work we need to do to live and more in freeing ourselves from heteronomy, that is, in reconquering spaces of autonomy in which we can *will what we are doing and take responsibility for it.*

Things have even reached the point where those aspiring to autonomy feel they can achieve this through the return to preindustrial modes of production of necessities and where, depending on which author one is reading, the adjective 'autonomous' applies either to craft production for one's own needs or to some form of self-managed or self-determined 'alternative' market activity. There is thus complete confusion. The examples which follow attempt to dissipate this confusion. We must not, in arguing that autonomy is defined principally by its opposition to heteronomy, forget the other dimension of the problem: autonomy also stands opposed to necessity, not because all necessary activity is inevitably heteronomous (*this is not the case at all*), but because the autonomy of an activity dictated by necessity is condemned to remain purely formal.

I will first of all recall therefore the definition common to both Marx and Aristotle: those activities are autonomous which are themselves their own end. In those activities, subjects experience their own sovereignty and fulfil themselves as persons. Commodity activities are therefore excluded by their very essence from this category. Their goal is commodity exchange which, as we have seen in respect of activities of assistance and caring, and also of prostitution, relativizes and contaminates the intrinsic, incommensurable value of the action and work performed. Thus painters do not paint pictures in order to sell them; they put them on sale to show them and to be able to continue to paint. If they paint to sell, they must paint to please and their quest will no longer be directed by an immanent necessity but by changes in fashion, taste and advertising style.

The same is true of craft production, which is wrongly equated with autonomous production. The craftworker or fashion designer who invents or produces pullovers for sale on the market has a large degree of technical autonomy. However, their activity remains broadly heteronomous: they must determine their style and their patterns not as a function of their own ideas and tastes like works of art, but with regard to the place (the 'gap') in the market that they hope to occupy and the most profitable price-to-cost relation. Their activity will thus largely be dominated by the kind of constraints that show up in economic and technical calculations. The situation will be quite different in the case of the neighbourhood association whose members create a knitwear workshop with semi-professional equipment, with the aim of making pullovers for their own use, their own pleasure and even perhaps for an exhibition or a non-commercial competition. These products which are made in their free time have no price. The time needed to produce them is not counted; a large part of it will, in any case, have been spent in discussion. Each product is a 'work of art' which people have taken pleasure in making and which they will take pleasure in wearing or giving.

This does not mean, of course, that these things will not be exchanged. But it rules out the possibility of that exchange taking a commodity form. The only form such exchange can take on within the sphere of autonomous activities is the form of the reciprocal gift. I give this to you without asking for anything in return; you accept this gift gladly and seek to give me something in your turn. It is not a question of giving me the equivalent of what you have received. This would be insulting and you know it. It is a matter of setting up a relationship of generosity in which each person regards the other *unconditionally* as an absolute end. We have encountered this type of relationship in respect of teaching or therapeutic activities, assistance or care. Artistic activities (whether they involve performance or creation), political campaigning, charitable work, worship, scientific or philosophical research are all by their essence of this same order. They are not ways of earning a living;

they involve an unconditional giving of oneself and this gift is recognized precisely in its *incommensurable* value when the public 'honours' it by a payment which never has the sense of a purchase, that is, as giving an equivalent amount in exchange: an audience shows its appreciation of an artist by standing ovations even when it has paid dearly for the opportunity to hear her or him.

To say that autonomous activities cannot have exchange as their goal is not a sufficient characterization. They also have to be free of necessity: they have to be motivated by nothing but the desire to bring the Good, the True and the Beautiful into the world. In other words, they have to stem from a conscious choice which nothing forces me to make. Thus auto-production of a part of life's necessities can only be an autonomous activity if it is not itself subject to necessity. Thus the community which, living under conditions of almost total autarky, has to produce all the bread it needs for its subsistence, is engaged in an activity which can only have at best a formal autonomy. By sculpting the tools employed, by carving ornate patterns on the loaves, by surrounding the removal of the bread from the oven with prayers and celebrations and so on, it is overdetermining work which simply has to be done by these optional activities, which serve no utilitarian goal. The dimension of autonomy here remains a subordinate one. The goal of the activity is to make bread. That process may provide an opportunity for rejoicing and artistic activity, but *the opposite is not true*: these rejoicings cannot emancipate themselves completely from the work that is necessary, nor transfigure this to the point where it would appear as an end in itself.

On the other hand, the inhabitants of a block of flats or a neighbourhood who get together to install a wood-fired oven so that, instead of buying their bread cheaply from the local baker, they can join together to produce organic bread in their free time, are engaging (as was the knitwear group mentioned above) in an autonomous activity: this bread is an optional product. They have chosen to produce it simply for the pleasure of making it, eating it, giving it as a present, or, through it, seeking a perfection whose norms they have defined for themselves. Each loaf is a work of art rather than a manufactured product; the pleasure of learning, co-operating and improving one's skills is predominant and the need to feed oneself merely a subordinate consideration. The time devoted to making bread is – like the time spent playing an instrument, gardening, campaigning, exchanging knowledge and so on – one's own living time. The activity is self-rewarding, both by its results and the capabilities which its accomplishment allows me to acquire.

We can see the political significance of these distinctions: auto-production and co-operative activities can only be autonomous activities if each person's necessities are secured for them elsewhere. The development of a sphere of autonomous activities can have no economic relevance. The idea of a 'dual economy' comprising a commodity or heteronomous sector and a convivial sector of autonomous activities is a nonsense. Economic activity in the modern sense defined above[32] cannot by its essence be its own end, even though it may contain – where it is co-operative, self-organized and self-managed – dimensions of autonomy which make it more fulfilling and pleasing.

But the development of a public space of autonomous activities may *give rise to* a limited reduction in the service and provision requirements of the welfare state. In other words, when free time ceases to be scarce, certain educative, caring and assistance activities and the like may be partially repatriated into the sphere of autonomous activities and reduce the demand for these things to be provided by external services, whether public or commercial. The opposite development is, on the other hand, out of the question. An expansion in the sphere of autonomous activities cannot, by definition, *come about as a result of* a policy which reduces state provision and state services, thus leaving those social strata least able to do so to fend for themselves. The expansion of a sphere of autonomy always presupposes that, time no longer being counted, individuals have chosen to repatriate into the domestic or microsocial sphere of voluntary co-operation activities which, for want of time, they had abandoned to external services.

Notes

1. Hilkka Pietilä, 'Tomorrow Begins Today. Elements for a Feminine Alternative in the North', *IFDA Dossier 57/58*, Nyon (Switzerland), pp. 37–54. The author goes on to call for the so-called primary economy to be made to serve the invisible economy, thus increasing the confusion: to the notion that all activity is 'work' is added the notion that all activity is economic. What she is really calling for is an economic system in the service of the private, family sphere, which 'also produces things (sic) that cannot be bought on the market, such as intimacy, encouragement, the sense of being somebody, recognition and the meaning of life.'

2. See above, p. 109–12.

3. Cf. Part I, Chapter 1.

4. These letters refer to parameters defined on pp. 138–9.

5. These letters refer to the parameters defined on pp. 138–9.

6. [Trans.] The French system operates along the following lines: all forms of medical treatment are codified by the social security department, which reimburses the patient for the treatment she or he has received at a nationally fixed standard rate.

7. The advantage of health-maintenance organizations (HMOs) is that they separate the doctor–patient relationship from the commercial relationship, whilst at the same time avoiding the centralization and anonymity of state health services. Doctors and ordinary citizens both have an equal interest in the self-limitation of the use and provision of treatment. Preventative health care is thus accorded importance and may take a number of different forms: eliminating health-endangering practices, public debates on hygiene,

nutrition, personal responsibility for one's own health, environmental awareness, and so on.

8. Among the pioneers of proposals of this type, we should mention Werner Geissberger, a deputy in the regional parliament of Aargau, who, in the early 1970s, promoted the idea of 'small networks' (*kleine Netze*) – types of co-operatives providing neighbourhood services for groups of about fifteen households; and Ego Matzner, an Austrian socialist, whose idea of 'self-organization of public services' was applied in various parts of Vienna. For more details, see his extremely interesting, *Wohlfahrtsstaat und Wirtschaftskrise*, Reinbek 1978, particularly chs 5, 6 and 10.

More recently, Ulf Fink, the Berlin senator in charge of social affairs, produced a series of original proposals for the mutualization of voluntary activities for the care of the disabled elderly. He envisages, in particular, a system whereby the volunteers providing these services will be entitled to these services themselves when they need them in the future. The supply and demand of these voluntary services would be co-ordinated by agencies on the lines of the British 'houses of volunteers'* and the voluntary services performed would be registered by the public social services so that if the volunteers move to a different area, they will still be eligible for the services provided in their new area. See Ulf Fink, 'Der neue Generationenvertrag', *Die Zeit* (Hamburg) 15, 3 April 1987, p. 24. See below p. 159 for the example of apartment block co-operatives in Scandinavia.

9. These letters refer to the parameters defined on pp. 138–9.

10. This is exactly what Sartre refers to as 'bad faith' in *Being and Nothingness*.

11. A copulating machine was developed in West Germany by Beate Uhse, whose company runs a network of sex shops, Eros Centers, pornographic cinemas and magazines. The demand for permission to market this 'love machine' was sent to the federal hygiene services in 1985. The latter have yet to make known their decision.

12. Two people who belong to each other are always a danger to the social order: its rules cease to be valid in the context of their relationship. Orwell gave a perfect demonstration of this, from the point of view of the state, in *1984* as did Baxter and Sade before him. In their commentary on Sade, Horkheimer and Adorno write:

> Science and industry denounced as metaphysics not merely romantic sexual love, but every kind of universal love, for reason displaces all love: that of woman for man as much as that of the lover for his sweetheart, parental affection as much as that of children for their parents . . . The family, held together not by romantic sexual love, but by mother love, which constitutes the ground of all tenderness and social emotions, conflicts with society itself.

And they quote Sade:

> Do not think you can make good republicans so long as you isolate in your family the children who should belong to the community alone . . . If it is wholly disadvantageous to allow children to imbibe interests from their family circle which are often quite different from those of their country, it is wholly advantageous to separate them from their family.

> Conjugal ties [Horkheimer and Adorno continue] are to be destroyed on social grounds; acquaintance with their fathers is to be '*absolument interdite*' to children. Sade conceived the full course of the state socialism with whose first steps St. Just and Robespierre tumbled.

Dialectic of Enlightenment, trans. John Cumming, New York 1972. Second British publication, London 1979, pp. 116–17.

13. This is what this text which comes from dogmatic Marxist-feminist literature suggests: 'A woman's body and her labour power have always been used *free of charge* for

---

*Local centres for the free exchange of services. The idea originated in Quebec. [Trans.]

alien needs. It is therefore crucial that she retake possession of them and be paid for their use.'

14. G. Gilder, a neo-Liberal ideologue and author of *Wealth and Poverty* among other works, maintains that an economic recovery could be established on shoeshining and selling flowers on street corners.

15. In *Revue française d'économie*, 3, summer 1987.

16. Cf., for example, Michel Drancourt and Albert Merlin, *Demain la croissance*, Paris 1986; and Octave Gelinier, *Le chômage guéri . . . si nous le voulons*, Paris 1986.

17. Philippe Seguin, article quoted.

18. CFDT, *Activités en friche . . . gisements d'emploi*, March 1987, p. 9.

19. '*Hausfrauisierung*', a term coined by Claudia von Werlhof.

20. The great majority of jobs created in the last twelve or so years in the United States are irregular, under-paid servants' jobs.

21. I will examine this in greater detail in Part III.

22. For further details, see *Scandinavian Housing and Planning Research*, 2, 1985, and 2 and 3, 1986; and Cornelia Cremer, Hans-Joachim Kujath, 'Wohnreform als Reform des Alltagslebens', *Neue Gesellschaft/Frankfurter Hefte*, 2, 1988.

23. Hence the extraordinary success, in Denmark and Norway, of a movement called 'The future in our hands', whose aim is the self-limitation of consumption, with the sums of money saved being used to aid the Third World.

24. It should be remembered here that the labour movement itself was originally a mutualist, co-operative (in England) and cultural movement, centred on working-class housing areas. On the potentialities of the new co-operativism in the United States, see Harry C. Boyte, *The Backyard Revolution, Understanding the New Citizen Movement*, Philadelphia 1980.

25. See Ivan Illich, *Gender*, London 1983.

26. Illich, *Gender*, p. 59. The same theory is maintained in West Germany by Claudia von Werlhof.

27. Illich, *Gender*, p. 105.

28. In *Love and Power in the Peasant Family: rural France in the nineteenth century*, Oxford 1983, Martine Segalen (quoted by Illich, *Gender*, p. 109) notes that, in the French countryside, even in the nineteenth century, men and women performed their daily tasks more as members of their respective gender than as partners united in marriage. 'The coupled pair carried little weight in the nineteenth-century French peasant household . . .' If they 'do not act in accordance with the demand of their respective genders, then the community will discipline the offending individual directly.'

29. See, on this subject, Guy Aznar, *Tous à mi-temps!*, Paris 1981.

30. See Ivan Illich, *Shadow Work*, London 1981.

31. To recap, the heteronomy of a job *does not lie* merely in the fact that I must submit to the orders of a superior in the hierarchy, or, which amounts to the same thing, to the rhythm of a preprogrammed machine. Even if I control my own time schedule, rhythm of work and the way in which I complete a highly skilled, complex task, my work is still heteronomous when the objective or final product to which it contributes is outside my control. Heteronomous work is not necessarily completely devoid of autonomy: it may be heteronomous because the specialized, even complex activities involved, which require a considerable degree of technical autonomy of the workers, are pre-determined by a system (organization) to whose functioning they contribute as if they were the cogs in a machine. Cf. above, Chapter 3, p. 32 and Chapter 7, pp. 78–9 ff.

32. Cf. pp. 109–12, 137–9.

The Limits of Sociology and Socialization
A Digression on the Notion of 'Lifeworld'

We have seen that economic rationality is applicable to the activities which meet four criteria and that the activities of the private sphere and those autonomous activities which are themselves their own end are by essence resistant to economicization. It is only by denying them their original meaning and by violating the internal logic of economic rationality itself that this can be extended to cover them.

If, following Habermas, we consider the activities to which economic rationality is applicable as activities that are or that can be regulated by money, we come to a conclusion which he has expounded with great care: regulation by money (as well as administrative regulation) is a hetero-regulation which dislocates the 'communicational infrastructure' in which the 'symbolic reproduction of the lifeworld' is rooted.[1] In other words, all the activities which retransmit or reproduce the cultural heritage – knowledge, tastes, manners, language, customs and so on, by virtue of which we orientate ourselves in the world as a site of familiar experiences and certainties, of self-evident norms and values – can only be regulated by money or the state, at a cost of 'pathologies of the lifeworld', or, in other words, the dislocation of that lifeworld. Clearly, the activities concerned here are educational, artistic, scientific and theoretical activities.

Habermas arrives at this diagnosis by an essentially theoretical procedure in which the activities resistant to hetero-regulation never appear themselves as practices lived and maintained by subjects, but in their *function of reproducing* the social system. Now, the impossibility of regulating this function by money is much less clearly evident than the impossibility of buying love, knowledge, care, or concern for the truth or any other disinterested form of behaviour. In other words, this impossibility of regulating the 'symbolic reproduction of the lifeworld' by money is only intelligible in the light of the *originary meaning* the relational and cultural activities which ensure the said 'symbolic reproduction' have for the individuals engaged in them. The impossibility of regulating this reproduction by money is merely the pale reflection of the impossibility of economicizing those activities. By 'forgetting' to interrogate these activities about themselves, that is, by not asking what lived meaning they have for the individual subject engaged in them, positivist thought 'forgets' the originary source from which the self-evidences spring which it is seeking to ground theoretically, whilst in reality these self-evidences preceded and motivated that theoretical effort. The rejection of the 'naiveté of lived experience' leads to the naiveté of thought without a subject, a thinking which is opaque to itself.

This is why I preferred to take lived experience as my starting point, in order to demonstrate, by existential (phenomenological) analysis, what it was in the originary meaning (the originary intention) of a certain number of activities that made them incompatible with economic rationality. This difference in method means that economic rationality has been shown to be inapplicable *from the subject's point of view* (that is, with a self-evidence grounded in lived self-understanding) to a set of activities and relations which it is impossible to subsume under the concept of 'symbolic reproduction of the lifeworld' or of 'communicative reason'. This difference of approach becomes important in a situation in which our historic task cannot be to *reproduce society* but to conceive it on a new base and with new perspectives which do not represent a mere continuation of received norms.

By examining activities only from the angle of their social function of reproduction, positivist sociological thinking acts as though these activities could be completely described in terms of their functions and as if the individuals concerned had no reality other than that which is socially constituted. In fact, they exceed their socially constituted reality by their autonomy and sensibility (and are exceeded by it). The activities and relations which can neither be hetero-regulated nor produced at will are situated both before and beyond speech. Verbal communication is incapable of expressing them in their entirety. The mother–child relationship or relationships between lovers or friends, therapist and patient, and master and pupil do not consist solely in the transmission of cultural knowledge nor in an act of comprehension or mutual understanding that is conveyed in language. On the contrary, these reciprocal relationships are situated as much, if not more, at the level of the unsaid and the unsayable, than at the level of speech.

Speech may indeed only serve to refer, beyond itself, to the originary silence of the incommunicable which each person is for themselves in so far as they are interiority. It is at the level of affective relations which always involves a lived understanding within my body of the life of another's body (of her or his way of being present in and *relating to* the world, of the timbre of the voice and not merely what is said) that bonds between persons are created and it is through these bonds, which are deeper than understanding or agreements about practical tasks or the values that should govern actions, that each person accedes to selfhood and to the world by acceding to the other. Thus the learning of speech depends on the child's affective attachment to its mother or to the person performing the mothering role; the acquisition of knowledge depends (if it is to be anything more than rote-learning and 'drill') on attachment to the person of the master; therapeutic success depends, to an extent that is never negligible, on the personality of the therapist, and so forth.

These affective relations between persons are both a prerequisite of and resistant to socialization. They are its prerequisite, for no one can *feel* they belong to a social group if that belonging is not rooted in an affective attachment to persons within that group. The opposite, on the other hand, is not true; attachment to persons does not depend on their social belonging. That is why an individual may detach him- or herself from his or her original group, 'betray' it – as, in the legends of all ages, do such characters as Hero and Leander, Tristan and Isolde, Romeo and Juliet – from friendship, love or humanity and why, as we have seen in respect of maternal love, love is by its essence a threat to any order. In short, in so far as it takes place, the social integration of the individual has its roots in an attachment that is not socializable: it is as incomparably unique individuals that we love one another or that parents and children love one another and socialization through the family in particular is the more successfully achieved if the child receives the impression that his parents make certain demands of him *because they love him as he is, unconditionally*, and does not feel that their love is conditional and in the service of some goal (socialization) other than himself. In a word the loved person may be the necessary mediator of my belonging to a group, but my love for that person can brook no mediation.

What is at stake in this discussion is nothing less than individual autonomy and, as a corollary, the autonomy of philosophy or the cultural sphere in relation to sociology or society. Philosophy cannot be the pursuit of the True and the Good, nor can it pose the question of the value of values and the meaning of goals unless the subject is capable of stepping outside the norms and values which govern social behaviour and questioning received truths. There can be no autonomous thinking, no artistic or intellectual creation or moral revolt unless an original rift prevents the individual subject from coinciding with the 'identity' its social belonging confers upon it. If I refuse payment for my affection, or refuse to be waited on by servants, this is not as a result of social norms or interpretations which by their essence can always be called into doubt or transcended, but by virtue of the meaning this relationship has in the absolute certainty of its lived intention (of its *cogito*). This meaning always *also* has determinations which a sociological interpretation will have to take account of, but it cannot be derived from that interpretation in the last instance.

Sociology is therefore overstepping its proper bounds when for example Habermas, commenting upon Mead, writes:

> Evidently, individuality too is a socially produced phenomenon that is a result of the socialization process . . . Mead conceives of personal identity exactly as Durkheim does, as a structure that results from taking over socially generalized expectations. The 'me' is the organized set of attitudes that one takes over from one's reference persons. Unlike Durkheim, however, Mead starts from the view that identity formation takes place through the medium of linguistic communication.[2]

All in all, then, society produces the individuals it needs to function as a society and reproduce itself through them. Because he sets out from society as his initial datum – a datum which cannot be arrived at by starting out from individual lived experience – the sociologist ends up by proposing society as the key to the understanding of the individual, which forces him to postulate that society understands itself and that it is the true subject (which poses the insoluble problem of the intelligibility of society for the individual, even if he is a sociologist). He thus makes it impossible for himself to understand that each individual is also for himself a reality which exceeds what society gives him the means to say and do and that no one actually coincides with what the sociologists call their social 'identity' or 'individuality' or 'personality'.

The reason for this is not that there exists a prior 'nature', resistant to any form of socialization, but the fact that it is impossible to exteriorize interiority, or objectivize the subjective. Each individual experiences this for him- or herself: language is a filter which always forces me to say more or less than I feel. Learning one's language is a form of original violence done to lived experience; that process forces those experiences for which there are no words to remain silent, while I am forced to express meanings which do not correspond to my experience, to have intentions which are not my own. It forces me to substitute a discourse which is not my own for the one it forbids me. It is a form of discipline and censorship and induces us into inauthenticity, pretence and play-acting.

All education is violence. Indeed, worse, it is rape. There is no need to refer to any notion of 'human nature' to understand this. The rape inflicted by education does not result from any violence done to what we are by nature, but from the obligation in which we find ourselves to fit in to a predetermined model, which, *no more than any other possible model*, does not entirely coincide with our innermost experience. Socialization prevents us from belonging entirely to ourselves, but we would not have belonged to ourselves if it had been different or even – though this is impossible – if there had been no socialization at all. It is the contingent form of the impossibility of our coinciding with ourselves, or, to put it another way, the contingent form of our genetically programmed aptitude to learn capacities which are not naturally our own, our genetic incapacity to have natural capacities. We are given to ourselves with the obligation of making of ourselves something which we are not by nature (in Sartre's formula, we are 'condemned to be free'). We learn in one and the same educative process that we belong to ourselves as unique subjects and that we are not allowed to belong to ourselves; that we are both condemned to be ourselves and unable to be entirely ourselves.

The non-coincidence of the individual subject with his social being can be seen, for example, in such simple situations as when I say 'I can't tell you what I feel', 'You don't understand what I mean.' The fact of being inexpressible or unsayable within the framework of a given culture does not prevent a lived experience from existing and manifesting itself, for example in the form of 'aberrations', 'deviations', 'neuroses', 'scandals', 'transgressions' and the like, or in works of art. This is one of the things Orwell was saying in *1984* and one of the shattering lessons of the appearance in China thirty years after the revolution of artistic creations which could only have been the fruit of clandestine, and most often solitary, work.

The non-coincidence of the individual subject with the 'identity' which society obliges him – or gives him the means – to express is at the root of both individual autonomy and all cultural creation. It is this that is thematized in the questioning or rejection of accepted values and norms – by the contesting of language, the subversion of clichés, the unearthing of meanings that are beyond all discourse and of the nonsense all discourse carries within it, in short in artistic or intellectual creation. It is the ferment of negativity at the heart of all culture, the ferment of doubt at the heart of practical certainties, the ferment of strangeness at the heart of familiarity and of nonsense at the heart of meaning.

The lived experience of the world thus has only a distant relation to the 'lifeworld' as sociologists conceive it. What they – unlike (existential) phenomenology – designate by that term is not in fact the world of original lived experience, but that of experience mediated by the social means of its formalized expression (by the stereotypes of language in particular) and shorn of its negativity. Thus Habermas defines the 'lifeworld' as 'represented by a culturally transmitted and linguistically organized stock of interpretive patterns'.[3]

The idealism of this definition drives out the sensory material reality through which the lifeworld exceeds all that can be said and known of it: it is both (and this is how phenomenological thinking apprehends it) the ground of all certainties and an inexhaustible stock of uncertainties, of doubt. And it is so to such a degree that Merleau-Ponty could conclude that 'certainty is doubt'.[4]

What sociology calls 'lifeworld' corresponds much more closely to what Heidegger in *Being and Time* described as the world of 'the "they"' [*das Man*], the banality of the everyday, inauthenticity. For phenomenology, from which this notion is borrowed, the lifeworld is admittedly the organized world, which is informed and interpreted by our knowledge, our habits, our customary relations, our familiar techniques, but it is so in the certain knowledge that *this is not all that there is* and that its familiar reality is a patterned formalization of a felt materiality which infinitely exceeds it, picked out from an undifferentiated background which threatens its permanence and coherence. The lifeworld has as its permanent potentiality the dislocation of the organization which makes it familiar, just as all knowledge contains the certainty of its inadequacy and its possible revision.

We can see what is at stake in this discussion of the notion of 'lifeworld': if we confine ourselves to the sociological conception, it is essentially a sediment of pre-modern and pre-rational meanings and relations, the questioning of which would be a questioning of the individuals themselves in their 'identity' and their fundamental convictions. The lifeworld seems then nothing more than a heritage to be defended against the changes which render custom, tradition, habits and received norms irrelevant. On this view, it is of no consequence what the content of the traditions, norms, customs and so on which constitute the lifeworld might be, and one cannot even ask the question *how* it is lived, or, in other words, at what cost in terms of repression, self-denial, violence against oneself and others, censorship and neurosis individuals fit their existence into the predetermined model through which society demands that it mediate their lived experience. With the subject's negativity and the negativity of the lifeworld the possibility of a critique that is not merely traditionalistic and conservative disappears, as does the possibility of autonomous actions.

Now this conception of the 'lifeworld' is neither pertinent nor operative in a situation in which 'all that is solid melts into air'; in which the traditions, values and norms inherited from the past have become obsolete; in which the 'stock of culturally transmitted models of interpretation' is empty; in which nothing is self-evident; where there are no longer any 'certainties' to be preserved and defended. When the colonization of society by the apparatuses and the crisis of these apparatuses themselves have destroyed what was familiar and taken for granted; when the lifeworld has become an unliveable world in its sensuous materiality, by reason of the structural violence which its arrangement and its continual mega-technological revolutionization inflict upon our senses, our bodies and the biosphere that surrounds them; when the sterotypes of culturally transmitted discourse have become obstacles to communication and traditional interpretations travesties of realities which they mask from knowledge and action; when, in a word, lived experience is reduced to silence by the accepted forms of its expression and the tissue of social relations torn to formless shreds, then the very object of positivist sociology becomes dislocated and transformed into mystification.

For society is no longer to be found where it institutionally proclaims its existence, nor the political in the struggles which the various apparatuses engage in for the control of other apparatuses. Society now only exists in the interstices of the system, where new relations and new solidarities are being worked out and are creating, in their turn, new public spaces in the struggle against the mega-machine and its ravages; it exists only where individuals assume the autonomy to which the disintegration of traditional bonds and the bankruptcy of received interpretations condemn them and where they take upon themselves the task of inventing, starting out from their own selves, the values, goals and social relations which can become the seeds of a future society. What is important in this situation is not what is happening centre-stage, but what is going on in the interstices of the system and expressing itself in the interstices of language. And, as Alain Touraine has so admirably demonstrated, this is not accessible to objective knowledge, but only to a research-intervention[5] through which an underlying, initially formless discourse will be brought to expression and turned into an articulate, methodical consciousness of the possibilities for action which are ultimately at issue. What is at issue today is not the protection and defence of a sphere where the self-regulation of our modes of social co-operation and the self-determination of the contents of our lives may prevail, but the reconquering and the extension of such a space.

Notes

1. Jürgen Habermas, *Theory of Communicative Action*, vol. 2. Cambridge 1987, ch. 6.

2. Habermas, p. 58.

3. Habermas, p. 124. Similarly Pierre Bourdieu refers to the knowledge which 'makes explicit the truth of the primary experience of the social world, i.e. the relation of familiarity with the familiar environment, the apprehension of the world as a natural, self-evident world' as 'phenomenological' (*Esquisse d'une théorie de la pratique*, Paris 1972, p. 163). But the relation of familiarity with a self-evident world is *never* primary experience, the experience of the child. That primary experience is one of wonder at things and living beings and astonishment at cultural conventions which are so unnatural that one has to make enormous efforts to learn them.

4. Merleau-Ponty, *The Phenomenology of Perception*, London 1962, (trans. modified), p. 383.

5. A lively résumé of this can be found in Alain Touraine, ed., *Mouvements sociaux d'aujourd'hui, acteurs et analystes*, Paris 1982.

PART III

Orientations and Proposals

Search for Meaning (4)

From all the foregoing analyses, there emerges, between the lines as it were, a vision of a possible other society. The progressive diminution of work for economic ends will have made it possible for autonomous activities to become preponderant in that society; 'free time will have gained the upper hand over unfree time, leisure the upper hand over work'; 'leisure will no longer simply be rest or compensation but essential living time and the reason for living, work having been reduced to the status of a mere means.' 'It would then be this free time which would be the bearer of all common values. One only has to think of the upheaval there would be in our society if creativity, conviviality, aesthetics and play came to predominate over the values of efficiency and profitability involved in work.' 'This is a crucial question . . . It is nothing short of an art of living and renewed forms of social creativity that have to be invented.'[1] What is involved is the transition from a productivist work-based society to a society of liberated time in which the cultural and the societal are accorded greater importance than the economic: in a word, a transition to what the Germans call a 'Kulturgesellschaft'.

Only this fundamental transformation (which would deserve to be called revolutionary if the term had not been devalued and condemned by fashion) could give a meaning to the changes that are currently occurring. If it does not take place, those changes will give birth only to fearful technical barbarities. And the savings in work and gains in time engendered by the accelerated development of new technologies will bring only social exclusion, pauperism and mass unemployment on the one hand, and an intensification of the 'war of each against all' on the other.

183

Given that paid work requires increasingly less time, it is essential that we develop a culture centred on self-determined activities which will prevent the exploitation of people by the amusement and leisure industries. Work done for oneself about the house, gardening, care for the immediate environment and also social involvement in mutual aid activities may create value and, more importantly, develop capacities and penchants in individuals which paid work is causing to wither away or, at least, does not call for . . . We want to see maintained or developed within local communities a culture of conviviality, of festivity and thinking.[2]

There is a remarkable similarity between these lines with which the draft of the new SPD programme closes and the following remarks by the authors of *La révolution du temps choisi*:

There is no reason why we should not imagine the main areas in which these human activities engendered by free time might take place: one might expect that the tasks of local or neighbourhood administration would more easily be reappropriated by those who benefit from them; the work of maintaining objects or heritage – whether individual or collective – would be accorded new value; many kinds of associative militancy could develop; an artistic and cultural production, at last relying on amateurs, could develop and promote micro-cultures that are more generative of meaning than the current standardized material turned out by the media. This immediate culture would stimulate community life and the 're-enchantment of the world' and the 're-birth of feeling' which has been called for by certain eminent sociologists (Moscovici, Touraine).

These social dynamics . . . will open the way to those fine notions of activity or craft which modern work has condemned to oblivion. It seems a good bet that they will promote a resocialization of society and a greater involvement of each person in his or her environment.[3]

I have deliberately begun by stating this guiding vision (which other languages call a 'concrete utopia', though without the pejorative connotations currently attached to this term in French) in synthetic fashion, leaving questions of feasibility for later. What is important here, in fact, is that this vision indicates the *possible meaning* of the technical transformations currently under way and that these transformations can have no other meaning but this: if savings in worktime do not serve to liberate time, and if this liberated time is not·used for 'the free self-realization of individualities,[4] then these savings in working time are totally devoid of meaning.

If, on the other hand, we choose to *give* the processes currently under way the emancipatory meaning they could have, the question of the means to that end arises in a concrete and positive way: the question is no longer the impotent, speculative one of deciding 'where we are going', if indeed we are going anywhere, but *how* to go in the only direction that is open to us, if our lives are to have a direction or meaning. And in its essentials we know the answer to this question: the programmed, staged reduction in working hours, without loss of real income, in conjunction with a set of accompanying policies which will allow this liberated time to become time for free self-realization for everyone.

All in all, what is needed is to take control of processes already under way and orientate them in a direction which corresponds with their own inclinations. This is not a process which will happen of its own accord. We know why this is the case: the development of the productive forces may, of itself, reduce the amount of labour that is necessary; it cannot, of itself, create the conditions which will make this liberation of time a liberation for all. History may place the opportunity for greater freedom within our grasp, but it cannot release us from the need to seize this opportunity for ourselves and derive benefit from it. Our liberation will not come about as a result of a material determinism, behind our backs as it were. The potential for liberation which a process contains can only be realized if human beings seize it and use it to make themselves free.

The problem is then, by its very essence, a political one. In the future, the Left will mainly be distinguished from the Right by the emancipatory goals towards which it seeks to guide technical change; or, as Peter Glotz has written, by its ability to 'wrest a utopia from technology'. It will be distinguished from the Right by its will to use savings in working time for societal and cultural ends, which will relegate economic objectives to the second rank. Here we come back to the essence of socialism, as we have defined it with Karl Polanyi: as subordination of economic activities to societal ends and values.

On this definition, socialism has never been more urgently on the agenda. The difficulty, however, as we have seen, comes from the fact that the traditional class base of the socialist Left has disintegrated under the impact of the transformations currently taking place and the direct link between the interest of the *workers* and their 'need for society' has been broken. But the problem is also that this need for society has never assumed the form it should have according to socialist theory. The workers had a self-evident need to contain economic rationality, to withdraw the sale of their labour from the laws of the market. This was a class need upon which their class organizations were built. But the limitations these imposed on the free play of market mechanisms were never the expression of an overall conception of a different *society*. To put it another way, the class struggle has never (except at the height of the Owenist movement) taken the form of an openly revolutionary enterprise for substituting a society based on the union and the voluntary collaboration of the producers for liberal capitalist non-society.

We have seen the reason for this political (or, more exactly, societal) deficit of the labour movement: the means of production and the organization (which is also a force of production) of the division of labour on a continental scale had acquired such a nature and such complexity that it was materially impossible for the united workers to take control of them and subordinate them to their own ends. The class struggle, though it was creative of social relations, could not produce a society for self-governing producers.

This is why the labour movement and the Left have gradually come to accept the 'Fordist compromise', which relieved the labour movement of the endeavour to promote a different society and simultaneously masked the society deficit specific to liberal capitalism. It delegated to the state – a state equipped with means of action and instruments of regulation lying to a large extent outside social and political control – the job of regulating the social system as an *autonomized system*, according to criteria of rationality which did not coincide with the particular interests of any of the classes in struggle, whilst procuring tangible gains and satisfactions for all of them.

The welfare state – more aptly termed social-statism by Pierre Rosanvallon[5] – must therefore be understood as a *substitute for society*.[6] In the absence of a society capable of self-regulation, it has, over twenty-five years of Fordist compromise, regulated economic growth and the working of the market, institutionalized collective bargaining between classes (redefined as 'social partners') and made the deployment of economic rationality socially tolerable and materially viable by virtue of the very rules and limitations it has imposed upon it.

It has, however, never *managed to produce a society* and it could not do so. The fiscal redistribution of the 'fruits of growth', the systems of social welfare, statutory insurance and protection and so on, served more or less to compensate for the dissolution of social solidarities and bonds, but they did not create new solidarities: the state, acting as indirectly and surreptitiously as possible, redistributed or reallocated a part of the socially produced wealth without any bond of *lived solidarity* being established between individuals, strata and classes. Citizens were not the active subjects of social-statism; they were the objects of its policies, as national insurance contributors, tax-payers and recipients of benefits.

This divorce between the welfare state and the citizenry was inevitable since the causes of the society deficit specific to market capitalism remained intact. Social-statism in fact saw itself expressly as a type of political management of market capitalism, intending to encroach neither upon its substance nor the hegemony it exercised over social relations. These were to remain essentially commodity or market relations, even if the markets within which they operated were administered from afar – and from on high – by the regulative interventions of the state. Now the market is fundamentally the place where scattered individuals confront one another, each pursuing their own advantage. Market and society are fundamentally antinomic. The right of everyone sovereignly to pursue her or his own advantage implies that no constraint or restriction should be imposed upon them in the name of the 'higher interests of society' or of transcendent values. 'Market society' is a contradiction in terms. It is supposed to come about as a result of the struggle of each against all. An external product of individual manoeuvres, independent of any human will, it has no reality other than the statistical.

Since, however, the market is incapable of perpetuating the conditions of its own autonomous working, and since the sovereign right of each to pursue his or her own advantage can only be generalised through limitation by legal rules, 'market society' has to have a state: it cannot do without a legal machinery which circumscribes individual sovereignties in such a way that the sovereignty of each has as its limit the rights of others. This legal machinery must necessarily be independent of the individuals themselves and independent from the political authorities. Thus, by its very nature, 'market society' demands that there be a split between law and custom, that the state be separate from civil society, and that it be autonomous in relation to individuals and the political government. The *rejection of the state* in liberal ideology must therefore be recognized as an indirect expression of the *rejection of society* inherent in liberal capitalism.

The 'Fordist compromise' thus constituted a fundamentally unstable arrangement. The state had equipped itself with instruments of intervention and regulation which, though they conformed to the interests of free-market capitalism as a whole, were nonetheless contrary to the interests of each individual capitalist. This high-handed, technocratic, interventionist state was only accepted by the bourgeoisie because it was able to ensure economic growth in a framework of relative social peace. In a system that was continually expanding, each person's advantage in fact becomes compatible with the interests of all: everyone wins. But when there is no growth, the market economy becomes a zero-sum game once again: each person can only gain an advantage at someone else's cost. When economic growth was halted, the 'Fordist compromise' therefore became obsolete. The technocratic state which was the indispensable broker of that compromise lost its legitimacy in the eyes of the bourgeoisie. It could only retain its powers of regulation and arbitration by restraining the play of the market more than it had previously done and by substituting an administered capitalism, ever closer to state capitalism, for the free-market variety. Which meant the state would have to engage in a head-on clash with the bourgeoisie.

The rest is history. The trial of strength with the bourgeoisie was never actually attempted or was aborted rapidly in the few instances in which it was. The regulatory power of nation states had, in the event, been overcome from another direction, namely by the internationaliz-ation of capital and, most importantly, by the development of a financial market on a world scale. To maintain their powers of economic inter-vention, the national technocracies would have had to confront not just their own national bourgeoisies, but the financial bourgeoisies and the central banks of all the industrialized capitalist nations. The opening up of national economies to the world market and the exacerbation of international competition thus became a sovereign weapon for the national bourgeoisies against a state interventionism operating only on the scale of a single country. Only a transnational Left coalition based on common political objectives could have resisted the internationalism of capital for any length of time. No such coalition emerged. The sole ambition of the majority of parties of the Left was to seize or retain control of the state apparatus. The members of the party machines thought in terms of positions of power within national power structures, without seeing that these national structures were being emptied of all substance and decisions were now being taken elsewhere.

The market – or rather the opening up of national economies to a world economy beyond the regulatory power of national states – thus recovered its original *political* function, which was to prevent the political control of the economy. 'Balance of payments pressures', which were nothing less than the law of the market in an apparently irresistible form, seemed to impose themselves on individuals, peoples and states as a *force majeure*.[7] Since they were apparently beyond human control, one simply had to submit to them. No one, neither governments nor industrialists, nor finance capital could be held responsible for the constraints imposed by competition on the world market.

The market and 'balance of payments pressures' thus became once again, as Bernard Manin has ably demonstrated, 'principles of order and governability'.

> If there is no one individuals can hold responsible for their fate, the social actors will come to accept what happens to them, whatever it may be . . . The market thus provides a very effective principle for limiting political power since it constitutes a regulatory agency which lies beyond the control of the different agents.[8]

This explains the crisis, retreat and malaise of the European Left. Once one allows the market to impose 'competitiveness' as the prime and irresistible imperative, then, as Karl Polanyi observed, 'society has to be managed as an auxiliary of the market.' The welfare state thus has to be dismantled and the economy 'deregulated', liberal capitalist ideology tends to become hegemonic and the Left, to the extent that it is identified with social-statism, finds itself on the defensive, without either programme, project or perspective. Where it does remain in power, it often owes this fact to its ability (in Austria, Italy and Spain) to make the labour movement accept the need for liberalizing reforms (or counter-reforms). It governs in the name of efficiency and technocratic coherence. It embodies the art of mediation between 'balance of payments pressures' on the one hand and the interests of the wage-earning strata on the other. In short, it is Left or socialist only in name – a name which it merely discredits. We can derive the conditions for a rebirth of the Left from this analysis.

The first of these conditions is internationalism or, in other words, a trans-, supra- and inter-national conception of the actions and policies to be carried out. 'Either the Left will be revitalized as a *European force* or it will disappear from the scene, leaving only its name on the role of honour',[9] notes Peter Glotz. In other words, it will either unite to bring about the birth of a 'European social space' on the basis of a system of legislation, protection and social policies common to all countries and developing towards common objectives, or it will be reduced to submit to – or endorse – social regression in each country, with 'balance of payments pressures' continuing to serve as an alibi for this.

The second condition is that the Left should present a vision of what society is to be which transcends, towards common goals, the immediate divergent interests of the various strata of workers and the unemployed. This is not a new task. It is one which the labour movement and the political Left which emerged from it have had to assume throughout their history. And they have only ever been able to do this by appealing, above and beyond the most direct corporative interests, to the moral, cultural and political motivations of men and women, to their need to give meaning, to their need for an 'ideal'. Currently, this need is only being expressed in campaigns which aim to affirm the founding values of the Left (peace, freedom and integrity of persons, equality of rights and opportunity and so forth). It can only be expressed outside the framework of political parties, so greatly have these merged with governmental and administrative machines which block off any possibility of debate on societal objectives. Thus political machines without guiding values are left facing guiding values with no political expression. The founding values of the Left are looking to create a space within the

churches and other types of association, rather than traditional parties.
Now (I am quoting Peter Glotz once again),

> the European Left has within its grasp a concrete utopia which could mobilize
> millions of people: the reduction in working hours. A reduction conceived not
> merely as the technocratic instrument of a fairer division of labour, but as the
> way towards a different society which will give people *more disposable time.*
> The historic opportunity we have before us has never before existed in human
> history: to create a situation in which the time each person may dispose of for
> their own search for meaning is greater than the time they need for their work,
> their recreation and their rest. You say the Left no longer has a goal? Then
> here is a goal for it and not just a goal on paper, but one that is already being
> fought out in social struggles . . . It ought to be possible to turn the struggle of
> the German metalworkers for a systematic reduction in working hours
> *without* any loss of wages into the theme of the entire European Left, to make
> this not merely a particular question of social policy but the terrain of a major
> political, cultural and societal undertaking. A new politics of time: this is not a
> side issue from some sectional struggle, but a humanist idea which transcends
> social divisions. It would be the most important objective in the programme of
> a political movement which would not be ashamed to claim emancipation as
> its goal.[10]

The convergence is almost perfect on this point between the German
SPD, the PCI and the main Italian trade unions, which have the
objective of achieving the thirty-hour week by the end of the century,[11]
and the Left parties (including the Social Democrats) and the trade
unions in the Netherlands whose goal is a twenty-five-hour week,
accompanied by the development of activities that have no economic
ends and a redistribution of domestic tasks between men and women.

There still remains the question of the ways and means of achieving
this. And this is the crux of the debate between the various components
of the Left on the one hand, and between Left and Right on the other.
Depending on the form in which it is achieved, the reduction of working
time may, in fact, reduce inequalities or increase them, increase
insecurity or security, be a factor of social insertion or exclusion. It may
be (1) equal for all or differentiated; (2) general or selective; (3) calculated on a weekly, annual or career basis; (4) accompanied by an
increase, maintenance or reduction of income; (5) sever or maintain the
link between the right to work and the right to an income, or make that
link more flexible. The ways in which this reduction in working time can
occur imply basic choices about what kind of society we are going to live
in. I shall try to illuminate the issues involved here by examining in turn
the five variables listed above.

THE REDUCTION IN WORKING TIME: ISSUES AND POLICIES

1. The Target-dates Strategy

Until now, the length of working time has been reduced in an extremely differentiated manner: for some workers, it has fallen to zero; for others, it has not changed. This differentiation has been produced by an extremely high degree of selectivity in dismissal and employment policies. It has produced new forms of social differentiation and exclusion; it has exacerbated inequalities. It is as though the reduction in working time had been concentrated entirely within one limited fraction of the population.

Obviously, one can envisage less extreme forms of differentiation. This is done by those authors who, from a strictly economic perspective, make the length of working time depend upon productivity gains achieved in the different enterprises. In their view, working time could be reduced, with whole or partial wage compensation, in those industries where productivity is progressing rapidly, but not where that progress is slow or non-existent. One can imagine the results of such a policy: society would continue to be split with, on the one side, an aristocracy of labour earning, for a twenty to thirty-hour week, as much as or more than the great mass of workers – particularly women – who, in hospitals, education, and the catering and distributive trades would remain subject to the traditional full working week.

One of the functions of a politics of time is precisely to share out savings in working time following principles not of economic rationality but of justice. These savings are the work of society as a whole. The political task is to redistribute them on the scale of society as a whole so that each man and woman can benefit from them.

This distribution or, in other words, this equal reduction for all in the *average* working week obviously involves a continual redistribution of labour between the different branches of industry: those in which productivity gains are at a low level will have to increase their work-forces, the others will have to reduce them, *as indeed they have been doing. But they will reduce them less quickly than in the past, whilst the branches with low productivity levels will increase theirs more quickly.*

The redistribution of workers between the various branches will obviously not come about spontaneously. It requires a planning policy and a training policy, which will have to be laid down in terms of target dates: for example, a reduction in the working week in four-hour stages every four years. What quantitative and qualitative staffing needs will this entail in the different branches? What types of programmes of training? What reforms of teaching methods and curricula will be necessary in the fields of education and training for people to be able, and willing, to acquire the necessary skills? This is a set of problems which all the major programmes (armaments programmes at the beginning of major wars, the military and civilian atomic programmes, the space programme, the computerization programme and the successive MITI programmes in Japan and the like) have had to resolve and have resolved. Today, *there is no industry, administrative body, public service or enterprise worthy of the name which does not have to plan its qualitative and quantitative personnel needs four years ahead*; and if there are any that are not capable of doing this, it is time that they were.

The planning policy would be based on the sum of these forecasts and endeavour to translate them into productivity contracts, the implementation of which would be a matter of negotiation with the trade unions at branch and enterprise level. The obvious effect of such a policy would be to mobilize the whole of society towards an outcome that concerns everyone. It will not be possible to determine and carry out the different policy programmes and their objectives technocratically, by issuing decrees from above. The elaboration of these programmes will have to call upon imagination, co-operation and the capacity for innovation and self-organization at all levels, in workshops, offices, schools, local-council services, trade-union branches, quality circles, works committees, parents' association meetings and so on: 'How do you see your work-station, your workshop, office or service after the introduction of a thirty-five-hour (or thirty-two- or twenty-eight-hour) week? What changes in work organization, equipment, hours and staffing do you consider desirable, useful or necessary, taking into account the foreseeable technological changes?' The collective discussion of these kinds of questions will produce a renewal of political debate and participation among employees – and also a mobilization of hidden stores of creativity and ability.

2. Less, Better, Differently

The *generalized* reduction of working time amounts to a choice as to the kind of society we wish to live in. This can be seen from its two inseparable objectives: (a) that everyone should work less, so that everyone may work and may also develop outside their working lives the personal potential which cannot find expression in their work; (b) that a much greater proportion of the population should be able to have access to skilled, complex, creative and responsible occupational activities which allow them continually to develop and grow. It is in these latter activities in fact that rises in productivity have been slowest in coming. It is therefore in skilled activities that a reduction in working time would create the most extra jobs, at the same time enabling areas of competence monopolized by elitist bodies to be democratized.[12]

This second objective will obviously be combated by occupational elites who derive their power and privileges from the monopoly hold they have on certain spheres of competence. Thus Albin Chalandon, when he was chairman of the Elf group of companies, wrote in an article in *Le Monde* that a manager who does not work sixty hours a week cannot be doing his job properly. We may translate this as follows: there can only be a selective reduction in working time for those jobs that are Taylorized and routinized. But of course, it is precisely these jobs which the technological revolution will tend to eliminate. The split in society between a hyperactive elite controlling all the skills and holding all the power and a mass of workers condemned to do temporary, discontinuous and low-paid jobs would therefore be inevitable.

This thesis which Chalandon was implicitly defending is explicitly defended by some trade-union representatives of the workers' elite. According to them, wherever work involves thinking, innovation, responsibility and personal commitment, work would continue fully to occupy all the time available to the technical and managerial staff. There would be no room for anything else in their lives. The price paid for creativity would necessarily be an exclusive passion for professional work. The reduction in working time would thus have the effect, on the one hand, of killing off innovation and creativity and, on the other, of preventing the reskilling and reprofessionalization of jobs; in other words, of preventing Taylorism from being superseded. The conclusion is that we should not reduce working time, since this would mean frustrating those for whom 'work is regarded as a pleasure'.[13]

Thus the glorification of the work of occupational elites serves as an alibi for the refusal to redistribute work and skills better. The fragmented specialist culture (German: *Expertenkultur*), totally wrapped up in their specialisms, is considered irreplaceable and the only image of the worker we are offered is that of a 'specialist without spirit and sensualist without heart'. In the end, then, only a selective reduction in working time could be envisaged, covering monotonous, unpleasant, unhealthy or nervously exhausting jobs, in other words a reduction for just those people whose low level of skills and income makes them least equipped to derive benefit from their disposable time in a way that contributes to the enrichment of civil society and culture.

Now the central thesis on which the elitist argument is based is an erroneous one. It is not true that continuous relentless application to one's work leads to professional success and creativity. The more skilled a type of work, the more time the people who do it need to spend updating their knowledge, trying out new ideas, and allowing themselves to remain open-minded and receptive by diversifying their interests. This is the case with teachers, medical staff, scientists and technicians, business managers and so on. And it particularly applies in the case of high-tech companies. To prevent tedium and mere routine working, the management in those companies demands that its workers take trips, have breaks in their rhythm of life, periods of leave: study trips, periods working in foreign subsidiaries, international seminars, sabbatical years. These seminars or periods abroad are not aimed at giving each worker a more complete knowledge of their particular specialism. On the contrary, they are, more often than not, not directly work-related, but are designed to encourage them to take on fresh ideas, to get a fresh perspective on their own situations, broaden their horizons, liven up their imaginations.[14]

All these are substantial, though disguised, reductions of working time. Working hours in fact tend to become shorter and shorter as one ascends the ladder of skills and creativity (especially in research and design). Or could it be argued that, for high-ranking staff, trips, seminars, art or manual work, or walks in the forest or reading science fiction are an integral part of their work? The argument would backfire on its proponents. For this would mean postulating that the time and activities necessary for the 'reproduction of labour power' – which, as it happens, consists in imagination, critical thinking and form – were an integral part of work itself. And therefore I am working as I sleep, while walking or talking with friends or listening to music or (like Seymour Cray) while I am digging out underground galleries with a spade and a pick, since it is at these moments that ideas sometimes come to me. And that therefore one's salary or wage should be paid not in terms of a *measurable quantity of direct labour* but in terms of one's *personal needs* which are much more varied and complex than one's direct professional work. *But this is precisely what I am arguing*: working less (in terms of the number of hours devoted directly to one's occupation) means working better, especially in innovative or continually evolving jobs. It is therefore *also in these jobs* that the reduction of working hours is possible and desirable (on condition, of course, that the way it is brought about be broadly self-determined and self-managed – a point to which I shall return below). In these jobs *also*, the work can be divided up among a much greater number of people.

This is very important, because it is on the diversification of the interests of the more skilled workers that the development of a culture capable of situating work performed for economic ends within a wider conception of the meaning of life *initially* depends.

3. Intermittent Work, Self-managed Working Time

The reduction of working hours takes on very different characteristics depending on whether free time is created on a daily, weekly or annual basis, or over the worker's entire active life – and depending particularly on whether the periods of free time created can be freely chosen by the person concerned. The linear reduction of working time, with rigid and uniform daily hours of work being maintained, is the least effective of the possible ways of liberating time and the one with the least potential. For it is clearly impossible to introduce into companies a uniform week of thirty-five, thirty, or twenty-five hours spread over five days for the whole of the staff. It is, however, quite possible to introduce for everyone a working year of 1,400 or 1,200 or 1,000 hours per year (instead of the current 1,600) spread out as desired over 30, 40 or 48 weeks or else over between 120 and 180 days which the staff members would share out among themselves in each workshop, office, service or enterprise during quarterly or monthly meetings, where both technical constraints and the needs or desires of each person would be taken into account: age, family situation, distance from the workplace, or life project and so forth, bestowing a prior right over the choice of certain working hours or days of the week or months of the year.

The implication of this will be clear: the *desynchronization* of working hours and periods is an indispensable precondition for a substantial reduction in working time. If the object is to spread a decreasing volume of work out among an increasing (or even a constant) number of people, it is practically impossible that they should all be present at the place of work on the same days and at the same hours.[15] The shorter everyone's hours become, the more likely work is to become *intermittent* for everyone either on a weekly basis (four days at first, then three) or on a monthly, quarterly, annual or even five-yearly basis.

The current *annual* average working hours, which are 1,600 for a full-timer, correspond to 200 working days or 40 weeks or $9^{1}/_{4}$ months of normal full-time working, but this in no way prevents employees from receiving their full wage or salary every month throughout the year. There is no reason why the reduction of working time to 1,400, 1,200 and subsequently to 1,000 hours a year should not allow those men and women who wish to to organize their timetable over the whole year for example, in such a way as to free up more substantial periods of time for themselves in which they will still be guaranteed their full income, just as they currently are for periods of various kinds of paid leave.

There is an obvious advantage in this: if disposable time is created in short, fragmented periods – a few hours a week, a few days a month, a few weeks spread out over the whole year – this will mainly give rise to an extension of passive leisure activities and time devoted to household jobs; if a longer period of time (several weeks or months) were made available to workers at one go, it would enable them to set in train or accomplish some project. And it is the development of individual or collective, artistic or technical, family or community projects and the like which a 'society of culture' will endeavour to facilitate, notably through the network of cultural facilities it will set in place.

I am not proposing any radical innovation in envisaging an increasingly marked discontinuity in work performed for economic ends. This increasing discontinuity is a tendency that is already showing up. It takes the form of an increasing casualization of work, of temporary and seasonal work, training or retraining periods, the employment of contract workers and so on. It also takes the form of a shorter working week or month: for example thirty hours per week over three days paid at full-time rates; or twenty to twenty-four over two days (Saturday and Sunday) entitling the worker to a full week's wage (a formula particularly appreciated by students and artists); or, again, of one week's holiday per month, a pattern introduced by the large Japanese companies. I am therefore proposing that the trade unions and the Left should lay hold of this tendency towards discontinuity and, by conducting negotiations and collective struggle around it, transform it from the source of insecurity which it largely is at present into a source of new freedom.

In fact, as an excellent study by Christian Topalov has shown, the right to intermittent work was perceived as an important freedom right up to the period in the 1910s when the notion of 'unemployment' was invented:

> Being employed on a permanent basis by the same company and working regularly throughout the year, or even in some cases throughout the week, was an experience unfamiliar to most of the craft workers in the big city factories . . . The same workers who protested about a shortage of work did not, on the other hand, seem to desire the permanent employment and continuous work which the coming industrialization process would signify for many of them. The employers' complaints about 'St. Monday' in England or 'Saint-Lundi' in France were just one symptom of the extremely common practice of absenteeism during periods of employment. In certain trades, the best workers seemed resolved to do their week's work in three or four days of intensive effort and only to return to the workshop or the site when they decided to. In the Parisian metalworking industry, these men were the *sublimes simples* whom Poulot informs us only worked when their money had run out and the *vrais sublimes* who earned their living from a three-and-a-half-day week.[16]

The notion of unemployment, as Topalov reminds us, was invented expressly to combat the practice of discontinuous work and to eliminate those intermittent workers who often preferred to lose wages to 'gain independence from the employer and, more generally, from the condition of wage-labour.' The aim of the national network of public labour exchanges, the creation of which was advocated in 1910 by William Beveridge, was 'quite simply to destroy a category of the population', the category of intermittent workers: they had either to become regular full-time wage-earners or else be completely unemployed. The labour exchange found work for those who would work a six-day week; it refused to give work to those wishing to work discontinuously.[17]

The reader will have noticed that, contrary to what the employers argued and Beveridge insinuated, the intermittent workers were not necessarily 'incapable and undeserving' idlers. Intermittent work was a 'way of life' which many craftworkers pursued more out of personal preference than necessity. Among those in the British ship repair yards who 'preferred to work night and day for short periods', then not work for a certain time, 'the majority were the best workers' observed a trade-union secretary and Labour MP in 1907.[18] What we find here is that taste for spasmodic work which is very widespread nowadays among computer software technicians. The abolition of the right to intermittent work was expressly directed at abolishing a particular freedom enjoyed by workers, the self-management of their own time, the self-determination by the individual workers of the rhythm of their lives.

The aspiration to such freedoms has by no means disappeared. Thus an Italian study on young people indicates that,

> even among university students from less well-off backgrounds, recent surveys have shown that the desire for education is most often disinterested and quite free of any concern for employment and career opportunities, and that the most sought-after jobs are those which leave one a lot of time for cultural activities ... Young people thus often express a preference for part-time work, for precarious or fixed-term contracts, for the possibility of changing jobs frequently or alternating between different types of work ... A certain precariousness of employment is no longer solely a source of anxiety, but may also enable the young person to feel freer, more open to change, less 'locked into' a job which threatens to absorb them totally and thus to define their identity in an irreversible way.[19]

What is true of the freedom to organize one's time over the course of a year is true, *a fortiori*, of the freedom to organize one's time on a daily, weekly or monthly basis. That is to say, there is here too an aspiration to determine one's own work schedule freely. In fact, the best way of organizing working time over a day, a week or a month will not be the same for a person living alone as it will for a young couple, for parents with children of school age or pre-school age, or for people who wish to pursue or resume their studies alongside their work, or build their own house, or engage in an artistic, campaigning or associative activity and so on that is not connected with their work.

Thus the civil servants in Quebec have managed to achieve a 140-hour month with practically total freedom as regards their daily or weekly hours. Certain large German companies have removed all control on hours for their employees: the week's work is handed out on a Friday and simply has to be handed in on the following Friday. A system of totally free time schedules has also been introduced in medium-sized mechanical or electrical engineering companies: each work-station is made independent of the others and is given its own stock of components. People can clock in at any hour of the day or night as long as they do their number of working hours during the week. Admittedly, fixed daily and weekly work schedules cannot be abolished across the board at the moment. But intermittent working on a monthly or yearly basis can, on the other hand, be generally introduced and it will have to be if a time-liberation policy is to be made possible.

I know that some trade unionists will object that the desynchroniz-ation and discontinuity of work will make trade-union activity impos-sible. But it is in any case already becoming impossible *in the form we are used to*. The introduction of 'flexi-time' (the employers' version of desynchronization) and increases in the number of temporary-contract workers, ephemeral subcontractors, seasonal mini-enterprises (the employer's versions of intermittent work) are making it increasingly difficult to organize, disseminate information and hold workplace meetings. The big Taylorized factory with its tens of thousands of workers all present at the same workplace at the same time throughout the year is disappearing. Mass trade unionism, factory occupations and strikes by rota (*grèves tournantes*) will inevitably disappear with it. Trade unionism will only survive if it changes. And changing means framing the tendencies to individualization and desynchronization of working hours in a structure of safeguards and collective security measures so as to create new kinds of freedom for the workers rather than for the employers. To oppose these new freedoms on the grounds that they will take workers out of trade-union control is to look at the problem the wrong way round: the union is there to serve the workers, not the other way about. If it cannot reach them all at the same time at the workplace, then it must reach them elsewhere. Let the unions open up buildings in the towns and the local neighbourhoods which people will wish to frequent because they find things they need there, things that interest them, that meet their need for solidarity, for mutual consultation, exchange, personal fulfilment and cultural creation. The trade unions will no longer be able to confine themselves to having forbidding offices sited in cities or big companies and open only at fixed times. They will need to create 'open centres' which people can go to late into the night, offering a meeting place, acting as an exchange for services and products, providing courses, conferences, film clubs, repair shops and the like, both for workers and the unemployed – and their families – for people taking time off work, for pensioners, adolescents and young parents, after the fashion of the 'popular universities', Britain's 'community centres' or Denmark's 'production schools'. They will have to oppose *in a practical fashion* the idea that outside paid work there can be only inactivity and boredom; and they will have to offer a positive alternative to the consumption of commercial culture and entertainment. In short, they will have to get back to the traditions of the co-operatives and the associations and circles of working-class culture from which they originally emerged and become a forum where citizens can debate and decide the self-organized activities, the co-operative services and the work projects of common interest which are to be carried out by and for themselves.

4. With or Without Loss of Income?

Since the beginning of the present crisis, social production has risen constantly but the quantity of paid work has steadily decreased. An increasing amount of wealth has thus been created with a decreasing quantity of work. But both the increase in wealth and the savings in working time have come to be more and more unevenly distributed. A *policy* of reducing working time will have as its objective to allow the whole population to benefit from the increase in wealth created and in the savings in working time achieved throughout society as a whole. In other words, the reduction in working time and the growth in the purchasing power of households could continue to accompany one another, as indeed they have done so far: working time could be reduced by between 8 per cent and 10 per cent every four to five years while real incomes could rise at the same rate.[20]

But one might also envisage a slower increase or even a nil growth in real incomes in exchange for a greater reduction in working time and therefore a distribution of the quantity of socially necessary labour over a greater working population. If the latter grows at the same pace as social production (for example 2 per cent per annum), it will no longer be possible to increase purchasing power, *though it will be possible to maintain it.* It is only if the working population grows at a faster rate than social production, as a result of very heavy reductions in working hours, that purchasing power will have to diminish: the sharing of work between a rapidly growing number of people will then be accompanied by a redistribution, in the favour of the newly employed workers, of a fraction (albeit a very small one) of everyone's previous income.[21] It will, however, be possible to resume the growth of purchasing power when unemployment has been reduced and the reductions in working time have reached a normal yearly rate once again, equal to the rate of growth of the disposable productivity.[22] But these reductions will have to continue *at least* at this latter rate to avoid unemployment reappearing. In short, it must be possible for the reduction in working time to occur *normally* without loss of income. Loss of income only has to be seen as necessary in an emergency, and then solely as a temporary measure.

Total wage compensation thus poses no insurmountable problems at the macro-economic level. The difficult thing, however, is to transpose on to the micro-economic level something which, from the point of view of the economy as a whole, seems self-evidently necessary. This is where many trade unionists get confused: they start out from the reality of a particular company and see a reduction in working time as an isolated measure which has, at a given moment, to redistribute a determinate quantity of work and money among a larger number of persons. The reduction in working time, particularly when it is intended to create extra jobs or prevent laying off workers, seems to them like a *sharing out* among a greater number of people of a fixed volume of work and resources. In this perspective, wage cuts seem inevitable.

This is why I emphasized from the outset that the reduction in working time without loss of income has to be understood not as a *measure* but as a coherent general *policy*. The point is not to redistribute existing jobs and resources but to *manage an ongoing dynamic process which demands less and less work but creates more and more wealth.* Micro-economic logic would want these savings in working time to be translated into *savings in wages* for those companies where such economies are achieved: producing at lower costs, these companies will be more 'competitive' and will be able (in certain conditions) to sell more. But *from the macro-economic point of view, an economy which,* because it uses less and less labour, *distributes less and less wages, inexorably descends the slippery slope of unemployment and pauperization.* To restrain its slide, the purchasing power of households has to cease to depend on the volume of work which the economy consumes. Though they perform a decreasing number of hours of work, the population has to earn the wherewithal to purchase the growing volume of goods produced: *the shortening of working time must not bring about a reduction in purchasing power.* We still have to discover how that result can be achieved.

A first point, as I have already mentioned, is that the reduction in working time should occur by stages every few years, following a pre-set timetable. It must be decided ex-ante and not ex-post. It must be the goal society sets itself and therefore the independent variable to which the other variables will be called to adjust themselves over a determinate period of time. This is how the eight-hour day was introduced, as were paid holidays, social insurance, the minimum wage and, in other fields, pollution control, which is very strict in Japan and the USA, or the 'European Single Market' which would never come about if it had to wait until everyone was ready for it. To announce that working time would be reduced by four or five hours per week or two hundred hours per year in four or five years time would be to stimulate efforts of imagination, self-organization, and innovation which would not be made if everything continued as before.

The second point is that it is obviously impossible to expect all businesses to pay constant or increased wages to people doing less and less work. This would not be a problem for those enterprises which are already highly automated in which, even today, the payroll represents only 5 per cent to 10 per cent of total production costs. But, long term, it would hugely increase the *relative* prices of products and services that are very labour intensive and have low rates of productivity growth: agriculture and stockbreeding, the building industry, medical care, teaching, council services, repair work, the hotel trade and so on.

This distortion of prices and the handicapping of labour-intensive enterprises can be avoided by the kind of solution Michel Albert suggested for part-time working:[23] each time the length of the working week is reduced, wages are reduced at the same rate. The resulting loss for the employee is, however, made up from a guarantee fund. This is what Guy Aznar calls '*the second cheque*'.[24]

This second cheque will have to cover the hours in which the employee now does not work at the same rate as the hours worked. Collective wage agreements will therefore bear in practice upon levels of income of which, as working time is reduced, enterprises will pay a diminishing part. In an increasingly automated economy, in which work is no longer the principal source of wealth, nor the number of hours worked its measure, the second cheque will tend to become by a long way the most important source of income. We arrive back then, by this route, at a system reminiscent of the 'distribution money' theorized by Jacques Duboin and the distributist movement in the 1930s, and the idea of a 'social wage', the function of which is not to give 'to each according to his work', but to ensure the distribution of socially produced wealth.[25] I shall return later to the question of the link between social wage and work and the conditions in which such a wage,

which already exists in one form or another in almost all the industrialized countries, can be paid. What will distinguish the Left from the Right
will not be the size of this social wage, but whether or not it is linked
with a right to work.

Various formulas have been suggested for financing a social wage or
second cheque. Guy Aznar takes up the idea of a 'revenue from robots'
which was given wide circulation in France by the Taddei Report and
which is supported, in Austria for example, by the Minister for Social
Affairs, Alfred Dallinger. This is a 'revenue paid by the machine, the
collection and distribution of which is organized by the state.'[25] In other
words, it is a tax on the productivity gains attributable to robotization.
But such a tax obviously has the effect of increasing the cost to the
enterprise of introducing robotized production: it is as if the companies
which invest in robotics were then expected to finance the second
cheque for everyone.[26] This system cannot but dissuade companies from
investment that would raise productivity levels; it is also an obstacle to
the accurate calculation of the real costs of production.

This is why I have proposed an indirect tax which would be raised,
like VAT or the duty on alcohol, fuel, tobacco and motor vehicles, not
on the means of production, but on products and services, at a differentiated rate.[27] This system of taxation would therefore put a brake on the
continuing fall in the relative prices of products that can be rapidly automated. It would hit them at a higher rate (whether they were produced
domestically or overseas) when they are not considered socially desirable. These taxes being deductible from export prices, competitiveness
would not be affected.

In this way, a system of political prices would come gradually to be
substituted for market prices. This is simply an extension of practices
that already occur within all modern economies. Every economy
corrects the system of market prices by a set of taxes (on fuel, cars,
luxury goods and the like) and subsidies (public transport, agricultural
production, housing, theatres, hospitals, nurseries, school meals and so
forth). As the unit costs of automatable products tend to become
negligible and their exchange value is threatened with collapse, society
must inevitably provide itself with a system of political prices reflecting
its choices and priorities as regards individual and collective consumption. Choices as to what is produced will ultimately have to be made in
terms of the use value of products and the system of prices will be the
expression of these choices.

5. *The Right to an Income and The Right to Work*

When the production process demands less work and distributes less and less wages, it gradually becomes obvious that the right to an income can no longer be reserved for those who have a job; nor, most importantly, can the level of incomes be made to depend on the quantity of work furnished by each person. Hence the idea of guaranteeing an income to every citizen which is not linked to work, or the quantity of work done.

This idea haunts all the industrialized capitalist world of today. It has as many supporters on the Right as on the Left. To look only at recent history, it was (re)launched in the USA at the end of the 1950s by left Democrats and libertarians on the one hand and by neo-liberals (principally Milton Friedman) on the other. Since the end of the 1960s, several local experiments with a local basic income guarantee have been conducted in the USA. Richard Nixon tabled a bill to introduce a measure of this kind in 1972 and it was narrowly defeated. In the same year, George McGovern, the Democratic presidential candidate, included the guaranteed income in his programme. The object was to find a cure for poverty, which showed up more in the USA than elsewhere on account of the absence of a nationwide statutory social-insurance system. The guaranteed income was meant as a substitute for such a scheme. European neo-liberals now dream of substituting such a basic income guarantee for the existing welfare-state institutions.

In Europe, discussion of an income dissociated from work revived in the early eighties. The Netherlands, Denmark and Great Britain had already implemented the idea. It was in the Federal Republic of Germany that the most sophisticated debate developed, after 1982, at the instigation of the Greens, who were soon joined in the debate by conservatives and social democrats. Everyone was agreed on the principle, formulated in these terms by Claus Offe: 'We must break with a development which has led the majority of the population to depend for their subsistance on the labour market.' The labour market, quite obviously, could no longer guarantee to everyone the possibility of earning their living. In other words, the right to an income could no longer be equated with the right to a wage. It was to be decided, however, whether the right to an income was also to be dissociated from the right to work (in the economic sense).

It was on this latter question that the Right/Left dichotomy gradually reappeared, at least in Germany. In France, where the guaranteed basic income was still being rejected, even in 1983, as utopian (in the pejorative sense of the term), the greater part of the Left, Right and centre suddenly found themselves in agreement on the necessity for it (if not on the form it should take): Aide à Toute Détresse, the abbé Pierre, the 'Restaurants du Cœur'[28] and the increasing spread of begging and poverty had made their mark. There were men and women who had never worked, and others at 45 who would never work again; there were the handicapped, the sick, the unstable, single-parent families of varying sizes, and so on. They could not simply all be allowed to sink; something would therefore 'have to be done' and, since it was an emergency, one would have to attack the effects without trying to locate the causes.

The emergency thus served as an alibi for avoiding any debate on the societal implications that are involved here: will the guaranteed minimum be a temporary palliative whilst we wait to see the policies of redistributing work come to fruition? Is it to begin the transition towards a society where work (in the economic sense) will become intermittent for all and where the second cheque will ensure a normal standard of living during the periods when one is not working? Or will it be the 'opium of the people which allows a third of the population to be reduced to inactivity and silence so that the other two thirds can between them enjoy society's wealth in peace'?[29] Will it serve to render an extension of unemployment and marginality socially tolerable, these things being considered inevitable consequences (if not indeed conditions) of economic rationalization?

The question is as old as the industrial revolution itself or, in other words, as the disintegration of society by capitalism. For the first forms of guaranteed minima reach back as far as the beginnings of industrialization: to the Speenhamland decision in 1795 followed by the Poor Laws which took a great variety of forms over the years[30] and the traces of which are still discernible in British social legislation today. These Poor Laws, introduced from the end of the eighteenth century onwards, were supposed to ensure each inhabitant of the rural parish received a minimum subsistence income indexed to the price of bread. Just like certain forms of social minimum envisaged by today's neo-liberals, the Speenhamland decision was accompanied by the suppression of the forms of social protection which the landless workers in the rural areas had enjoyed up to that point. They had in the past always had the right to grow a little grain and some vegetables on the common land and to graze a few sheep here. This right was taken away from them when common property was abolished and lands were enclosed and allotted to landowners. This measure had a dual objective: to develop commercial farming at the expense of the growing of foodstuffs for one's own consumption and to force the landless countryfolk to sell their labour to the landowners.

These latter had no need, however, to employ a permanent additional labour force. The Poor Laws would relieve them of the need to do this and, by ensuring the survival of the unemployed, spare them any bad conscience. There was an even worse side to it: whereas in the past the landowners had maintained a labour force that was large enough so that they would not be short of hands during ploughing or harvesting, the Poor Laws would allow them to replace their permanent workers with journeymen whom they packed off back home once the harvest was in to live on the subsistence minimum which the parish was required to pay to the poverty-stricken. We can see the parallel with the present situation. Today, too, the reduction of the proportion of permanent waged workers and the increase in the number of casual or temporary workers, consigned to unemployment for part of the year, presuppose that a subsistence minimum be paid to those men and women who cannot find work for long enough periods to qualify for unemployment benefit.

This is why the debate on the amount of the guaranteed minimum, however important it may be in the short term for the victims of 'rationalization', masks the deep significance of the very principle of this form of guarantee. It is not, in fact, paid out of solidarity, but as an act of institutional charity. And like every charitable institution, it is conservative in intention: instead of combating the segmentation and South Africanisation of society, it tends to make these things more acceptable. The guaranteed minimum functions as the wages of marginality and social exclusion. Unless it is explicitly presented as a transitional measure (and the end situation to which the transition was directed would have to be clearly specified), the guaranteed minimum is a Right-wing idea.

From this we may discern what the Left's alternative must consist of. It will not accept the growth of unemployment as something inevitable and will not accept that its goal must be to make this unemployment and the forms of marginalization it entails tolerable. It must be based on the rejection of a splitting of society into one section who are by rights permanent workers and another which is excluded. It is not therefore the guarantee of an income independent of work that will be at the centre of a Left project, but the *indissoluble bond between the right to an income and the right to work. Each citizen must have the right to a normal standard of living; but every man and woman must also be granted the possibility (the right and the duty) to perform for society the labour-equivalent of what she or he consumes*: the right, in short, to 'earn their living'; the right not to be dependent for their subsistence on the goodwill of the economic decision-makers. This indissoluble unity of the right to an income and the right to work is the basis of citizenship for every man and woman.

In effect, as I have shown in relation to work in the economic sense as emancipation,[31] one belongs to society (more exactly to modern democratic and not slave-owning society) and one has rights in that society or is partially excluded from it according to whether or not one participates in the process of production organized on the scale of the whole society. The work one exchanges not with society as a whole but with the members of a particular community (one's family, habitat, village, district) remains particular work, subject to particular rules, which are themselves the result of a particular relation of forces, interests or particular bonds. Conversely, work in an economic sense, socially determined and remunerated, is governed by universal rules and relations which liberate the individual from particular bonds of dependence and define her or him as a universal individual, that is, as a citizen: her or his paid activity is socially recognized as *work in general* having a *general social utility*. I can sell this work to an indefinite number of enterprises without having to form any personal and private relationship with those who are paying me. They pay me for the general social utility of my skills and not for a personal service I am rendering. They are, in a sense, merely the intermediaries between an *impersonal demand* on the part of society as a whole (whether it be expressed through the market, the plan or an order from a public body) and the work by which I can contribute to satisfying that demand.

The emancipatory character of work in the economic sense derives from this: it confers upon me the impersonal reality of an abstract social individual, as capable as any other of occupying a function within the social process of production. And precisely because what is involved is a *function* which is impersonal in its essence,[32] which I occupy as an interchangeable person among others, work does not, as is generally claimed, confer a 'personal identity' upon me, but the very opposite: I do not have to engage the whole of my person, the whole of my life in it; my obligations are circumscribed by the nature of my occupation, by my work contract and by social legislation. I know what I owe to society and what it owes me in return. I belong to it by virtue of social capacities which are not personal, during a limited number of hours specified by contract and, once I have satisfied my contractual obligations, I belong only to myself, to my own family, to my grassroots community.

We should never lose sight of the dialectical unity of these two factors: work in the economic sense, by its very impersonal abstractness, liberates me from particular bonds of dependence and reciprocal belonging that govern relations in the micro-social and private sphere. And this sphere can only exist as a sphere of sovereignty and voluntary reciprocity because it is the obverse of a clearly circumscribed sphere of *clearly defined* social obligations. If I am relieved of any social obligation and more precisely of the obligation to 'earn my living' by working, be it only for a few hours, I cease to exist as an 'interchangea-

ble social individual as capable as any other': my only remaining existence is private and micro-social. And I cease to experience this private
existence as my personal sovereignty because it is no longer the obverse
of compelling social obligations. The customary balance of living in a
macro-socially organized society is upset: I no longer negate myself as
private individual by my 'work in general' nor do I negate myself as an
individual in general by my private activity. My existence collapses into
the private sphere where, being subject to no general social obligation,
to no socially recognized necessity, I can only be or do or not do what I
have decided myself, without anyone asking anything of me: 'Excluded
from every group and every enterprise, a pure consumer of air, water
and other people's labour, reduced to the boredom of living, an acute
consciousness of my contingency', I am a 'supernumerary of the human
species'.

This is the condition of those who are involuntarily unemployed; and
the guarantee of a social minimum will do nothing to change that (nor
indeed will giving him or her an *unreal job*, a job which is not needed by
society, but which has deliberately been created to occupy people for
whom there are no real jobs and to justify the allowance allocated to
them). Whatever the size of the guaranteed minimum, it can do nothing
to alter the fact that society expects nothing of me, thus denies me a
reality as a social individual in general. It pays me an allowance without
asking anything of me, thus without *conferring any social rights upon
me.* By this payment, it holds me in its power: what it grants me today, it
can take away bit by bit, or altogether, tomorrow, since it has no need of
me, but I have need of it.

It is for all these reasons that the right to an income and the right to
macro-social work must not be dissociated or – which amounts to the
same thing – that the right to an income must be linked to the duty to
work, however little, to produce that income. I do not propose this in
order to save 'work-based society', the work ethic or biblical morality,
but to maintain the indispensable dialectical unity between rights and
duties. There can be no rights without corresponding obligations. My
duty is the basis of my rights and to relieve me of all duties is to deny me
the status of a person having rights. Rights and duties are always two
sides of the same coin: my rights are the duties of others towards me;
they imply my duty towards these others. In so far as I am *one of them*
(one among others), I have rights over them; in so far as I am *one of
them*, they have rights over me. It is through these rights – and therefore
through the duties they give me – that they *recognize me* as one of them.
In so far as I belong to society, it has the right to ask me to do my appropriate share of social labour. It is through the duties it gives me that it
recognizes me as belonging to it. If it asks nothing of me, it rejects me.

The right to work, the duty to work and one's rights as a citizen are inextricably linked.[33]

In a Left conception, the point is therefore not to guarantee an income independent of any work; what must be guaranteed is *both* the income *and* the quantity of social labour corresponding to it. In other words, the point is to guarantee an income which does not diminish as socially necessary labour time is reduced. *Income should not become independent of work itself, but of working time.*

In this way, however intermittent work may become and however short the time spent on it, the income guaranteed to each person throughout their lives in exchange for a corresponding quantum of work will always be an earned income to which she or he has acquired a right by her or his labour.

I shall attempt to give a more precise account of this proposition in order to distinguish it from the forms of guaranteed minimum and universal grants.

(a) Guaranteed Income. Rightist Version

The guaranteed minimum is an income *granted* by the state, financed by direct taxation. It starts out from the idea that there are people who work and earn a good living and others who do not work because there is no room for them on the job market or because they are (considered) incapable of working. Between these two groups, no lived relation of solidarity emerges. This absence of solidarity (this society deficit) is corrected by a fiscal transfer. The state takes from the one group and gives to the other.

The legitimacy of this transfer will always be more or less openly contested, since through it those who do not work appear to be making the others work in their stead. The state will therefore always be suspected of promoting parasitic behaviour and idleness. It will always tend to disarm that suspicion by spicing the right to a social income with more or less humiliating and harassing checks and controls. The recipients of these benefits will remain at the mercy of a taxpayers' revolt or a political change. And this will be the case even if the income guarantee takes the form of the universal, unconditional payment of a basic allowance, as the Charles Fourier collective[34] and the German eco-libertarians have suggested. This basic income runs the risk, moreover, of serving as a pretext for the unchecked growth of low-grade and badly paid casual jobs, regarded by employers as a top-up income. It also runs the risk of serving as a justification for increased discrimination against women. There will be a tendency to confuse the guaranteed minimum with a 'wage for housework' or a maternal wage, justifying the confinement of women to the domestic sphere and (to borrow a formula used by Jacques Chirac in 1987) the official recognition of the 'profession of housewife and mother'.[35]

The guaranteed minimum or universal grant thus form part of a palliative policy which promises to protect individuals from the decomposition of wage-based society without developing a social dynamic that would open up emancipatory perspectives for them for the future.

(b) Guaranteed income. Left version

From a Left perspective,·the guarantee of an adequate income to those whom society marginalizes must neither be the final goal nor the starting point of the political project. The starting point must be the diminution of the quantity of economically necessary labour; the objective must be to eliminate not only poverty and involuntary unemployment, but also the lack of time, harassing working conditions and the obligation to work full time throughout one's entire working life. The point is not to ensure that there are welfare benefits for those who are excluded from the production process, though these may have to be provided as a temporary measure. The point is to do away with the conditions which have led to the exclusion of those people.

This objective demands, as we have seen, a policy of redistribution of the economically necessary quantity of work. This will gradually, by stages, reduce the *full-time norm* from the current 1,600 hours per year to an average of 1,400, 1,200 and, finally, 1,000 in the space of some 15 to 20 years. These annual 1,000 hours will be considered the *normal* extent of full-time working and will entitle you to a normal wage which corresponds to your level of skills or qualifications, just as the current 1,600-hour year is considered the full-time norm and gives you the right to draw a full wage (which is four or five times greater in purchasing power than that received by a worker putting in some 3,200 hours per year at the beginning of the century).

I have demonstrated above that, as the length of annual working time decreases, work tends to become more and more intermittent. A thousand hours in a year may be done as two days' work a week, ten days a month, two fortnights every three months, one week in two, one month in two or sixth months a year, and so on, entitling you to a full wage (in the form of two cheques) throughout the year, just as you do today for 1,600 hours spread over two hundred days a year.

The idea of determining the number of working hours that entitles a person to receive a full income not over a year but over a five- or ten-year period follows logically from this new organization of time. This idea is not as 'utopian' (in the pejorative sense) as is commonly thought in France. The Swedish economist, Gösta Rehn, was the first to propose it on the occasion of the 1960 reform of the Swedish old-age-pension system: he proposed that everyone should be free to take an extended period of leave at any age which would be counted as an instalment of their retirement, the beginning of which would be correspondingly delayed. This 'drawing right', he explained to me, 'means the right to exchange one form of life for another during selected periods . . . For me this means freeing man [woman] from the obligation to be "economically productive" all the time.'[36]

It is precisely such a liberation which the determination of working hours on a yearly or five-yearly or career scale at last allows, when the norm for full-time working has greatly diminished. Just as 1,000 hours a year will be a normal full-time quota and will entitle you to a full income throughout the year, 3,000 hours over three years or 5,000 hours over five years will be a normal full-time quota entitling you to a full income for three or five years, even if the work concerned has been performed in a discontinuous fashion with breaks of six months of even two years. Your income during these breaks will be your normal income, sometimes paid in advance, sometimes in arrears, the income to which normal work entitles you, in no way different in principle from the income you are entitled to today during paid holidays for example, though the mode of financing it will be different. This possibility of periodically interrupting your working life for six months or two years at any age will enable anyone to study or resume their studies, to learn a new occupation, to set up a band, a theatre group, a neighbourhood co-operative, an enterprise or a work of art, to build a house, to make inventions, to raise your children, to campaign politically, to go to a Third World country as a voluntary worker, to look after a dying relative or friend, and so on. And the same reasoning which applies over the three-year or five-year period holds good over the period of one's entire life with its twenty or thirty years of work (20,000 to 30,000 hours): there is no reason not to envisage these being spread out over forty or fifty years of one's life or concentrated into ten or fifteen years. There is also no reason not to let people plan their lives or a second (or third) start in life.

One could elaborate endlessly upon this type of system, refine it and make provision for bonuses or penalties and for fiscal incentives or disincentives to work either uninterruptedly or intermittently. One could stipulate whether there would or would not be a ceiling to the amount of the second cheque, whether it would or would not be reduced if your break from work lasted beyond a certain time, and so forth. And one might also raise a whole host of objections: some may fear that this will require excessively cumbersome bureaucracy (quite wrongly, since the management of a work-time account is no different from the management of a pension fund, family allowances or a current bank account); or others might be concerned about 'those who just don't want to work at all' fearing that a guaranteed income linked to the right (and obligation) to work, however intermittently, will bring about 'compulsory labour', as if the right to be paid for doing nothing were a well-established constitutional right which I had somehow had the bad taste to violate. This last objection ('what will you do about those who don't want to work at all') could be raised in respect of any type of obligation (paying your restaurant bill, stopping at a red light, taking a shower before entering a swimming-pool). It is a particularly specious objection in this case since the compulsion in question is merely *alleviated*; it is not something new that would require new forms of surveillance or repression. If someone got particularly into arrears with his working hours, he would receive a first and possibly a second warning letter informing him that his right to receive his second cheque would expire on such and such a date. The letter would be sent by the computer managing the social account of the person concerned, which regularly sends him a statement just as one receives a monthly or bi-monthly statement for a bank account. Everyone knows the rules: you can't have an unlimited overdraft at your bank, nor could you at the social fund paying the second cheque. The openness and fairness of this rule mean that it cannot be considered oppressive and authoritarian. It is the rule for everybody. It seems to me greatly preferable to the blind constraints of anarcho-liberal non-society and to the social-statism which grants a 'civic income' to everyone and then leaves them to 'slug it out'.

   The essential aspect of an obligation to work in exchange for a guaranteed full income is that this obligation provides the basis for a corresponding right: by obliging individuals to produce by working the income which is guaranteed to them, society obliges itself to guarantee them the opportunity to work and gives them the right to demand this. The obligation it imposes on them is the basis for the right they have over it, the right to be full citizens, individuals like any other, assuming their – increasingly light – share of the burden of necessities and free, by that very token, to be unique persons who, during the rest of their time, may develop their multiple capacities, if such is their desire. I do not claim here to have responded to all the questions and objections that may be raised. I do not know if there is a need to set an age limit for entry into active life; or whether the person who at 35 has already done all the work that is due must be discouraged from continuing at the same rate nor whether one should continue to advocate, as Gunnar Adler-Karlsson does, a division into two economic sectors, a socialized sector ensuring that all necessities are provided in the most economical conditions for workers and users, and a free sector providing the optional goods and services and so on,[37] but I know that the vision of a society where each person may earn their living by working, but by working less and less and increasingly intermittently, in which each person is entitled to the full citizenship which work confers and to a 'second life', whether private, micro-social or public, enables workers and the unemployed, the new social movements and the labour movement to join together in a common struggle.

Unlike the 'universal grant' or social assistance to non-workers, which depend entirely on central government, a project for a society in which everyone may work, but work less and less while having a better life, may be carried through by a strategy of collective action and popular initiatives. Unlike the formulas of the 'guaranteed minimum' or 'universal grant', this project does not break with the traditional logic of trade-union struggle, since full payment during occasional and annual holidays and during maternity or paternity leave and training periods or sabbaticals, and so on is prefigured in a number of collective agreements. And lastly, I know that a policy of a staged reduction in working hours, accompanied by a guaranteed income, cannot fail to enliven thinking, debate, experimentation, initiative and the self-organization of the workers on all the different levels of the economy and therefore to be more generative of society and democracy than any social-statist formula. This is the essential point: that control over the economy should be exercised by a revitalized society.

Here then is the reasoning behind my proposals. They are not the only possible proposals. You could make other ones based on other reasoning, but you could not avoid, in the name of realism, all debate about the future society which will no longer be a work-based society. Evading the issue and the need for radical innovations and change implies that you simply accept the fact that society, as it decomposes, will go on engendering increasing poverty, frustration, irrationality and violence. 'If you don't want Gorz's model or mine', said Gunnar Adler-Karlsson at a recent trade-union seminar, 'then build your own models. But please suggest something new. If you gave me one hundredth of the staff and the economists who are working on conventional employment theories to work out my theories and Gorz's, we would find solutions to a whole host of problems.'[38]

Notes

1. Échanges et Projets, *La révolution du temps choisi*, Paris 1980, p. 107.

2. SPD, *Entwurf für ein neues Grundsatzprogramm der Sozialdemokratischen Partei Deutschlands*, ch. XII, 'Auf dem Weg zur Kulturgesellschaft', Irsee, June 1986.

3. Échanges et Projets, p. 109.

4. See above, Chapter 8.

5. Pierre Rosanvallon, *Pour une nouvelle culture politique*, Paris 1978.

6. See above, p. 132.

7. On the possibility and the political means for getting round this apparent obstacle, see Alain Lipietz, *L'audace ou l'enlisement*, Paris 1984, chs. 10 and 11.

8. Bernard Manin, 'Les deux libéralismes: marché et contre-pouvoirs', *Intervention*, 9, May–June 1984.

9. Peter Glotz, 'Die Malaise der Linken', *Der Spiegel*, 51, 1987.

10. Ibid.

11. At the communist workers conference of 3 March 1988, Antonio Bassolino, speaking in the name of the PCI leadership, declared the thirty-five-hour week to be an immediate objective and the thirty-hour week an objective for the end of the century 'in a European perspective'. He presented a reduction in working hours as the 'link between the struggle for liberation *in* work and the struggle for liberation *from* work: the point is to liberate ourselves from the domination of the economy over our lives.'

12. On the technical possibility of this democratization of skills (or making them 'commonplace' and interchangeable), see above Chapter 7, pp. 76–7.

13. See in particular Daniel Mothé, 'Faut-il réduire le temps de travail?', *Autogestions*, 19 April 1985, pp. 16–17.

14. Cf. Bruno Lussato, *Bouillon de culture*, Paris 1987.

15. The extremely interesting work of a neo-liberal libertarian economist, Jean-Louis Michau, is fundamental as regards the feasibility of desynchronization. 'If the use of the impressive industrial capacity we have built for ourselves and individual fulfilment are recognized as common goals, then the choice of how one divides one's time between work and other activities is fundamental and represents our chief freedom . . . Let us organize work so as to allow individuals more liberty; very important transformations should then follow quite naturally. This method of arranging work is known as the 'modular timetable'. The principle is that the work is divided up into modules that are independent of one another and to arrange things so that several workers can follow one another at a single work station. Each worker plans their own timetable out of the modules that are available by choosing both the number of modules, that is, the length of their working hours, and how they are distributed, that is, the make-up of their timetable. Other techniques are compatible with the modular timetable: variable working hours, the compressed week, shift work, à la carte holidays or part-time working.' The author is careful to note, 'The arrangement of working hours, the shortening of the working week and the individualization of work are only possible if the workers are seriously organized.' J-L. Michau, *L'horaire modulaire*, Paris 1981, pp. 150, 164.

16. Christian Topalov, 'L'invention du chômage', *Les Temps modernes*, 496–7, November–December 1987, p. 65, 67–8. We must also remember here that when the Heath government, during the great miners' strike of 1974, decreed the closure of all enterprises for four days a week in order to save fuel, the British workers organized themselves in such a way as to maintain production at its normal level. This was one of the most astonishing demonstrations of worker self-management in industrial history.

17. In this regard, Topalov (p. 60) quotes this astonishing and quite explicit text by William Beveridge:

> For the man who wants to work once and lie in bed for the rest of the week the labour exchange will make their wish unrealisable. For the man who wants to get a casual job now and again the exchange will gradually make his mode of life impossible. It will take that one day a week he wanted to get and give it to another man who has already four

days a week and so will enable that other man to get a decent living. Then the first man will be thrown on your hands [Beveridge is replying here to a question by Professor Smart] to be trained and disciplined into better ways.

Royal Commission on the Poor Law and Relief of Distress, Appendix Vol. 8, Q 78153, London 1910, p. 35.

18. Topalov, p. 68.

19. Sergio Benvenuto and Riccardo Scartezzini, 'Verso la fine del Giovanilismo?', *Inchiesta* (Bari), November–December 1981, p. 72.

20. See note 3 of Introduction on p. 8.

To give some clear idea of these developments, production has been increasing since the beginning of the crisis at an average rate of 1 per cent to 3 per cent per year, while productivity per hour of work has been increasing, for the economy as a whole, by 3 per cent to 4 per cent per year. The total annual number of hours (the volume of work) is diminishing in consequence at an annual rate of 1 per cent to 2 per cent. A part of this decrease is concealed by various artificial means, notably the increase in the number of paid activities for which there is no economic rationality, including servants' jobs.

An average annual reduction in working hours of about 2 per cent could thus be accompanied by an increase in purchasing power, also of about 2 per cent. However, since a shortening of working hours accelerates the growth of productivity and since insignificant, fractional reductions in working time (2 per cent represents a reduction of less than ten minutes per day) would be largely compensated for by a slight intensification of labour, it is preferable to reduce working hours in stages every four or five years. Both workers and enterprises would be motivated to prepare for the event and derive benefit from it.

21. In this regard, cf. Alain Lipietz, *L'audace ou l'enlisement*, Paris 1984, pp. 284–6, where he insists in particular that a 'compromise over wage compensation can be negotiated' on condition that the 'shortening of working hours really does open up possibilities for a new life, and really does provide jobs for the unemployed.'

22. Disposable productivity is the difference between the rate of growth of productivity (for example, 4 per cent across the whole of the economy) and the rate of growth of economic production as a whole (for example, 2 per cent).

23. See Michel Albert, *Le pari français*, Paris 1982.

24. Guy Aznar, 'Le deuxième chèque', *Futuribles*, 101, July–August 1986, pp. 66–67.

25. At first sight, this formula appears to perpetuate commodity relations, while a socialist (or, more precisely, communist) economy should abolish them by providing free goods. (On this subject, see the recent debate between Ernest Mandel and Alec Nove in *New Left Review*, 159 and 161, September–October 1986 and January–February 1987.) I have, however, demonstrated, where work-for-oneself is concerned, that the liberation of time will tend to increase considerably the space available for non-commodity forms of production and exchanges of goods and services, as well as non-individual forms of consumption, with work in the economic sense tending to become a secondary activity. This is the key point. The problem of transition does not arise in the same terms in this second perspective as it does in that of a communist economy based on free goods and services, the creation of which presupposes the existence of an extremely well self-organized, revolutionary working class within a society structured along the lines of a federation of kibbutzim. Now, as I have shown in Part I, industrial societies will, for a long time hence, remain dominated by the division and specialization of labour at the level of large economic spaces and, thus, by the *abstraction* (in Marx's sense of the term) of labour performed for economic ends. In these conditions, money remains, as Ivan Illich put it, 'the cheapest currency', which does not imply that the final prices have to be market prices.

26. Unless the second cheque were limited solely to waged workers in the robotized enterprises, which would lead to the creation of a society that was cut in two.

27. The development of taxes on consumption will, in any event, become inevitable with the contraction of the volume of labour and incomes derived directly from work. It is already impossible to finance retirement pensions from earnings-related contributions.

28. (Trans.) French charitable organizations which have particularly come to prominence during the unemployment crisis of the late 1970s and 1980s.

29. Alfred Dallinger, Introduction to 'Basislohn/Existenzsicherung, Garantiertes Grundeinkomme für alle?', *Forschungsberichte aus Sozial- und Arbeitsmarktpolitik*, Frauenrat des Bundesministeriums für Arbeit und Soziales, Vienna 1987.

30. On this subject, see E.P. Thompson, *The Making of the English Working Class*, Harmondsworth 1980, and Karl Polanyi, *The Great Transformation*, Boston, Mass, 1957.

31. Cf. above, pp. 139–41.

32. Cf. above, Chapter 3, pp. 31–3.

33. I purposely speak of *belonging* to society rather than social *integration* here. Indeed, I have demonstrated at length (in Chapter 3, p. 33 ff), that in its socially divided and specialized form, work is no longer a source of *social* integration, but of *functional* integration: through it we become integrated into a social system which remains external to us, and not into a web of co-operative relations established for the purpose of attaining common goals. It gives us an identity as citizens, as defined in a series of codified rights and duties, not as 'members' each assuming the goals sought by all as our own. At best, it only affords us a purely micro-social form of integration (in relations of mutual aid and comradeship).

34. See 'L'allocation universelle, une idée pour vivre autrement?', *La Revue nouvelle* (Brussels) 4, 1985. A more complex system, comprising 'a universal and unconditional basic civic income (70 per cent of the net minimum wage per person), together with additional components linked to the individual's current activity' and 'the quantity and quality of work' supplied, is proposed by Bernard Guibert in 'Un revenu minimum, et après?' in *Projet*, 208 (November–December 1987) and a related form of such a system is suggested by Michael Opielka (1,000 DM per person per month plus 20 hours' work per week for everyone). See, in particular, Michael Opielka and Georg Vobruba, ed., *Das garantierte Grundeinkommen*, Frankfurt am Main 1986.

35. On the subject of the distinction that must be made between a 'maternal wage' and a specific allowance for mothers, see above, pp. 161–2 and 150–52.

36. Personal letter, April 1982. For more details, see Gösta Rehn, 'Vers une société du libre choix', *L'Observateur de l'OCDE*, February 1973, and *On Incomes Policy*, Stockholm 1969, p. 167ff.

37. I outlined a two-sector model in *Farewell to the Working Class* and this was fleshed out in greater detail in *Paths to Paradise*, (where a micro-social co-operative sector served to balance out and arbitrate between the two sectors), without realizing at the time that Josef Popper-Lynkeus had proposed a similar solution (which admittedly included obligatory labour service in the socialized sector of basic production, in return for a guaranteed income for life) (see *Die allgemeine Nährpflicht* Leipzig 1912, partially reproduced in Norbert Preusser, ed., *Armut und Sozialstaat*, vol. III, Munich 1982); more importantly, I was not aware that the Swedish economist, Gunnar Adler-Karlsson, had published a brochure in Denmark in 1977 entitled, 'No to full employment – Yes to a guaranteed basic minimum', which anticipated my own 'model' on a number of important points. This work had a considerable impact in Scandinavia and West Germany, where it was published under the title of 'Gedanken zur Vollbeschäftigung' ('Thoughts on full employment'), in *Mitteilungen zur Arbeits- und Berufsforschung*, 4, 1979.

38. See G. Adler-Karlsson in *Weniger arbeiten, anders arbeiten, besser leben? Zukunft der Gewerkschaften*, Protokoll des 4. Hattinger Forums, 20–24 November 1985, DGB-Bundesschule Hattingen, pp. 47–8.

Appendix

Summary for Trade Unionists and Other Left Activists*

The Crisis of Work

1.1. The Ideology of Work

Work for economic ends has not always been the dominant activity of mankind. It has only been dominant across the whole of society since the advent of industrial capitalism, about two hundred years ago. Before capitalism, people in pre-modern societies, in the Middle Ages and the Ancient World, worked far less than they do nowadays, as they do in the pre-capitalist societies that still exist today. In fact, the difference was such that the first industrialists, in the eighteenth and nineteenth centuries, had great difficulty getting their workforce to do a full day's work, week in week out. The first factory bosses went bankrupt precisely for this reason.

That is to say that what the British and the Germans call 'the work ethic' and the 'work-based society' are recent phenomena.

It is a feature of 'work-based societies' that they consider work as at one and the same time a moral duty, a social obligation and *the* route to personal success. The ideology of work assumes that,

— the more each individual works, the better off everyone will be;

— those who work little or not at all are acting against the interests of the community as a whole and do not deserve to be members of it;

---

*This text was presented as a discussion paper for the international symposium on 'Trade unionism in the year 2000', organized by the Confederation of Christian Trade Unions (CSC/ACV) in Brussels in December, 1986, under the title, 'Trade unions between neo-corporatism and an expansion of their role'.

— those who work hard achieve social success and those who do not succeed have only themselves to blame.

This ideology is still deeply ingrained and hardly a day passes without some politician, be he Right- or Left-wing, urging us to work and insisting that work is the only way to solve the present crisis. If we are to 'beat unemployment', they add, we must work more, not less.

1.2. The Crisis of the Work Ethic

In actual fact the work ethic has become obsolete. It is no longer true that producing more means working more, or that producing more will lead to a better way of life.

The connection between *more* and *better* has been broken; our needs for many products and services are already more than adequately met, and many of our as-yet-unsatisfied needs will be met not by producing *more*, but by producing *differently*, producing *other things*, or even producing *less*. This is especially true as regards our needs for air, water, space, silence, beauty, time and human contact.

Neither is it true any longer that the more each individual works, the better off everyone will be. The present crisis has stimulated technological change of an unprecedented scale and speed: 'the micro-chip revolution'. The object and indeed the effect of this revolution has been to make rapidly increasing *savings in labour*, in the industrial, administrative and service sectors. *Increasing production is secured in these sectors by decreasing amounts of labour.* As a result, the social process of production no longer needs everyone to work in it on a full-time basis. The work ethic ceases to be viable in such a situation and work-based society is thrown into crisis.

1.3. The Neo-conservative Ideology of Hard Work

Not everyone is aware of this crisis. Some are aware of it but find it in their interest to deny its existence. This is true, in particular, of a large number of 'neo-conservatives', bent on upholding the ideology of work in a context in which paid work is becoming increasingly scarce. They thus encourage people looking for paid work to enter into increasingly fierce competition with each other, relying on this competition to bring down the cost of labour (that is, wages) and allow the 'strong' to eliminate the 'weak'. They look to this neo-Darwinian process of the 'survival of the fittest' to bring about the rebirth of a dynamic form of capitalism, with all its blemishes removed together with all or part of its social legislation.

1.4. Working Less so that Everyone can Work

It is in the common interest of waged workers not to compete with one other, to organize a united response to their employers and collectively negotiate their conditions of employment with the latter. This common interest finds its expression in trade unionism.

In a context in which there is not enough paid full-time work to go round, abandoning the work ethic becomes a condition of survival for the trade-union movement. To do so is no betrayal on the movement's part. The liberation *from* work and the idea of 'working less so everyone can work' were, after all, at the origin of the struggle of the labour movement.

1.5. Forms of Work

By work we have come to understand a *paid* activity, performed on behalf of a third party (the employer), to achieve goals we have not chosen for ourselves and according to procedures and schedules laid down by the person paying our wages. There is widespread confusion between 'work' and 'job' or 'employment', as there is between the 'right to work', the 'right to a wage' and the 'right to an income'.

Now, in practice, not all activities constitute work, and neither is all work paid or done with payment in mind. We have to distinguish between three types of work.

1.5.1. Work for economic ends

This is work done *with payment in mind*. Here money, that is, *commodity exchange*, is the principal goal. One works first of all to 'earn a living', and the satisfaction or pleasure one may possibly derive from such work is a subordinate consideration. This may be termed work *for economic ends*.

1.5.2. Domestic labour and work-for-oneself

This is work done not with a view to exchange but in order to achieve *a result* of which one is, directly, the principal beneficiary. 'Reproductive' work, that is, domestic labour, which guarantees the basic and immediate necessities of life day after day – preparing food, keeping oneself and one's home clean, giving birth to children and bringing them up, and so on – is an example of this kind of work. It was and still is often the case that women are made to do such work on top of the work they do for economic ends.

Since the domestic community (the nuclear or extended family) is one in which life is based on *sharing everything* rather than on an accounting calculation and commodity exchange, it is only recently that the idea of wages for housework has arisen. Previously, by contrast, domestic labour was seen as work done *by and for* the domestic community as a whole. This attitude, it should be stressed, is only justifiable if all the members of the domestic community share the tasks equitably. A number of activists have called for women to be given wages for housework in the form of a public allowance, in recognition of the social utility of such work. But this will not lead to the equitable sharing of household chores and moreover it poses the following problems:

— it transforms domestic labour into work for economic ends, that is, into a domestic (servant's) *job*;

— it places domestic labour in the same category as *socially useful* work, whereas its aim is – and should be – not social utility but the well-being and personal fulfilment of the members of the community, which is not at all the same thing. The confusion between the fulfilment of individuals and their social utility stems from a totalitarian conception of society in which there is no place for the uniqueness and singularity of the individual or for the specificity of the private sphere. *By nature* this sphere is – and should be – exempt from social control and the criteria of public utility.

1.5.3. Autonomous activity

Autonomous activities are activities one performs freely and not from necessity, as ends in themselves. This includes all activities which are experienced as fulfilling, enriching, sources of meaning and happiness: artistic, philosophical, scientific, relational, educational, charitable and mutual-aid activities, activities of auto-production, and so on. All these activities require 'work' in the sense that they require effort and methodical application but their meaning lies as much in their performance as in their product: activities such as these are the substance of life itself. But this always requires there to be no shortage of time. Indeed, the same activity – bringing up children, preparing a meal or taking care of our surroundings, for example – can take the form of a chore in which one is subject to what seem like oppressive constraints or of a gratifying activity, depending on whether one is harrassed by lack of time or whether the activity can be performed at leisure, in co-operation with others and through the voluntary sharing of the tasks involved.

1.6. The End of Utopia

The progressive domination of work for economic ends was only made possible by the advent of capitalism and the generalization of commodity exchange. We owe to it in particular the destruction of a great deal of non-commodity services and exchanges and domestic production in which work for economic ends and the pleasure of creating something of beauty were inextricably linked. This explains why the labour movement originally challenged the overriding importance industrial capitalism attached to waged work and economic ends. However, in calling for the abolition of wage labour and for the government or self-government of society by freely associated workers in control of the means of production, the demands of the workers ran directly counter to the developments that were actually taking place. The movement was utopian in so far as the possibility of giving substance to its demands had not emerged.

Yet what was utopian in the early nineteenth century has ceased in part to be so today: the economy and the social process of production require decreasing quantities of wage labour. The subordination of all other human activities and goals to waged work, for economic ends is ceasing to be either necessary or meaningful. Emancipation from economic and commercial rationality is becoming a possibility, but it can only become reality through actions which also demonstrate its feasibility. Cultural action and the development of 'alternative activities' take on particular significance in this context. I shall return to this point below.

Crisis of Work, Crisis of Society

2.1. Giving Meaning to the Changes: The Liberation of Time

Trade unionism cannot continue to exist as a *movement* with a future unless it expands its mission beyond the defence of the particular interests of waged workers. In industry, as in the classical tertiary sector, we are witnessing an increasingly accelerated reduction in the amount of labour required. The German trade-union movement has estimated that, of the new forms of technology which will be available by the year 2000, only 5 per cent are currently being put to use. The reserves of productivity (that is, foreseeable labour savings) in the industrial and classical tertiary sectors are immense.

The liberation *from* work for economic ends, through reductions in working hours and the development of other types of activities, self-regulated and self-determined by the individuals involved, is the only way to give positive meaning to the savings in wage labour brought about by the current technological revolution. The project for a society of liberated time, in which everyone will be able to work but will work less and less for economic ends, is the *possible meaning* of the current historical developments. Such a project is able to give cohesion and a unifying perspective to the different elements that make up the social movement since (1) it is a logical extension of the experiences and struggles of workers in the past; (2) it reaches beyond that experience and those struggles towards objectives which correspond to the interests of both workers and non-workers, and is thus able to cement bonds of solidarity and common political will between them; (3) it corresponds to the aspirations of the ever-growing proportion of men and women who wish to (re)gain control in and of their own lives.

2.2. *Regaining Control Over One's Life*

Workplace struggles have not lost any of their significance but the labour movement cannot afford to ignore the fact that other struggles, in other areas, are becoming increasingly important as far as the future of society and our regaining control over our own lives is concerned. In particular, the labour movement's campaign for a reduction in working hours cannot ignore the fact that the unpaid work done by women in the private sphere can be as hard as the labour which men and women have to put up with to earn their living. The campaign for a shortening of working hours must, then, go hand in hand with a new and equitable distribution of paid work amongst all those who wish to work, and for an equitable redistribution of the unpaid tasks of the domestic sphere. The trade-union movement cannot be indifferent to the specific women's movement campaigns on these questions and it must take these into account when determining its own courses of action, especially with respect to the arrangement and self-management of work schedules.

Nor can the trade-union movement be indifferent to people's campaigns against the invasion of their environment by mega-technological systems which upset or destroy the environment and subject vast regions and their populations to unchecked technocratic control, so as to meet logistical or safety requirements.

The right of individuals to sovereign control over their own lives and ways of co-operating with others suffers no exception. It cannot be gained in the field of work and work relations at the expense of struggles going on in other fields, any more than it can be gained in these other fields at the expense of labour struggles.

2.3. Towards 50 per cent Marginalization

A progressive and wide-scale reduction in working hours without loss of income is the necessary (though not sufficient, as I will go on to explain) condition for the redistribution of paid work amongst all those who wish to work; and for an equitable redistribution of the unpaid work in the private sphere. Everyone must therefore be able to work less so that everyone can lead a better life and earn their living by working. This is the only way the trend towards an increasingly deep division of society, the segmentation of the labour market and the marginalization of a growing percentage of the population can be checked and then reversed.

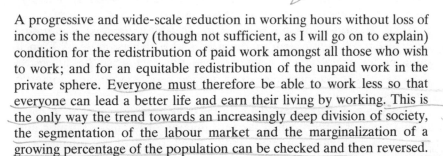

According to a study by Wolfgang Lecher, of the WSI (the Institute of Economic and Social Research of the DGB), the continuation of the present trend would lead, within the next ten years or so, to the following segmentation of the active population:

— 25 per cent will be skilled workers with permanent jobs in large firms protected by collective wage agreements;

— 25 per cent will be peripheral workers with insecure, unskilled and badly-paid jobs, whose work schedules vary according to the wishes of their employers and the fluctuations in the market;

— 50 per cent will be semi-unemployed, unemployed, or marginalized workers, doing occasional or seasonal work and 'odd jobs'. Already 51 per cent of the active population in France aged between 18 and 24 fit into this category (26 per cent unemployed, 25 per cent doing 'odd jobs'); and the percentage is even higher in Italy, Spain, the Netherlands and (especially) Britain.

2.4. The New Domestic Servants

The Right acknowledges and accepts the direction in which these developments are going. A new employers' ideology, the so-called ideology of 'human resources', is seeking to integrate the stable core of permanent skilled workers into modern enterprises which are portrayed as 'sites of intellectual and personal fulfilment', whilst advocating 'modest jobs' for a 'modest wage' in service enterprises, particularly 'person-to-person' services, for the rest.

In the United States, which is often taken as a model, of the thirteen to fifteen million new jobs created in the last ten years, the majority are in the personal-service sector and are very often insecure, badly paid and offer no possibilities of achieving professional qualifications or advancement – jobs as caretakers, nightwatchmen, cleaners, waiters and waitresses, staff in 'fast food' restaurants, nursing assistants, delivery-men/women, street sellers, shoeshiners, and so on.

These 'person-to-person' services are, in reality, the jobs of *domestic or personal servants* in their modernized and socialized guise. A French minister for social affairs acknowledged this fact when he suggested there should be tax incentives to encourage people to employ domestic servants.

This shows a striking parallel with the developments which took place during the last century when the introduction of intensive farming and the mechanization of the textile industry led to millions of unemployed people going into domestic service: 'personal and domestic servants' represented 14 per cent of the working population in Britain between 1851 and 1911. It is quite likely that 'person-to-person' services – and this includes jobs in massage and relaxation salons, therapy groups and psychological counselling bureaux, for example – today represent more than 14 per cent of the United States' working population.

As in the colonies in the past and many Third World countries today, a growing mass of people in the industrialized countries has been reduced to fighting each other for the 'privilege' of selling their personal services to those who still maintain a decent income.

2.5. The Dangers of Trade-Union Neo-corporatism

As a result of all this, a new dividing line is cutting across class barriers, a fact commented on by Wolfgang Lecher in the study quoted above:

> The opposition between labour and capital is increasingly coming to be overlaid by an antagonism between workers in permanent, well-protected jobs on the one hand and peripheral workers and the unemployed on the other . . . The trade unions run the risk of degenerating into a sort of mutual insurance for the relatively restricted and privileged group of permanent workers.

If they see their sole task as that of defending the interests of those with stable jobs, the trade unions run the risk of degenerating into a neo-corporatist, conservative force, as has occurred in a number of countries in Latin America.

The task of the trade-union movement, if it wishes to survive and grow as a movement promoting individual and social liberation, must, therefore, be to extend its sphere of action beyond the limited defence of workers as workers, in their workplaces, much more clearly than it has done in the past. Trade unions will only avoid becoming a sectionalist, neo-corporatist force if the segmentation of society and the marginaliz-ation of a growing percentage of the population can be prevented. If this is to happen, an ambitious policy for a continual, programmed reduction in working hours is indispensable. Trade unions are incapable of imple-menting such a policy on their own. But through their campaigns they can ensure that the necessity for such a policy is accepted and, more importantly, they can adopt it as the objective governing their actions and their social project. A project for a society in which each can work less so that all can work better and live more becomes, today, one of the principal binding elements of social cohesion.

It still remains for us to examine: (1) the extent of the reduction in working hours that can be envisaged; (2) the cultural changes and cultural tasks which trade unions will have to tackle as a result; (3) the changes it will bring about in the life of individual people; (4) how it can be programmed, realized and made compatible with an improvement in our standard of living.

WORKING LESS SO THAT ALL CAN WORK

3.1. Towards the 1,000-hour Working Year

The current technological revolution is giving rise to savings in labour, the extent of which are often underestimated. Productivity in industry has risen between 5 per cent and 6 per cent per year since 1978; in the economy as a whole it has risen by between 3 per cent and 4 per cent per year. Production of commercial goods and services has risen by about 2 per cent per year. In other words, though the economy keeps growing, the amount of labour it requires diminishes every year by approximately 2 per cent.

This *net saving in labour* is set to accelerate between now and the end of the century, thanks, mainly, to the improvements that can be predicted in robotics and information technology. Yet even without any acceleration, the amount of labour required by the economy will have diminished in the next ten years by about 22 per cent; in the next fifteen years it will have diminished by about a third.

The prospects from now until the beginning of the next century are therefore as follows: either current norms of full-time employment will be maintained and there will be another 35 per cent of the population unemployed on top of the current 10 per cent to 20 per cent; or else the number of hours spent in work for economic ends will be reduced in proportion to foreseeable savings in labour and the number of hours we work will decrease by between 30 per cent and 40 per cent – or even by half if everyone is to be guaranteed paid work. Evidently intermediate solutions can be envisaged, but the optimum solution is obviously the one which allows everyone to work but work less, work better and receive *their share of the growing socially produced wealth in the form of an increasing real income.* This presupposes a staged, programmed reduction in working hours from approximately 1,600 hours per year at present to approximately 1,000 hours per year in fifteen years' time, without any reduction in people's purchasing power. This calls for a whole series of specific policies, in particular a social policy which will make purchasing power dependent *not on the amount of working hours put in but on the amount of social wealth produced.* We will return to this later.

3.2. New Values, New Tasks

For the first time in modern history, *we will be able to stop spending most of our time and our lives doing paid work.* The liberation *from* work has become, for the first time, a tangible prospect. However, we must not underestimate the implications this has for each of us. The campaign for a continual and substantial reduction in the amount of paid work we do presupposes the latter's gradually ceasing to be the only – or main – occupation in our lives. It must, then, cease to be our principal source of identity and social insertion. Values other than economic values, activities other than the functional, instrumental, waged activities social apparatuses and institutions compel us to perform, will have to become predominant in our lives.

The cultural and societal change involved here demands from each of us a change in attitude which no state, government, political party or trade union can bring about on our behalf. We shall have to find a meaning in life other than gainful employment, the work ethic and productivity, and struggles centred on issues other than those implied in wage relations. The extent of these cultural changes is such that it would be futile to propose them *were it not for the fact that the changes presently under way are already heading in this direction.*

3.2.1. *Liberation* in *work and liberation* from *work*

Disaffection with waged work has been on the increase over the last twenty years or so, as shown by surveys conducted periodically by institutes in Germany and Sweden. Particularly prevalent among young workers, this attitude finds expression not so much in a lack of interest or a refusal to work hard but rather in a desire that work should fit into life instead of life having to fit into or be sacrificed to one's job or career. Workers, particularly young workers, aspire to (re)gain control of their lives and this increases their awareness of and openness to movements which have this specific aim.

This desire to liberate oneself from, or vis-à-vis, work should not be seen as opposed to the traditional union objectives of achieving liberation *in* work. On the contrary, past experience has shown that workers become more demanding with regard to their working conditions and work relations when their work leaves them time and energy to have a personal life. Conversely, personal self-development requires that the nature and hours of work should not be damaging to the workers' physical and psychic faculties. The trade-union movement must, therefore, keep campaigning on two levels simultaneously, just as it did in the past: for the 'humanization' and enrichment of work *and* for a reduction in working hours, without loss of income.

The traditional task of the trade unions is as relevant now as ever. For although the employers' ideology sets great store by the reskilling and personalizing of jobs and the policy of giving workers greater responsibility, in practice this revaluation of labour only affects a small and privileged elite.

For large sectors of industrial and service workers it entails not only redundancies, but the deskilling and standardization of numerous previously skilled jobs and the introduction of a system of constant electronic monitoring of behaviour and productivity. Instead of being liberating, computerization often intensifies labour by eliminating 'dead time' and forcing an increase in the pace of work.

Often accompanied by putting workers on short time or the introduction of flexi-time, this intensification of work masks, as if by design, the fact that the intensity of human effort is now just a *secondary factor* of increased productivity, the main factor being the savings in human labour due to the high technical performance of the equipment employed. This equipment *could* be used to ease the strain and monotony of work, as well as working hours. This fact makes the arbitrary and oppressive nature of the intensification of labour all the more acutely felt.

3.2.2. New forms of work, new responsibilities

In general, labour is tending to become a secondary force of production by comparison with the power, degree of automation and complexity of the equipment involved. Jobs in which the notion of individual effort and output still retain some meaning, in which the quantity or quality of the product depends on the workers' application to their task and in which their pride in producing something well-made is still a source of personal and social identity, are becoming increasingly rare.

In robotized factories and process industries in particular, work consists essentially in monitoring, (re)programming and, should the occasion arise, correcting and repairing the functioning of automatic systems. Workers in this situation are *on duty* rather than *at work*. Their work is by nature intermittent. It is as dematerialized and functional to the system whose smooth running it ensures as that of 'functionaries' or civil servants and, as in the case of the latter, often requires the worker to respect procedures whose minutest details have been laid down in advance and which preclude all forms of initiative and creativity. The control the workers exercise over their 'product' and over the purpose it serves is minimal. Traditional work values and the traditional work ethic thus seem destined to give way to an ethic of service and, possibly, of responsibility towards the community, in so far as one's professional consciousness can now only consist in identifying oneself with the value of the *function* one fulfils and no longer with the value of the *product* of one's labour.

It thus becomes essential to ask ourselves what purpose we serve by the function we fulfil at 'work'. Professional consciousness must therefore extend to include an examination of the effects technological, economic and commercial decisions have on society and civilization, and the issues that are at stake. This is especially necessary in the case of technical and scientific workers, whose associations and groups have been known publicly to question the moral and political aims, values and consequences of the programmes they are to implement.

This broadening of professional consciousness, this assumption of a reflexive and critical perspective on the implications of one's professional activities can obviously occur in associations and discussion groups, but should also be a central concern of the trade-union movement. In the absence of such developments, we run the risk of seeing the emergence of a technocratic caste which uses its expertise, or allows others to use it, to reinforce the domination of big business and the state over its citizens.

At a time when the economy has less and less need for everyone to be in full-time employment, the question of why we work and what our work consists in doing assumes prime importance. Asking this question is our only way of protecting ourselves from an ethic of 'hard work for its own sake' and 'producing for the sake of producing' which in the end lead towards an acceptance of the war economy and war itself.

3.2.3. The importance of non-economic aims and actions

The capitalist economy is no longer able to guarantee everyone a right to economically useful and remunerated work. Hence the right to work cannot be guaranteed for everyone unless, first, the number of hours everyone works *in the economy* is reduced and, second, the possibilities of working *outside the economy*, in tasks not performed for economic ends, are developed and opened up to all.

3.2.3.1. The trade union in everyday life: cultural tasks   As has been shown, we cannot all be guaranteed the possibility of working within the economy unless working hours are reduced to approximately 1,000 hours per year. *Waged* work cannot then continue to be the most important element in our lives. Unless people are to become passive consumers of amusements, who are fed on and manipulated by a deluge of programmes, messages and media games, they must be given the possibility of developing interests and autonomous activities, including productive activities. Their socialization, that is, their insertion into society and their sense of belonging to a culture, will derive more from these autonomous activities than from the work an employer or institution defines for them. (The same remarks would also apply, should society prefer to have a mass of reasonably well-compensated people out of work rather than reduce working hours.) The labour movement should not forget here that its origins lie in working-class cultural associations. It will not be able to survive as a movement unless it takes an interest in people's self-realization outside their work as well as in it, and helps or participates in the creation of sites and spaces in which people are able to develop their ability to take responsibility for their own lives and self-manage their social relations: open universities, community schools and community centres; service-exchange co-operatives and mutual-aid groups; co-operative repair and self-production workshops; discussion, skills-transfer and art and craft groups, and so on.

These are not tasks to be undertaken at some time in the distant future but objectives which should be given urgent priority now, for two reasons.

— The tendency of large-scale enterprises to sub-contract the maximum amount of manufacturing and services out to tiny enterprises employing an unstable, fluctuating workforce, or even people working from home, means it is essential that trade unions should exist in towns and suburbs and that they should be open to all who live in them. They must attract this floating workforce and the population as a whole, independently of their ability to organize waged workers at their workplaces.

— More than at any other time, the influence of the trade-union movement depends on its ability to contend with the cultural industry and the entertainment or leisure moguls, so as to break the monopoly they are aiming to acquire over consciousness-formation and our conception of future society, life and its priorities. The trade-union movement's cultural task is really a political one, if we give 'political' its original meaning of an activity relating to the organization, future and good of the 'city'.

3.2.3.2. Trade unionism as one movement among many   The trade-union movement should also not ignore the struggles which have developed in the last fifteen years or so in areas outside work. These campaigns, which are extremely varied in nature, are all characterized by the aspiration of individuals and communities to regain existential sovereignty and the power to determine their own lives. These campaigns have a common target: the dictatorial rule industry and the bureaucracy exercise in alliance with professions whose aim it is to monopolize knowledge in areas as diverse as health, education, energy requirements, town planning, the model and level of consumption, and so on. In all these areas, single-issue movements – the 'new social movements' – are attempting to defend our right to self determination from forms of mega-technology and scientism which lead to the concentration of decision-making power in the hands of a technocracy whose expertise generally serves to legitimate the economic and political powers-that-be.

These campaigns of resistance to the professionalization, technocratization and monetarization of our lives are specific forms of a wider, more fundamental struggle for emancipation. They contain a radical potential which has repercussions on workplace struggles and they mould the consciousness of a growing number of people. It is essential for the trade-union movement to be receptive to the aspirations contained within these movements and to adopt them as part of its struggle. It is equally essential that it should see itself as an integral part of a wider, many-sided movement of individual and social emancipation. The fact that the trade-union movement is – and will remain –

the best-organized force in this broader movement confers on it a particular responsibility: on it will largely depend the success or failure of all the other elements in this social movement. According to whether the trade-union movement opposes them or whether it seeks a common alliance and a common course of action with them, these other elements will be part of the Left or will break with it, will engage with it in collective action or will remain minorities tempted to resort to violence.

The attitude of the trade-union movement towards the other social movements and their objectives will also determine its own evolution. If it divorces itself from them, if it refuses to be part of a wider movement, if it sees its mission as being limited to the defence of waged workers as such, it will inevitably degenerate into a conservative, neo-corporatist force.

3.3. Working Less, Living Better

3.3.1. The field of autonomous activities

A progressive reduction in working time to 1,000 hours or less per year gives completely new dimensions to disposable time. Non-working time is no longer necessarily time for the rest, recuperation, amusement and consumption; it no longer serves to *compensate* for the strain, constraints and frustrations of working time. Free time is no longer merely the always insufficient 'time left over' we have to make the most of while we can and which is never long enough for embarking on a project of any kind.

If the working week were reduced to under twenty-five or thirty hours, we *could* fill our disposable time with activities which have no economic objective and which enrich the life of both individual and group: cultural and aesthetic activities whose aim is to give and create pleasure and enhance and 'cultivate' our immediate environment; assistance, caring and mutual-aid activities which create a network of social relations and forms of solidarity throughout the neighbourhood or locality; the development of friendships and affective relationships; educational and artistic activities; the repairing and production of objects and growing food for our own use, 'for the pleasure' of making something ourselves, of preserving things we can cherish and hand down to our children; service-exchange co-operatives, and so on. In this way it will be possible for an appreciable proportion of the services currently provided by professionals, commercial enterprises or public institutions to be provided on a voluntary basis by individuals themselves, as

Copy

members of grassroots communities, according to needs they themselves have defined. I shall return to this later.

These activities, taken as a whole, should not be viewed as an *alternative economic* sector which forms part of a 'dual economy'. These activities are characterized by an absence of economic rationality and have no place in the economic sphere. The act of performing them, is not the *means* to achieve an end, to achieve satisfaction. It produces that satisfaction itself; it is an end in itself. The time we devote, for example, to music, love, education, exchanging of ideas, to creative activities, to looking after the sick, is time for living, and cannot be bought or sold at any price. Extending this time for living and reducing the amount of time devoted to necessary tasks or work for economic ends has been one of humanity's constant aims.

3.3.2. From the self-management of time to the self-management of life

There is no reason why we should make this reduction of the amount of paid work a reduction in daily or weekly working hours. Computerization and the greater flexibility of decentralized units of production increase the scope for individual and/or collective self-management of work schedules. This is already happening in Quebec, where public employees are able to arrange their monthly quota of 140 hours as best suits them individually. Factories and administrative bodies have been reorganized so that employees are no longer obliged to put in a set number of hours per day, with work stations functioning independently of one another. Such possibilities for workers themselves to manage their own time should be mobilized against schemes which introduce flexi-time on the employers' terms.

One thousand hours per year could, for example, be divided into twenty per week, done in two and a half days, or ten days per month, or twenty-five weeks per year, or ten months spread out over two years – without any loss of real income of course (I shall return to this). Working hours could also be defined as the amount of work performed over a lifetime: for example, a person could do 20,000 to 30,000 hours over a lifetime, which would be completed within the fifty years of their potential active working life and guarantee them – throughout their lifetime – the full income which their 1,600 hours per year provides at the present time.

A form of self-management such as this which spans an entire lifetime presents a number of advantages and has been the subject of much debate in Sweden. By allowing people to work more or less during certain periods in their lives, this arrangement allows them to be ahead

or behind in the amount of work they have to do *per year*; to interrupt
their professional activity over a number of months or years *without loss
of income* in order, for example, to learn a new trade, set up a business,
bring up children, build a house, or undertake an artistic, scientific,
humanitarian or co-operative project.

The possibility of alternating between waged work and autonomous
activities, or doing the two simultaneously, should not be interpreted as
a devaluation of waged work. Personal development through autonomous activities always has repercussions on one's professional work. It
enriches it and makes it more fruitful. The notion that one must devote
oneself and one's time entirely and exclusively to a single job if one is to
succeed or be creative is erroneous. The creator and the pioneer are
generally jacks-of-all-trades with extremely diverse and changing
interests and occupations. Einstein's theory of relativity came to him
during the free time he had while working full-time job in the patent
office in Berne.

In general, innovation and creativity are the result not of continuous,
regular work but of a period of spasmodic effort (for example, twenty
hours or more at a stretch in computer programming; three hundred to
five hundred hours a month, over a period of several months, to set up a
business or perfect a new type of technology or piece of equipment),
followed by periods of reading, thinking, pottering about, travelling and
emotional and intellectual interaction.

Continual hard slog does not make work more creative or more
efficient; it only serves the will to power of those who defend the rank
and the position of strength their work affords them. It is rare for
pioneers, creators or high-level researchers to be *at work* for more than
1,000 hours per year on average. Experience has shown that two people,
sharing a single position of responsibility (for example, as a dean of a
university, a personnel manager, a legal adviser, a municipal architect or
a doctor) and doing two and a half days each, do the job better and
more efficiently than one person doing the same job full-time.

3.3.3 The democratization of areas of competence

A policy for the reduction of working time limited solely to unskilled
jobs will not avoid the division and segmentation of society it is designed
precisely to prevent. All it will do is displace the split. It will give rise on
one side to professional elites who monopolize the positions of responsibility and power and on the other to a mass of powerless deskilled,
peripheral workers on short time. If the maximum number of people are
to have access to creative, responsible, skilled jobs, then it is just as

essential for the amount of working hours to be reduced here as elsewhere. The current scarcity of jobs such as these can be explained less by a lack of talents and will to develop a career than by the fact that creative, responsible, skilled jobs are monopolized by professional elites intent on defending their corporate and class privileges and powers. Reducing the amount of time work takes up will enable these jobs to be 'democratized' and allow a larger percentage of the working population to have access to them, since it will create scope for people to acquire new skills and to study regardless of age.

AN INCOME UNCOUPLED FROM THE QUANTITY OF LABOUR PERFORMED

When the economy requires a decreasing amount of labour and distributes less and less in the way of wages for an increasing volume of production, the purchasing power of the population and their right to an income can no longer be made to depend on the amount of labour they supply. The purchasing power distributed must increase despite the reduction in the amount of labour required. The level of real income distributed and the quantity of labour supplied must become independent of each other, otherwise the demand for production will be insufficient and economic depression will deepen. The key question for all the industrial nations is not the principle of uncoupling the level of income from the amount of labour the economy requires, but the way in which to implement this dissociation. Three formulas can be envisaged.

4.1. The Social-Democratic Logic

The creation of jobs outside the economy proper is often advocated, especially by the Left, on the grounds that 'There is no shortage of work, since there is virtually no limit to the needs we have to satisfy.' The question remains, however, as to whether these needs will be best satisfied through the waged labour of people employed to that end. Two categories of inherently non-commercializable needs can be distinguished.

— The first group relates to the environment on which our quality of life depends, and includes our need for space, clean air, silence and styles of architecture and urban planning which make it easy for us to meet and interact. These needs cannot be expressed on the market in terms of effective individual 'demand' giving rise to a corresponding 'supply'. The resources to which these needs relate cannot in fact be produced and sold, whatever the price offered for them. These needs will be satisfied not by working and producing more but by working and producing differently. To this end, a policy of selective public incentives and subsidies is required so as to express a collective level of demand which would make it possible to furnish the corresponding supply (especially in the case of re-afforestation, pollution control, energy conservation, urban development or the prevention of illnesses, for example). This will create a limited number of jobs. But part of the jobs thus created will be lost elsewhere because the consumption of energy, medical services and pharmaceutical products will diminish, as will the demand for goods and services, since jobs created by public demand are financed from public, fiscal resources drawn from the economy.

— The second category of non-economic needs which cannot be expressed in cash terms concerns helping and caring activities (for the aged, the disturbed, children, the sick, and so on). Industrialization has resulted in a shortage of time and autonomy, and its growth has been based on compensating for this by turning activities which were traditionally part of the private, family or community sphere into professional, commercialized ones. This has resulted in the impoverishment and depersonalization of human relations, the disintegration of grassroots communities and the standardization and technicization of caring and helping services – all things which the 'new social movements' are reacting against at different levels. We must consequently ask ourselves to what extent our need for the care and help provided for by these services, whether public or private, is generated by our *lack of time*; to what extent, therefore, that need would not be better met if we increased the time we had available rather than employing people to take care of our children, ageing parents, mixed-up adolescents and distressed friends in our stead. A reduction in working hours without loss of income could allow the repatriation to grassroots communities, through voluntary co-operation and mutual aid on the level of the neighbourhood or block, of a growing number of services which will better satisfy our needs, and be better adapted to them, if we provide them for ourselves than they are when professionals are paid to administer them according to norms and procedures laid down by the state. It is not a question of dismantling the welfare state but of relieving it, as the amount of work we do for economic ends diminishes, of certain tasks which, apart from being expensive, also bring the tutelage of the state to bear on the beneficiaries.

4.2. The Liberal Logic

The second formula for uncoupling the level of income from the amount of labour supplied is the institution of a 'social minimum' or 'social income' unconditionally guaranteed to all citizens. This formula has its supporters on the Left as well as on the Right. In general, its objective is to protect an increasing mass of unemployed people from extreme forms of poverty. In the most generous variants of this scheme, the social income guaranteed to all citizens is to be fixed above the poverty line.

The neo-liberal variant, however, fixes the guaranteed social income at or below subsistence level, with the result that the recipients are practically forced to earn a top-up income by doing 'odd jobs', which will not prevent them receiving the guaranteed minimum income as long as their earned income does not exceed a certain amount. In this conception of the scheme, the guaranteed minimum is to allow the price of labour to change in keeping with the laws of supply and demand and, if necessary, to fall below subsistence level.

In all of the above cases, the guaranteed social income is essentially an *unemployment allowance* adapted to a situation in which a high percentage of the unemployed have never worked and have little chance of finding a regular paid job. It amounts to a form of social assistance provided by the state, which neither stems the tide of unemployment nor arrests the division of society into a class of active workers in full-time employment on the one hand and a marginalized mass of the unemployed and semi-employed on the other.

4.3. The Trade-Union Logic

The third formula for making the level of income independent of the amount of labour supplied is the reduction of working hours without loss of income. This proposal reconciles the right of everyone to have a paid job and the possibility for everyone to have a greater degree of existential autonomy and for individuals to exercise more control over their private, family and community lives. This proposal is most closely in keeping with the trade-union tradition. While the demand for a guaranteed social income is a *social policy* demand addressed to the state and one which trade unions can neither carry through by direct mass action nor implement themselves through workers' control, the demand for a reduction in the working week to thirty-two, twenty-eight, twenty-four or twenty hours, without loss of real income, can be campaigned for through collective action and, more importantly, can create solidarity between workers, the unemployed and those people – a significant number of whom are women and young people – who wish their jobs to fit into their personal lives instead of requiring the sacrifice of the latter.

Contrary to the social income, which is a more or less inadequate compensation for social and economic exclusion, a reduction in working hours meets three basic requisites of justice:

— the savings in labour which technological development has created must benefit everyone;

— everyone must be able to work less so that everyone can work;

— the decrease in working hours must not entail a decrease in real income, since more wealth is being created by less labour.

These are not new aims. There is no shortage of collective agreements, and sectoral or company agreements which have, in the past, made provision for a progressive reduction in working hours accompanied by guarantees of purchasing power and a stabilization, if not indeed an increase, in the size of the workforce.

What is new is the fact that the technological revolution is now affecting all fields of activity and bringing about highly differentiated savings in labour. This will continue over a long period. Trade-union action is indispensable if we are to achieve reductions in working hours which correspond to the predictable rise in productivity: indispensable, in particular, if the reductions in working hours are to lead to employees being able to *self-manage their time* and not merely to more flexible-time on the employers' terms. But trade-union activity *is not enough* to effect a planned reduction in working hours by stages across the whole of society. This calls for specific policies which very much concern the trade-union movement but which cannot be conducted and implemented by it. These specific policies must focus on four areas: forecasting and programming; employment; training; and financing.

4.4. Complementary Policies

4.4.1. Productivity contracts

Increases in productivity are neither unpredictable nor unforeseen. Enterprises, industrial sectors and administrative bodies generally plan investment programmes spanning several years which are intended to produce predictable productivity gains. Social control over the technological revolution consists in translating these productivity forecasts into, for example, company, sectoral or public-service contracts, which can serve as a framework for ongoing negotiations over the necessary adjustments and means of implementation.

4.4.2. Employment policy

Increases in *available* productivity are obviously not the same in all companies, sectors and institutions. Social control over the technological revolution consists in avoiding a situation in which there are redundancies and a surplus of labour power in some sectors of the economy, while there is plenty of overtime and a shortage of labour in others.

It thus becomes essential for labour to be transferred from enterprises and industrial sectors in which there is rapid growth in available productivity to those where there is little or no growth. Such transfers are the condition for an approximately equal reduction in working hours for everyone, proportionate to the *average* growth in productivity of the economy as a whole, in conditions as close as possible to full employment. An employment policy which offers incentives for professional mobility is therefore necessary. This evidently presupposes the possibility of learning or relearning a trade at any age, without loss of income.

4.4.3. Educational reform

Current training methods are often inappropriate and not particularly stimulating. There is an urgent need at all levels of the education system for a reform which will focus on the individual's ability to learn by her- or himself, on the acquisition of a range of related skills which will enable individuals to become polyvalent and develop their capacity to carry out a range of occupations. Schools also need to reverse their priorities: instead of giving priority to training 'human computers' whose memory capacity, abilities of analysis and calculation and so on, are surpassed and largely made redundant by electronic computers, they need to give priority to developing irreplaceable human capabilities such as manual, artistic, emotional, relational and moral capabilities, and the ability to ask unforeseen questions, to search for a meaning, to reject non-sense even when it is logically coherent.

4.4.4. Fiscal reform

From the point where it takes only 1,000 hours per year or 20,000 to 30,000 hours per lifetime to create an amount of wealth equal to or greater than the amount we create at the present time in 1,600 hours per year or 40,000 to 50,000 hours in a working life, we must all be able to obtain a real income equal to or higher than our current salaries in exchange for a greatly reduced quantity of work. In practice, this means that in the future we must receive our full monthly income every month even if we work full-time only one month in every two or six months in a year or even two years out of four, so as to complete a personal, family or community project, or experiment with different lifestyles, just as we now receive our full salaries during paid holidays, training courses, possibly during periods of sabbatical leave, and so forth.

In contrast to the guaranteed social minimum granted by the state to those unable to find regular paid work, our regular monthly income will be the normal remuneration we have earned by performing the normal amount of labour the economy requires each individual to supply. The fact that the amount of labour required is so low that work can become intermittent and constitute an activity amongst a number of others, should not be an obstacle to its being remunerated by a full monthly income throughout one's life. This income corresponds to the portion of socially produced wealth to which each individual is entitled by virtue to their participation in the social process of production. It is, however, no longer a true salary, since it is not dependent on the amount of labour supplied (in the month or year) and is not intended to remunerate individuals *as* workers. It is therefore practically impossible for this income to be paid and guaranteed by economic units or enterprises, either in the form of increases in salary per hour of work or through contributions paid into a social fund. In both cases, the reduction by half of working hours, without loss of real income, would raise the hourly cost of labour to double the present level.

Leaving aside problems of competitiveness, the result would be a prohibitive rise in the *relative price* of highly labour-intensive services and forms of production such as building, agriculture, maintenance and repair work, and cultural and educational activities. This difficulty could be overcome by implementing the following solution: enterprises would only pay for the hours of work completed, on a negotiated wage-scale, which would thus ensure that the real costs of production were known. The loss of salary resulting from a reduction in working hours would be compensated from a guarantee fund which would pay for the working hours saved due to advances in technology, at the rate set for hours of work actually completed. This guarantee fund would be paid for out of a tax on automated production, comparable to VAT or the duty on alcohol, cigarettes, fuel or cars, for example. The rate of taxation of products would rise as their production costs decreased. The less socially desirable or useful that production, the higher this tax would be. As these taxes would be deductible from export costs, competitiveness would not be affected. The real income individuals receive would be made up of a direct salary and a social income which, in non-working periods in particular, would itself be sufficient to guarantee their normal standard of living.

The implementation of a system of political prices, reflecting the choices society has made, and the creation of a social income independent of the amount of labour supplied, will in any case become necessary as the cost of labour in increasingly widespread robotized production is reduced to a negligible amount. The value of salaries distributed and the price of automated forms of production can only be prevented from falling through the floor by a price-and-incomes policy by means of which society can assert its priorities and give direction and meaning to the advance of technology. Nevertheless, there is nothing to guarantee that society will choose the emancipation and autonomy of individuals as its priority or its intended direction, rather than seeking to dominate and exert even greater control over them. What direction the present social changes will take is still an open question; it is today and will, for the foreseeable future remain, the central issue in social conflicts and the key question for social movements.

CONCLUSION

I have attempted to identify the meaning history *could* have, and to show what humanity and the trade-union movement could derive from the technological revolution we are witnessing at present. I have tried to indicate the direction in which we should advance, the policies we should follow if we are to bring this about. Events could nevertheless take a course which would miss the possible meaning of the current technological revolution. If this happens, I can see no other meaning in that revolution: our societies will continue to disintegrate, to become segmented, to sink into violence, injustice and fear.

Index